PROLOGUE

Whoever teaches you how to be a parent? You do the best you can. You give your kids everything they need, everything they want, everything you didn't have. Why, because you love them.

I had a perfect family, a wonderful wife and loving kids. Sometimes things aren't as they appear. Little did I know before long I would have to completely re-learn everything I had ever known about love and family?

I'd always thought putting my kids first was the best way I could show how much I loved them. Now I know true love for my kids' means I had to put myself first and teach them their actions are theirs not mine and the consequences of their actions are also theirs.

The best gift that I could give my kids was to teach them to function happily and responsibly on their own in the world. This is the story of how I learned what it really means to let go and be able to say to your kids, "Everything I do, I do to help you become the best people you can be, **because I love you**".

The best gift I hope to give you, the reader, is to make available the many villages that you may need to visit during your never ending parenting journey. On that path you will come to accept as I did, that Pain is Inevitable but it's the Suffering that is optional ………

DADDY I'M PREGNANT

CONTENTS

CHAPTER ONE

Let's Go Say Goodbye to Your Mother

"Daddy, I'm Pregnant," Lesli whispered in my ear, as
sadly we continued our solemn drive in the back seat of a
white fifteen foot limousine. Blankly, I looked down at
my daughter; her slender body crouched as close to me as
possible and her right arm entwined with mine. I could feel
her quivering as I took my arm from hers and put it around
her waist to hold her close to me. Lesli waited patiently for
a reaction. This poorly timed declaration by my fifteen-
year-old daughter would have pierced me, if I wasn't
already numb by the fact that this was the day I was
burying Joyce, my wife of seventeen-years.

I glanced at my thirteen-year-old son Ian, as he
nervously continued changing channels on the small

television built into the seat behind the driver. I realized I had no clue who these children were. In the moment, I

couldn't remember who was allergic to what. Did Ian know about the birds and bees? Who was Lesli's guidance counselor? Where did Joyce keep their birth certificates? I was all they had now and I had no idea how I was going to continue raising them without my wife, their mother, my lover. That fact scared the shit out of me. Joyce had been our anchor. Now I was left with up to this point I had never done, being a hands-on parent.

This was not how it was supposed to be. I always felt pretty much in control of my life. Everything seemed to be in place, with the exception of Joyce's reoccurring hospital visits. I was convinced I was doing a good job as a provider, a loving husband and a caring father for our two children. Okay, the business at my two retail dress shops was declining and the medical bills were growing by leaps and bounds, but what I never imagined was that I could be left with the responsibility of raising two teenagers all by myself. Why was this happening to me? Where did I go wrong? I believed strongly in God although I was never very religious. As a child, I remember our families had

6

always celebrated the traditional Jewish Holidays but I didn't have any formal religious education. I rarely went to

Temple and even escaped having a Bar Mitzvah, after a disastrous attempt with one of my grammar school buddies. We actually were asked to leave the classes because we were so disruptive, much to our parent's dismay.

Joyce and I were comfortable in following the same routines at our home as we both remembered in the homes of our childhoods. However, when our nieces and nephews were all attending Hebrew schools and my in-laws were planning on Bat and Bar Mitzvahs, we told Ian that we would welcome his following the traditions of our faith. He wasn't thrilled, but once he started the classes, he actually began to look forward to them.

I sometimes questioned the lack of religious education in our home. Would it have made a difference in our lives? I remember our house had always been decorated for the Christmas Holidays, which included a 6' tall pine scented tree with all the traditional decorations. We did place a big Star of David on the top of the tree in place of the usual angel and referred to it as our Chanukah bush. We also honored the tradition of lighting the candles during the seven nights of Chanukah as Lesli and Ian recited the

prayers. Joyce was very adamant that it be a tradition in our home. It really was not an issue with me one way or the other. Was I wrong?

Were my reasons for having live-in help, selfish ones? I told myself that it was to relieve Joyce from some of her daily chores, due to her failing health, and she seemed to welcome the assistance. Or could it have just been because I enjoyed having the built-in baby sitter who allowed Joyce and me to comfortably leave our kids at home while we pursued our active social life? We both loved to play Pan, a popular card game, and there was a local casino near our home which we frequented. I was ashamed to admit that I felt guilty of my choices. Wow, who was I? Emotionally, I was very confused? Was I the real loser here? I never stopped to think about all the times I spent away from the kids, not only to include the long hours at work, but also the many evenings out with Joyce and our friends. What was I thinking? I was feeling both ashamed and bitter at the same time.

Ashamed for not seeing the errors of my actions. Why did I shuck so many of my responsibilities as a parent and depend solely on Joyce's role as the authoritarian with our kids? Perhaps a more active role with my children could have prevented some of the trials and tribulations she alone had faced. I cannot change what had already happened but perhaps I would learn to cope with what was on the horizon.

The bitterness was towards Joyce for leaving me. I questioned my ability to manage this new role and if God will help guide me and my children through our storm. How will I explain all of this to Lesli and Ian? Will they understand? Will the pieces of this shattered puzzle of my life's plan ever be able to be put back together? I had a sick feeling in the pit of my stomach: kind of a hollow feeling much like a hunger pain. My thoughts were of continuous pleas for God's help. There was a weakness as well as a lack of control in my whole body. My hands were clammy and the sweat began to drip from my forehead. I tried desperately to pull myself together as I searched for an escape hatch from this confining MRI state of mind.

I leaned back on the seat of the limo with my eyes closed, as I wrestled with thoughts of the first time I laid eyes on Joyce. It was the second day of the semester at John Burroughs Junior High School in the Hancock Park section of Los Angeles where I first caught a glimpse of her. I was a junior and Joyce Goldstein was a newly arrived freshman. I worked as a cafeteria server during lunchtime, for extra credits. When Joyce came through the line, I couldn't stop starring at her. She was beautiful. She looked like today's version of Miley Cyrus. Same color hair and same shaped face. She smiled at me and I melted as I scooped an extra portion or two of mashed potatoes onto her plate.

I made it my business to meet her after my shift was over. Despite my lunchtime getup of white apron and hairnet, I had become one of the most popular guys at John Burroughs. I intended to cash in on my status and confidence. What did I think made me so popular? It

10

certainly wasn't my looks. I was not tall and considered myself extremely over weight through most of my junior high school years. I certainly had no athletic ability, which

is why I was always one of the last chosen for any team. Though humiliating, I learned at an early age to laugh at myself, along with everyone else. Having a fantastic sense of humor became my most valuable asset. For some unknown reason, I was always the one who everyone would confide in or could depend on as a shoulder to cry on. Being blessed with an innate talent for organization, I was constantly volunteered as the chairperson of many school functions as well as numerous off campus parties and notable charity fund raisers. Perhaps this fed my continuing desire to someday be a part of the entertainment industry and it allowed me the courage to bring some of my dreams to fruition.

As an example, at eleven-years old, I was already producing and directing local community charity shows for the March of Dimes. With the help of many friends who I accumulated along the way, I successfully raised a great deal of monies for this charity. I was even able to pursued Jerry Lewis to appear in one of my shows. That whole experience was a real trip for a then thirteen-year old chubby little kid. I remember how big of a fan I became of Martin and Lewis after seeing their first few films. I was

determined that I was going to get him to appear in my next fund raiser.

I remember riding my Schwinn bicycle over ten miles to the heart of Beverly Hills on Sunset Boulevard where I had often seen the guys on the streets selling maps to the homes of the stars. Hopefully Jerry Lewis' home would be listed.

There it was, on Tower Drive, not too far from where I purchased the map. After obtaining the directions from the map seller, I once again was on my way. I remember it being a very warm day as the sweat began pouring from my forehead while I continued peddling through the hills of Beverly.

Finally I arrived in front of one of the most beautiful mansions I had ever seen. It was a two story, white stucco trimmed in brick with plush surroundings of exotic plants and trees. I was so excited, especially when I saw a few cars on the massive brick driveway and assumed that one or more of the vehicles were Jerry's.

Okay Dennis, get yourself together and have some sort of a plan ready. Too late, because as I climbed the few steps to the decorative double door entry, it opened and standing in front of me was an elderly gentleman dressed in a black suit and tie with a stern look upon his face.

"Can I help you?" he said with an authoritative tone.

With a trembling voice, I responded, "My name is Dennis and I am Mr. Lewis' cousin from Chicago. I would like to speak to him, please."

Before his butler, I guess that's who he was, could answer my request, Jerry Lewis hollered from somewhere inside the house "I don't have any cousins named Dennis in Chicago or any state" My first instinct was to turn around and run, but I stood my ground. I was trying to compose myself and to stop the excessive shaking. Before I was able to do or say anything in response, Jerry Lewis was standing in front of me in living color. I must be dreaming.

13

I continued my shaking but was able to hold back the nervous laughter at the site of seeing him. "Okay Dennis, what's your story? You want an autograph, a signed picture, passes for my TV show, a coke, a pizza" and the list kept coming until I burst out in a relieved state of laughter.

"I'm so sorry Mr. Lewis, but I was really hoping that I could convince you to appear in my charity show that I am producing for The March of Dimes in two months."

"Come on in and tell me all about this show that you are producing" he answered as he led me through his huge marble entry way and into an office that was about the size of our apartment. The room was covered in mahogany wood paneling, with framed photographs of Jerry and Dean, along with other recognizable celebrities who were scattered about. Four oversized brown leather swivel chairs lined the front of his desk which I am sure was the size of my parent's king size bed. It was covered with family pictures and some opened script that he must have been reviewing before my unscheduled interruption. He instructed his butler to bring in some cold drinks while he motioned for me to take a seat.

I kept pinching myself to make sure I wasn't dreaming. Oh my God, I thought, I am sitting in the home of Jerry Lewis, sipping a coke and he is actually here with me. Even if he won't appear in my show, this will go down as one of the most exciting days of my life. I will never forget it.

"So now let's get down to the business of what brought you here today" Jerry inquired. I proceeded to tell him all about the two annual charity shows which I had already put on for The March of Dimes. I explained even though the shows were always a sellout, the venues were small and therefore, so were the monies raised. I made up my mind that I was going to expand my event this year by renting a much larger hall and traveled to most of the high schools around my neighborhood to enlist their best talent for a variety show. The hall I obtained could comfortably seat 500 people, which was about five times larger then any other place I had used in the past. I knew very well that if I planned on filling the place, I would need a draw much bigger then just local talent. "That's why I need you, Mr.

Lewis. Nobody would be a bigger draw today then you and I am seriously running out of time. Can you help me?" I surprisingly blurted out.

"What's the date of your big production?" Jerry asked as he thumbed through what appeared to be a date book. I gave him the date and he immediately picked up his phone, dialed a number and then I heard, "Dean, it's Jerry. See if we have anything booked for the evening of June 10th? Good, you enjoy your golf tournament and I will be doing a charity show for The March of Dimes that evening, so mark it down in your calendar." Now I was sure I was dreaming as I attempted to act cool and collected.

He also shared that when he was my age, he used to put on various charity shows back in New Jersey and invite the whole neighborhood. With thankful tears running down my cheeks, I was out the door.

Well, we sold out that evening to an SRO crowd. Jerry arrived on time along with his friend Tony Curtis and they did a full hour of comedy. We had newspaper and radio coverage. It was the talk of John Burroughs Junior High School for weeks and after that show, I became a star on the campus.

I did one more show a year later with the Lancers, who sang with Kay Starr, and was given an award from The March of Dimes for the youngest continuing fund raiser for their charity. With all this notoriety, you would have thought that my self confidence would have been off the chart, but it really wasn't.

The image I secretly carried of myself though still in the cellar, allowed me to improve my self esteem by being the leader of the pack. As the accolades continued for my services to the community, so did the gathering of new friends. It was as if someone was coating my stomach with whipped cream. Sort of like the Pepto- Bismol ad that you would see on TV. I loved being the one in control which I continued throughout my life. I was never again going to be the last one picked for the team. Instead, I became the captain of the teams.

Was I cocky? Maybe, in a perverse way, but perhaps it was my need to exude self confidence. I also anticipated that someday I would be a famous performer on the stage. Not sure in what capacity, but I felt certain I would be doing something that would keep me in the public's eye. Having come from a Vaudevillian family, music always permeated our home. Never could I imagine I had to accept myself first and the audience would follow. So in this transitioning period of my early teens, I had the audacity to approach Joyce with a grand charm.

"My name is Dennis Poncher and I want you to know I think you are very cute" Joyce responded with a big smile. I convinced her on that first day to let me walk her home after school.

In meeting Joyce, I felt I had met the girl whom I wanted to be partnered with. She was witty, charming and she loved to dance. I fancied myself as one of the better dancers on campus, so we became a natural pair on the dance floor. What really stood out about
Joyce was her incredible laugh. It was sweet and had a contagious element to it, which made it easy for me to develop a crush on her. Although she was not interested in going steady, she did seem to enjoy our hanging out together. We socialized a lot with a large group of friends

which went along with being popular. We enjoyed trips to the beach, movies and picnics in the park as a regular part of our weekend plans.

By the following year, we were an official couple and I took her to my senior prom. We dated off and on during high school, usually between other relationships and even went to college together. Eventually, we lost track of each other. I left college to join the Army and did not see or hear from Joyce for almost four years.

Back from the service, I was alerted by a friend that Joyce had gotten married, but it did not work out for her. She was going through a painful divorce, after discovering her husband and her best friend were involved in an illicit affair. She suffered both physically and emotionally as she tried to pick up the pieces of her life. She fell into a deep depression and experienced several diabetic seizures. She had been able to keep her juvenile diabetes under check for many years, a fact she chose not to share with anybody. The added stress and unpredictable eating habits took their toll on her. She withdrew more and more from her family and friends and couldn't seem to pull herself out of a deep despair. She was working in the collection department of the Diners Club and was struggling to make it to work ever day. She felt like a failure and did not want anyone around her for any support.

After hearing many rumors of what Joyce was going through, it was suggested that I pay Joyce a visit. Her West Hollywood apartment was very close to the one that I was sharing with my best friend Chad, so I agreed to check in on her. On our first phone call, I found Joyce rather distant and very unresponsive to my offer of renewing our friendship. Her frosty edge did not deter me and I continued calling until she finally agreed to let me come over and visit with her.

When Joyce opened her apartment door, it was clear to me that she was in a great deal of emotional pain. The open cheer that had always been her calling card was replaced with a tight face and rounded shoulders. She wasn't interested in our going out for a drink, so we sat on her couch. Initially, we did some small talk, but once I asked her about her rocky marriage, the tears came tumbling down. She poured her heart out to me. We talked about how she felt betrayed, confused and stupid. Why did she marry him? Why did she allow that bitch into their lives? Why did this happen to her? She barely took a breath as she continued on how she found out about the affair, and how her ex- husband acted like an ass, saying some very mean and hurtful things to her when she confronted him. I just sat there and allowed her to vent. I was happy that I could create this opportunity for her to release all she had penned up for the past few months. I was glad to see my old friend and help her start feeling better.

After that first night, I called on her regularly. We talked a lot, had dinners together and went for long drives. We rebuilt our childhood friendship. Soon I found myself feeling more for Joyce then just a casual friendship. I had always liked the way we interacted with one another and I wanted a serious relationship with her. But Joyce was not at all interested. She was still working on healing from her failed marriage and didn't want to disrupt what we had as friends. She made it clear to me that she was not in love with me and she encouraged me to date other girls. I told her that I was seeing other girls, the question was, am I going to keep seeing her? This however did not stop my pursuing a romantic relationship with Joyce.

We went along as friends for a few more months when I received the devastating news that my father was rushed to the hospital with a massive heart attack. I was in no condition to drive, so Chad drove me to the hospital in the San Fernando Valley. Shortly after we arrived, we met my mom and brother in the waiting area of the emergency room. After a few hours, we were ushered into another room where we were to receive the devastating news that my father, at the age of 62 years old, had passed away. I was crushed and dazed and had a hard time accepting this loss. I turned to Joyce for comfort and she was amazingly loving and supportive.

As I moved through the grief process, she was always there by my side and never let me get too dark or distant. She also was a great comfort for my mom and they grew very close over the next few weeks of mourning. She was as much a friend to me as I was to her in her time of need. Eventually that kind loving space became romantic again. Like that time at John Burroughs, we again began a real and totally consuming relationship.

By Christmas, I decided that I was going to ask Joyce to marry me. We had fallen deeply in love with each other. Since my father's death, Joyce had become very close to my family, especially my mom. She thought nothing of it when I invited her to join me and my family spending a weekend in Palm Springs to celebrate New Years Eve. I told my mother what I was planning and she thought it was a wonderful way to bring in the New Year and wipe away some of the sorrow we had been experiencing for the past few months. She gifted me the diamond from her wedding ring along with her blessings. I had the diamond set into an awesome platinum design and then visited Joyce's parents, while she was at work, to ask them for her hand in marriage. They were thrilled and soon Joyce and I joined my brother and sister-in-law for the ride to Palm Springs.

Shortly before we rung in the New Year, I got on my knees in the middle of the crowded Sorrentinos Italian Restaurant in Palm Springs. I pulled the diamond ring from my pocket which I had been obsessing over for most of the early evening. Joyce looked perplexed as she gazed around the beaming faces at the table and then back to mine. She returned my wide smile with a smaller one, her eyes searching for mine. For a moment, it crossed my mind that she might say no, in front of everyone. But this is the woman who I would take any risk for. "Joyce, will you marry me?" The stunned look on her face caught me off guard. There wasn't a time I hadn't let her know I wanted nothing else but to someday marry her.

I wasn't sure how long I held my breath, when she reached over and touched my cheek, as she softly replied "Yes." The dining room erupted into applause. In the middle of raised champagne filled glasses, we kissed and hugged.

Our life as a couple was as perfect as it appeared to others We had an awesome wedding at the University Synagogue in Brentwood where Joyce, having been married before, made a statement by wearing a light pink wedding gown. She looked so beautiful as she was walked down the aisle by her mom and dad. After a fantastic evening, we were off to the Hawaiian honeymoon that I had promised Joyce when I was still trying to convince her that one day she and I would get married

We were a great team and nothing was too hard for us to tackle. Even when we returned home from our honeymoon to find our apartment had been broken into and most of our wedding gifts and jewelry were stolen. While I was busy lamenting our loss, Joyce was setting up a post-honeymoon brunch and inviting some friends and family over for the following Sunday.

I grew up in a happy home and I was pleased that my new wife would be carrying on the tradition. Joyce and I felt we had the most incredible marriage any two people could possibly have. We laughed all the time. We never went to bed angry. We were best friends above all and could talk to each other about anything. She was my soul mate and I was so blessed to be a part of such a loving relationship.

A few months after we were married, Joyce surprised me with the news that we were going to have a baby. We were overjoyed, but complications set in pretty early due to Joyce's pre-existing diagnosis as a diabetic. By her seventh month, an emergency Cesarean section had to be performed, because the complications were putting both Joyce and our unborn child's life in danger. I had no idea diabetes would affect her well being until the fifth month when the complications of her pregnancy began. For two months, I was worried sick about her and the baby. What if something happened to them? This was my first experience with how deadly the disease was and how it could effect Joyce and our future children.

Lesli Renee Poncher came into our lives October 31st, 1965 at 8:30AM with a shock of black hair, big black eyes and weighing seven pounds. She was also born with a rare hyaline membrane disease, a respiratory difficulty common in babies born to diabetic mothers. It was the same disease which had taken the life of Patrick Kennedy, the son of President John F. Kennedy and First Lady Jacqueline Bouvier Kennedy, as he only survived two days after his birth.

I stood in front of the thick glass window of the nursery, my first born child on the other side, and faced the real possibility that we could lose her. The doctors were giving Lesli a 50/50 chance of survival and the first seventy-two hours of her life were critical.

With such a fragile prognosis, I refused to leave the nursery. I stationed myself in front of the window at the special section where preemies were cared for. I was so sure Lesli was looking at me and I kept talking to her as if she understood every word. Because she was the only one in the special area, she was receiving much attention from all the nurses and doctors on the floor. I felt so helpless as I watched her little chest jumping with each heart beat. So many tubes were inserted in the fragile little body of hers. My heart was aching as I watched her struggle to stay alive. I cried each time she cried. There was nothing Joyce or the staff could say to make me leave the area. Joyce had made the painful decision that she would not see Lesli until she was out of danger. She felt it would be too hard for her if Lesli didn't pull through. I continued to send messages back to her with nurses and family members while I continued my vigil.

For the first three days, Lesli had my undivided attention. I was there for every feeding and diaper change, willing her little lungs to keep working, I talked to her continually, describing her bedroom which was waiting for her with all the stuffed animals and toys and her beautiful crib with hot pink trimmings. I told her about her crazy but

27

loving family members and about how much her mother and I loved her. As the hours passed, I assured her of how anxious her mother was to hold her and nurture her. I must have looked pathetic as I continued to give her pep talks about her role as a Poncher which meant she was a fighter. There were times when I thought she understood as she continued to stare at me with those piercing black eyes, letting me know she wanted to live as much as we wanted her to live. When she slept, I prayed. I made all kinds of deals with God which I would break over the years, but all I wanted was for my child to survive.

On the third day, Doctor Brooks determined Lesli was out of danger. Just like that, her lungs had miraculously healed. When the nurses finally brought Lesli to Joyce for the first time, there wasn't a dry eye on the wing. As I watched my sobbing wife tenuously stroke our daughter's dark hair, it was in that moment I truly understood how scared we both had been. The thought our baby might not have survived continued to race through my mind. It was two days later when we were able to bring Lesli home. First born children have a way of scaring the hell out of you and I am convinced those three days of vigilance created a bond to be tested for decades.

The doctors warned us Joyce should not get pregnant again, so about a year later we applied at Vista Del Mar to adopt a son to round off our family. Joyce had an IUD inserted and we were sure she was now protected from once again conceiving. Nearing six months of waiting to hear from the adoption agency, we discovered somehow the IUD must have slipped and Joyce was once again pregnant.

Against her endocrinologist's strong recommendation to terminate the pregnancy, Joyce insisted, "I want this baby".

I refused to process in my mind that we could even consider the risk of having another frightening experience and put my wife and baby in jeopardy once again. I insisted on a second opinion. We got one from her obstetrician who assured us that with the proper care and his watchful eye, we could avoid the same experiences. Nothing was written in stone and I was still not completely sold on our decision, but we moved forward with extreme caution.
Unfortunately, Joyce once again became ill. Come on God; don't put us through this again.

As Joyce entered her seventh month, Doctor Brooks gently informed us he could not hear the heart beat of our baby. Joyce was rushed to the hospital to undergo her second emergency Cesarean. The doctor determined that the pregnancy was no longer viable and there was a possibility she was carrying a dead baby. They needed to relieve Joyce of the serious health issues which she was experiencing. Once again I began my bargaining with God only this time it was with anger. Why was he allowing this to happen?

I camped out in the waiting room with my in-laws, my stomach tied in knots, waiting for the ordeal to be over and preparing myself to console my wife over the loss of our child. The universe had other plans for us. A smiling Doctor Brooks arrived in the waiting room and I nearly jumped out of my skin just to hear Joyce was doing fine. I wasn't prepared for what I heard next. We were blessed with a healthy baby boy. A son, I had a son. He was completely unaffected by the complications during the pregnancy.

We named our son Ian after my beautiful mother Isabel who six months after Lesli was born, had been killed by a hit and run driver while on her way to our home. It was only three years after the death of my father and I was devastated that my children would never know their grandmother, who introduced me to music, the art of making friends and who loved me unconditionally. Losing my mother was horrific for me. We were extremely close and if it wasn't for Joyce and Lesli, I would have never survived the intense grief which I suffered in her lose. Not a day goes by that I don't, at sometime, think about her and continue to miss her.

A mutual decision made by us that our immediate family was complete, Joyce had her tubes tied and shortly thereafter, we purchased a home in the San Fernando Valley. I took a second mortgage on our home so I could purchase two retail dress shops from Joyce's aunt and uncle, who were about to retire. They continued to work in the shops for about a year as I learned all the tricks of the trade. With a successful business under my belt, I planned on giving my family the best possible life. We hired a nanny to assist

31

Joyce and she traveled everywhere with our family. Our children were the focal point of our lives and I was proud as can be to show them to the world.

When our kids were small, they seemed to be perfect. They were polite, easily redirected and obviously inherited their parents' penchant for instantly making friends. But somewhere along the way, they started developing their own personalities by the time they were six and eight years old. I am not proud of the fact that I only wanted them around when they were willing to do what I wanted them to do and when their behavior was stellar... Perhaps this would lead to other problems later on. Who ever heard of parenting classes other then what we learned and remembered from our own childhood?

As the years went by, the kids began to have behavioral issues but Joyce did her best to keep the peace. I would not learn until after her death, how out of control our kids had become once they hit their teens. She handled every school suspension, fight, outburst and meltdown. When I came home from work at the end of the day, my perfect family was in place which is all I seemed to care about. I only wanted to see what I wanted to see. When I look back now, many of the signs were there but it was not in my line of vision of the perfect family. I left it up to Joyce who would always clean up any mess. I grew up in a home where my mom was the disciplinarian and my father would sit back and let her handle any issues with my brother and myself. It seemed natural for me to allow Joyce the same freedom. These were the only parenting skills I was familiar with, a fact which would haunt me throughout their adolescence.

We wrapped ourselves in the cloak of a good life. We were blessed with many special friends and had a fantastic social life. Joyce loved to entertain. She was very much like my mother, in that way. I can't remember a time when our home wasn't buzzing with one social event after another. Even though we had the smallest house in our family, all the holidays were always spent at our home. Our New Years Eve parties were legendary. They were always a catered affair, with an open bar, attracting no less then 200 friends and family every year. Our den was turned into a disco, complete with a jukebox, rotating disco ball and even a fog machine keeping the crowds dancing until the wee hours of the morning. Back then, it really felt like everyday was a party.

Suddenly in 1976, at the age of 37, Joyce had a massive heart attack. One minute we were planning our day with the kids, and the next I was pacing the floor of the Intensive Care Unit at St. Josephs Medical Center in Burbank.

As I sat by her bedside, my whole world had been turned upside down. I was not used to seeing her look so fragile. She was ghost white under all the tubes and wires that were keeping her alive. I felt so helpless, but there was nothing I could do. The doctors were openly concerned that she would not survive the day and made it very clear to me, there was nothing more they could do. We simply had to sit and wait, and of course do a lot of praying. I could not think about anything except I might lose Joyce. I didn't even think about Lesli or Ian, my only concern was Joyce. I refused to entertain the thought that she might not pull through. She was a fighter and she just had to make it through this horrible ordeal. Once again a dark cloud circled our family. Yes, I have heard that God does not give you more then you can handle. But this time I was proving him wrong. I was delirious as I tried to reason why I was being tested. I pleaded with God to take me, not Joyce.

Miraculously, Joyce did survive the first critical 72-hours. I rarely left her side and by day four, she was on the phone making appointments with her manicurist and hairstylists to come to the hospital, before she would see any visitors. That was my Joyce, my rock. To me, she was bulletproof. To our family and friends, she was a shining star. The "No Visitors Sign" did not deter the downstairs lobby from filling up with concerned friends and family members, as the word spread of Joyce's untimely attack. I was up and down the elevator every hour with a health update. Our friends were so supportive. By the time she was moved to a private room, there was a steady stream of cards, plants, stuffed animals and of course, visitors. Everyone on the floor thought Joyce was a celebrity. Lesli and Ian were shuffled from relative to friend, allowing me more time to spend with Joyce at the hospital. Either I would pick them up and bring them to visit Joyce everyday, or someone else would bring them.

Initially, her recovery appeared to be immediate and complete, but her doctors informed me that her juvenile diabetes had been taking a toll on her body. Her heart was in pretty bad shape and it was the first of many of her organs to suffer. I was told they did not expect Joyce to live more then five more years. I was in a state of shock. At first, I requested they not tell Joyce of her declining condition, but then I felt I was wrong and she needed to know.

The brutal news was not taken lightly; still Joyce refused to accept her fate. We had small children and a full life in front of us. Joyce was determined to see her children grow up and grow old with both their parents by their side. But this would mark the beginning of the end; we just couldn't see it then.

As predicted, her health did begin to deteriorate and her hospital admissions increased. Small infections turned into amputations of some toes and a portion of a heel. Circulation issues kept her in the hospital for weeks at a time while they removed veins from one spot to another in her legs. In front of Joyce, I kept up a positive attitude, but I was in tremendous pain watching my beautiful wife fade away. I surrounded myself in fear. I was so afraid of losing her and being alone. The thought continually made me sick to my stomach. I found comfort in denial. I refused to discuss her fate with anyone.

Well not anyone, because there was always Michel, Joyce's best friend, who was my sounding board and shoulder to cry on. When the kids asked about their mom, I would always tell them she was a fighter and she would pull herself through this terrible ordeal as she had in the past. That always seemed to comfort them. But where was my comfort zone?

By the end of 1980, Joyce realized she was not going to beat the clock. She started having horrible headaches and was fatigued all the time. Her hospital visits became more frequent. But there were two major events in our children's lives she had every intention of being present for; Ian's Bar Mitzvah and Lesli's Sweet Sixteen party.

Planning the Bar Mitzvah was a good deterrent for Joyce and she made it through the affair in January, with flying colors. Even though it was Ian's night to shine, Joyce held so much of the attention that evening. You would not have had any idea she was ever sick a day in her life. Being in the garment industry, I was able to provide Joyce with an exquisite gown to add to her evening's festivities. She looked so incredibly beautiful on that evening and a smile never left her face. She danced the evening away as she camouflaged her pain. She could always carry off that façade.

But we both knew she was not going to make it to Lesli's birthday in October. Her hospital stays became more frequent and the severe headaches were uncontrollable. The doctors were unable to pinpoint the cause of those headaches. My visits to the hospital were draining. Our communication was limited because she was unable to carry on a coherent conversation, due to the heavy doses of Morphine which were being fed through her veins. I never had such a feeling of helplessness as I watched my beautiful wife begin to fade away. It was so hard to leave her bedside but I needed to be home for Lesli and Ian. I promised Joyce I would always keep a positive attitude when the kids asked about their mom. All of this seemed so unreal to me. There were times I even believed that Joyce would survive this terrible ordeal and we would be able to once again resume a normal life. I forgot what a normal life was.

Lesli was unsure about having her birthday party three months before her actual birthday. She anticipated her sweet sixteen party would carry out the theme of Halloween as all her previous birthday parties had done. Joyce was able to convince her to move the date and have a wonderful pool party at her Uncle Howard and Auntie Jo's home. They had a beautiful back yard with an inviting pool.

"Maybe we should tell Lesli and Ian just how serious your condition is and start preparing them for what appears to be the inevitable" I tried to persuade Joyce.

"That is not an option, honey" was her reply

There was no negotiation when it came to this discussion. Joyce acted as if she truly believed she would once again bounce back and she almost had me convinced. But as I looked at her face and watched the continuing wincing from the uncontrollable pain she was going through, reality would overtake my hopeful thoughts.

So from her hospital bed, she planned Lesli's Sweet Sixteen Party. Joyce had no intentions of telling Lesli or Ian that she was dying and carried on as she always did. The kids were oblivious to the seriousness of their mom's illness. They were so accustomed to their mom's visits to the hospital, always fully confident that she would return back home. Each day I would arrive at the hospital and pick up a new list form Joyce of needed party supplies. In all her pain, she still was able to contact the caterers and party supply rentals. She went over the guest list with Lesli and they spent time together in the hospital addressing the invitations.

In order for Joyce's release from the hospital to attend the planned party, she had to convince her doctors she was out of pain for at least 24 hours. She decided she was going to lie to them and everyone else, including me. It meant not taking any Morphine, which had become her lifeline. This was an amazing sacrifice because her pain was excruciating. She seemed to have added a sense of urgency to her life.

The party was a huge success. Joyce beamed as she watched Lesli splashing in the pool with all her friends, her cousins and of course her brother Ian. No details were left out and it was amazing how Joyce had been able to cover all bases from her hospital bed. The decorations were very festive and the food and drinks were never ending. Joyce and I ran around making sure everyone was having a good time. No one, not even me, suspected that Joyce was in crucial pain all day. That was her talent; to disguise her distress and make us all believe everything was okay. I even let myself believe she was back to her old self, as I listened to her infectious laughter which made me fall in love with her some thirty years ago. Unfortunately, as the last guest left, Joyce collapsed and was rushed to the hospital. We didn't know then, it would be her final stay.

On September 28th, we celebrated her 42nd birthday in the intensive care unit. She was so heavily medicated she didn't even know we were around. It didn't stop the immediate family from being there to offer their birthday wishes. She was still our shinning star.

But stars too, are extinguished. A grave-looking Dr. Sherman Holvey entered the intensive care waiting room as I was just about to have my 5AM cup of coffee. It was the day of reckoning. He counseled me to contact the family

41

and get them to the hospital immediately. Joyce was not going to survive the day.

I began to shake as I made my way to the phone booth in the corner of the hallway. In a panic, I could only remember my sister-in-law Sydney's phone number. When she heard my voice, we both started to cry. Unable to talk, I left it up to her to contact the rest of the family. I wanted to be with Joyce. When I entered her room, there were several medical personal working on her. Her face was swollen and her arms black and blue from all the needles and treatments which had extended her life up until then. They wouldn't let me near her, so I just stood in the doorway in a state of shock. I knew I was losing her, but I still prayed to God not to take her.

The first to arrive was Michel, Joyce's best friend and also the ex- wife of Michael, one of my closest buddies. I knew how much Michel meant to Joyce and how close of a relationship they had nurtured over the years. What I didn't know was of the many hours and days that Joyce would attempt to escape from her pain and suffering by hiding out at Michel's home while the kids were in school and I was at work.

I first met Michel, when Michael brought her to our West Hollywood Apartment, about a year after Joyce and I were married. She had a warm and winning personality. There was instant chemistry with the four of us and we continued what I was sure would be a life long friendship. Even when Joyce and I were relocated by my then employer, to Daly City just outside of San Francisco, we remained very close. I was in the wig business then and I had to move up there to assist in opening a new location. After six months of training the staff, we moved back to Los Angeles and continued our friendships. We spent almost every weekend with Michael and Michel and they agreed to take care of our children in the event anything ever happened to both Joyce and me.

After several years of marriage and two beautiful daughters, Michel and Michael got a divorce. I was devastated. How could they break up this foursome we had shared for so many years? We were there for each other during the happy times and the sad times. When they got divorced, we managed to maintain our close relationships although it seemed that we were seeing much more of Michel.

I never expected Michel's and my friendship to flourish as it has. She became my confidant and we began to see each other with or without her newly acquired boyfriend, Rick. I would speak with her daily, just to check in.

Michel keeps me grounded and in some ways, fills the gaps of my loneliness due to the loss of my beloved Joyce. There will never be more to our relationship other then what we have but what we have could never be more complete I am truly blessed to have her in my life.

When Michel arrived at the hospital, I just lost it. She managed to pull me away from the doorway and back into the small waiting room. She just held on to me and tried to give me some comforting words. "She will finally be at peace and out of so much pain," Michel attempted to comfort me with. I cried harder. What was I going to do without Joyce in my life?

Shortly thereafter, Joyce's brothers and sister-in-laws arrived with Lesli and Ian. My kids ran up to me and hugged me and I didn't know what to say to them. I felt as if I had betrayed them by not being totally honest about their moms' condition. They were both crying.

"Is mom going to die?" Lesli managed to get out, through her tears.

I was so nauseous as I tried to hold it together for them. "God has some wonderful plans for your mother and she is going to be one of his special Angels who will be watching over us until the day when we will all be together again in Heaven"

Her face crumbled. I rocked her in my arms while Ian sat stone faced next to his Aunt Jo. How do you explain this to your children who had been accustomed to seeing their mom go into the hospital so many times and yet return home to a normal life?

A solemn-looking Dr. Holvey came into the waiting room. He gestured for me to follow him. My brother-in-law Howard helped me from my chair. Lesli and Ian started screaming as I followed Dr. Holvey down the hall to Joyce's room to say my final good bye. I later discovered that each family member had a chance to go in and see Joyce to say goodbye and everyone took that time, except for Ian. He just could not handle it and held onto his Auntie Jo until we all left the hospital and made our way back to my home. On Wednesday, September 30th at 8:30AM, Joyce Goldstein Poncher passed away.

"Daddy, did you hear me? I'm Pregnant", she repeated once more as I took Lesli's hand and ushered her and Ian out of the Limousine on our way to the Mortuary where the services were going to be held.

"Let's go say goodbye to your mother" I quietly requested.

CHAPTER TW0

Crisis Never Sends a Save-The Date

Over five hundred friends and relatives came to Eden Memorial Park in Granada Hills to say their final goodbyes. I appreciated the support and comforting words of Rabbi Goldring, who was our Rabbi on our Marriage Encounter weekend, yet it did not seem to help the healing process of my pain in the loss of my beloved Joyce. Back in the limousine, I could feel myself becoming overwhelmed.

I asked Ian to close the window but he was somewhere off in space. I reached over to him and touched his knee to give him some sign of assurance that everything was going to be okay, although in my heart I knew it was not. He didn't acknowledge my gesture and just turned on the TV in the back of the limo. I wasn't surprised that he had emotionally stopped communicating. At the hospital, he refused to go in and say goodbye to his mother and would not talk to anyone on how he was feeling. No matter how much anyone asked him, Ian completely shut down. Maybe this was the norm for a thirteen year old boy in this kind of a situation, I just didn't know. I did remember the pain I had in losing my mom but I was in my late twenties. Ian was still a child experiencing this great loss.

Lesli, who was extremely emotional at the hospital and today at the services, was now sitting subdued in the corner of the limo, just gazing out at the crowd. It had been a little over two hours when she first told me that she was pregnant. Did I really hear that or did I just imagine it? I was no closer to confronting her. No closer to storing that fact in my soggy brain.

The limo arrived at the end of our block now jammed with cars trying to find available parking spaces. The sidewalks on both sides of the street had people walking towards the corner, where our house was awaiting the deluge friends and family. People were carrying plants, flowers, pastries and covered foil pans which were soon to overload our freezers. A small table was set at the front door with a pitcher of water and some rolls of paper towels. I watched as people sprinkled their hands with the water and wiped off with the towels, honoring the Jewish tradition of not taking death into the house of mourning.

I briefly glanced to the corner of my driveway where my car no longer was parked. Joyce's car now claimed that spot. The finance company saw fit to reclaim my car after I failed to make the last few payments. Over the past year, I had to close one of my retail shops because the business had dropped excessively. Running back and forth to the hospital, I found myself devoting less and less time to my remaining store. It was also losing business and the area was on a rapid decline due to an increase in crime. It's not that I didn't want to continue payments on my car, but the business soon went into bankruptcy partially due to my accumulating medical bills. I used what little monies that I had left in the bank, to pay for more important things like food and my mortgage.

As the limo made its way into my driveway, Lesli asked "Why is everyone here? Can't they leave us alone? We need some time by ourselves to talk"

For a split second, I wasn't sure what she was referring to. Grief has a way of blocking out reality. If breathing wasn't involuntary, I probably would have forgotten how to do that. I hugged her and gave her a kiss on the cheek while I assured her that we would have plenty of time to talk after the crowds subsided. I had no idea it would take months. Right now, I had to attend to my guests. Isn't that what Joyce would have expected me to do?

Lesli and Ian exited the limo, rushed by me and ran up the front stairs, disappearing into the crowd. I turned to the door and paused briefly, expecting or perhaps hoping to see Joyce come through the archway and into my arms. Once again my eyes filled with tears and I began to sob as I leaned against the wall of the porch. How can I go on living knowing I will never see Joyce again? How will I survive without her? Will I be able to hold myself together? I was terrified of being alone.

Michel was already in the house with my sister-in laws, getting the tables set and ushering in the crowds. Her friend Rick, who I did not recognize at that moment, was making his way up the path and stopped to help me in to the house. I was grateful for his ability to effortlessly move people out of the way as he guided me to my bedroom. I glanced over to see Michel and could sense she was not happy to see Rick. I found out later she had asked him not to show up at my house. But I was soon to discover Rick does what Rick wants. I needed a minute to get myself together before I began to face the huge crowds.

Rick politely maneuvered the guests off my bed and out of the room. As he closed the bedroom door, he asked me if I wanted to be alone. I didn't respond. I peeled off my jacket and loosened my tie, then sat down on the edge of the bed. He asked me if I wanted something to drink. Michel knocked gently on my bedroom door to see if we needed anything.

"I have it all under control" Rick replied as he reached into his coat pocket and pulled out a slender joint. He immediately lit it. "Here, take a hit off of this, it will help to relax you" Rick insisted.

I looked at him like he was out of his mind. He continued to push the joint towards me. I relented and took it from him. It had been years since I smoked pot. I never kept it in the home or near my children. Nevertheless, I took a few deep hits and lay back on the bed while Rick proceeded to finish the bud. In a matter of a few minutes, my head was spinning and I started to giggle uncontrollably. Obviously this was some really good shit Rick had.

For five minutes, this stranger and I laughed at absolutely nothing. We stopped abruptly when Lesli knocked on the door. "Daddy, can I get you something to eat?" she asked.

"Don't come in" I yelled back as I scrambled off the bed and into the bathroom trying to regain my composure. "I will be out in a minute"

Rick just sat there with a big grin on his face. I was beginning to discover he was a very unique character and in the next few weeks he was just what I would need, as my aching depression would bare down on me. I returned from the bathroom with a can of Lysol and began to spray the room as I opened the window to the outside for some fresh air. Back in the bathroom, I threw some cold water onto my face, brushed my hair and rinsed my mouth with Listerine to remove any trace of the pot smoking. I took a quick look into the mirror and let out a long breath. All right Poncher, here goes...

People were beginning to leave, but only to make room for the next group of waiting friends to enter the house. The dining room table was covered with many platters from Brent's and Wieler's Delis while the bar in the downstairs den, was covered with cold drinks and some bottles of liquor. People were milling around in the house and out in the yard, carrying plates of sandwiches, coleslaw, potatoes salad and the likes. The kitchen table was set up with dozens of desserts and the coffee table had two opened boxes of See's Candies, a very popular line of chocolates in California.

My sisters-in-laws, Jo-Ellen and Sydney were busy walking from room to room, picking up half empty plates and cups while other friends were manning the kitchen area. My brother-in-law Howard was playing bartender and unloading some of the ice which my good friend Chad had just returned with from the liquor store. It was wall-to-wall people in every room. Molly, a dear old friend from the North Valley Jewish Community Center who Joyce and I met shortly after we were married, motioned for me to come sit next to her on one of the couches in the living room. We fell into each others arms and both began to cry. People kept coming over to me and after awhile, everyone looked the same. I tried to be strong and even forced a smile now and then,

By 7PM we were down to a small group of about fifty and the noise level became a little more bearable. But now it was time for the night shift to arrive and arrive they did. I was terrified at the thought of being alone as I welcomed the visitors. Everyone walked in with boxes of desserts and trays of food. Where was it all going to go? Seriously, I really didn't care. By this time, the freezer in the kitchen was full and the giant freezer in the garage was reaching capacity. I was curious why people always thought to bring food to a house of mourning. I could think of something that I would rather have and that was Joyce. Now that would trump any deli platter.

Greg and Chad brought in all kinds of paper goods from their catering supply company, which was slowly being used up. The 100-cup coffee pot was on its second go-around. Ian and his cousin Jake finally came out of the Rumpus room/Garage breaking away from their marathon Nintendo game long enough to ask if Jake could spend the night. In a matter of a few minutes the boys were undressed and on Ian's floor of his room in sleeping bags, watching TV. I looked around for Lesli who was no where in sight.

"Does anyone know where Lesli is?" I asked. I heard someone say they saw her leave the house and get into a white van with some boy and drive away. This was the first time it popped into my head that maybe what I heard in the Limo from Lesli was really a fact. I got up from the couch and made my way into Ian's room.

"Do you have any idea where your sister went and with who?" I quizzed Ian.

"She probably went with Billy" Ian casually responded.

"Billy who" I asked.

"I don't know. It's just some guy she has been hanging with lately. I think he is a roadie for some heavy metal bands Lesli has become friends with."

This was not a good time for me to hear all of this nor to deal with it, so I closed Ian's door and returned to my guests wondering if Joyce had any knowledge of this Billy person and what Lesli's relationship was with him?

Finally around 10PM, all that remained in my home besides Ian and Jake were my in-laws plus Rick and Michel who were in the kitchen doing a final clean-up. Aunt Beverly, who was my mom's sister and lived in Palm Springs, was going to stay with us for a few days to help out. She was fast asleep in Lesli's room. Lesli was going to camp out with Ian but since Jake was here, I will have her stay in my room. That is if she returns home tonight. We needed to talk.

My in-laws looked exhausted, so I insisted they leave and take some of the overflow of deli platters and desserts home with them. We wrapped up some care packages and they were on their way. They assured me they would return tomorrow evening before sundown for the evening prayer which was conducted while sitting in my home by Rabbi Goldring earlier that evening. I agreed to one more evening of the prayer session and that would have to accommodate certain relatives.

It was now closing in on 11PM and Michel and Rick were keeping me company until Lesli arrived home. About fifteen minutes later, we heard the key in the door and in strolled Lesli.

"Where have you been?" We all asked.

She casually put her keys into her purse, completely unfazed by the cluster of stern-looking adults staring at her. "I needed some time by myself and couldn't take the crowd so I called Billy to pick me up" Leslie informed us.

"Billy who?" I replied.

"I don't want to talk now Daddy; I'm tired and need to go to bed"

There was a hint of guilt in her voice but I didn't really want to deal with it in front of Michel and Rick. I told her that Jake was sleeping over and she needed to sleep in my room for tonight. She quickly made her exit to avoid any further questioning.

Michel and Rick came in separate cars. I watched as Rick walked Michel to her car and then he came back into the house. Rick was unlike any guy I had ever encountered in my life. He definitely made a tremendous impact, but was it just for the moment? I had no other single friends who were not either engaged or committed to some type of relationship, with the exception of Michael and it was my subconscious goal to scc he and Michel get back together.

This of course was never going to happen and I was soon to learn that Michel's feelings for Rick would overshadow any hopes of reconciliation. It suddenly donned on me that Rick was the guy who I met once when he was with Michel in Vegas, several months ago.

"I'm spending the night on the couch" Rick announced, not even waiting for an invite. I was soon to learn Rick never asks, he just does what ever he says he is going to do. He had a way about him which made me laugh or was it still the effects of the pot.

He took off his shoes and socks and made his way down the hall to the linen closet where he picked up a sheet, pillow and blanket. Don't ask me how he knew where to go for the linens and why he decided to spend the evening at my house. When Joyce had first met Rick, after Michel and Michael had been apart for sometime, she couldn't stop raving about what a nice guy Rick was. I refused to renege on my position that Rick was the reason why Michel and Michael were not getting back together. I was not interested in hearing anything positive about Rick.

Michel and Joyce even went out of their way to force a meeting between Rick and myself. During a weekend vacation in Las Vegas, Rick and Michel flew up without my knowledge. Joyce had me paged in the casino and asked me to meet her in the coffee shop where she was sitting with Michel and Rick. I was pissed off and extremely rude. After all, Michel and Michael were our closest and dearest friends and when they broke up, I was devastated. Rick was a barrier, as far as I was concerned, in getting Michael and Michel to reunite; even though there was no evidence they wanted to ever get back together.

After a few minutes, I excused myself and returned to the casino. Embarrassed, Joyce made all kinds of excuses for my shitty behavior but it was the last time they ever attempted to bring us together. As usual, Joyce was right and it took this terrible tragedy in our lives for me to see

Rick was genuinely sincere. I needed to give him a chance to prove he was indeed a candidate for being a good friend of mine.

As I made my way around the house, closing things up and shutting off many of the lights, a rush of realization once again flooded over me. The kind that makes your heart beat fast and your hands feel clammy. Joyce was never coming back. My life as I knew it, was over. No time machines or miracles to take me back before I lost the one person I loved the most. A lump rose up in my throat as I willed myself not to cry. I leaned against the wall in the cool dark hallway to steady myself. As I stood there with my eyes closed, I wondered how many times I would have to be reminded of this cruel fact. I knew then and still do today; I will never stop loving her.

I went into Ian's room to check on the boys. They were fast asleep. I turned off their TV. As I made my way back to the living room to say goodnight to Rick, I stopped dead in my tracks. There he was in the middle of the living room floor doing push-ups, as if it was the most natural thing in the world. Once again, I started to laugh when I witnessed his bizarre behavior which was becoming an entertaining break to the sadness now surrounding my being.

Back into my bedroom, I found Lesli fast asleep on Joyce's side of our cal-king bed. For a split second, I thought it was Joyce because Lesli was all wrapped up in our blanket with her back to the door. I watched her for a few minutes. We would have to talk in the morning. Now, I also needed to get some sleep. Just kicking off my shoes and emptying my pockets, I laid down on top of the small piece of blanket which Lesli allowed me to have. I was asleep within minutes of my head hitting the pillow.

It was a deep sleep with no dreams until about 4 AM when I suddenly awoke with hunger pains. Perhaps the pot was causing the need for the munchies. I quietly got out of bed and tiptoed past Lesli's room where Aunt Beverly was snoring like a Lumberjack. I checked on the sleeping boys and all was fine there, so I closed their door and continued on to the living room. Rick was supposed to be sleeping but he was sitting up reading the newspaper.

"Can't sleep?' he asked.

I explained that hunger pains had interrupted my sleep. I made my way to the kitchen and began rummaging through all the wrapped packages of deli trying to find something that would satisfy my hunger. Rick joined me in the kitchen.

He took a quick look at all the food and declared, "I want an In-N-Out Burger"

I chuckled at his outlandish request. It was four in the morning, but before I knew it we were cruising down Ventura Boulevard in Rick's powder blue Rolls Royce. Rick had a way about him making it almost impossible to say no to any of his requests. As we pulled into the drive-through, I wondered how practical it would be to become this mans friend. We had nothing in common except for Michel, but I was beginning to suspect that this guy had a good heart.

We finished our food in front of my house and continued sitting there until the sun began to peek over the horizon. I did most of the talking and it was to answer many questions Rick was throwing my way. He wanted to know about how Joyce and I met and all about our life together. How did we meet Michel? Did Joyce ever talk about Michel's feelings for Rick? I was able to get him to disclose a bit of his history, like he was married before and had a son. He didn't seem comfortable speaking about his past so I dropped the questioning. Mostly, he wanted to assure me how much he loved Michel. Finally at 7AM we quietly entered the house.

Ian and Jake were just leaving the kitchen with much the same response as I had. "I don't want deli for breakfast" Ian squawked.   Jake echoed his feelings. Rick volunteered to take them to IHOP. I watched as the three of them pilled into the Rolls Royce and pulled away from the curb.

After a quick shower, I walked down the hall towards my bedroom. Lesli was already dressed and exiting in what seemed to be a planned escape from the house She looked like a streetwalker in her outfit; a pair of super tight Capri's and an equally tight tube top that barely covered well endowed breast of a girl her age. Her eyes were heavily made up with fuchsia eye shadow and gobs of black eyeliner.

"Lesli, go change your clothes now" I demanded.

She looked at me with recrimination. "Why?" she objected. Before I could answer, a white van pulled into our driveway and she headed for the door. I followed after her.

"We have people coming over all day and you need to be here with your brother and me"

She grabbed her bag. "I'm hanging with Billy".

Before I could protest, she ran out the door and jumped into the van. What was going on here? Who was this Billy and who was this little girl who just left my house? I think it's time for me to find out.

Aunt Beverly was in the shower now, so I made my way into Lesli's room to see what I could find. I searched through every drawer in hopes of finding something which might explain this Billy character. I found her Diary under her mattress and took it back to my room so Aunt Beverly would not see how upset I was. Skimming through the pages, I felt guilty invading her privacy. But if she was in trouble, I needed to know how and what this Billy's involvement was in her life. The last few entries were all about Billy.

Cutting school and going with Billy. Told mom that I was sleeping at Roxie's house, but really will be spending the night in the van with Billy.

Boy did she have the wool pulled over our eyes.

I told Billy that I was late with my period. He just laughed and said for me to take care of it and not to mention it again to him

I could feel my pulse racing and the blood rushing to my head. I wanted to put the book down but I needed to know more.

I don't know how I am going to go on without my mom. She was my best friend. How could she leave me when I need her so badly now? Dad wouldn't understand. He will probably disown me, which is why I have to take care of this real fast. I can't take the chance of Billy leaving me. He is the most important person in my life. I love him so much.

I couldn't read anymore. I had a sick feeling in the pit of my stomach as well as the beginnings of a first rate migraine. I closed the Diary, went down the hall and returned it under the mattress, just as I found it. I glanced around her room and suddenly realized that this was no longer the room of my little pumpkin. I didn't recognize the person who lived in this room now, but I guess it was time that I found out who she has become. When did all this start and how could I have been so oblivious to all of this?

CHAPTER THREE

Is Blood Really Thicker Then Water?

For the next two weeks, I never left my house. We
welcomed hundreds of visitors over those fourteen days.
Even two of my brother's ex- wives, but not my brother.
He had been estranged since he divorced his second wife,
several years ago. He did show up at the hospital when
Joyce had her heart attack. He didn't get in to see her but
said he would visit her when she returned home. Five years
later and he still had not shown up nor did he ever call
either one of us to see how Joyce was doing. Jo-Ellen did
call his office and leave a message on the morning of
Joyce's passing. The following day, I received a short note
in my mailbox saying that he would not be able to make the
funeral but would come by after the crowds subsided. I
guess he figured that the crowds never did subside because
he never did come over or call. It's well over thirty years
since we last spoke.

Lesli took full advantage of the fact our home was always filled with guests, by sneaking out of the house right under my nose on a regular basis. My demands she stop seeing this Billy, who I learned was almost eighteen, fell on deaf ears. His white van became an on-going fixture in my driveway and Lesli made no attempt to hide the fact she was leaving without my permission. Obviously he must have known how I felt about him and the whole situation since he had never entered my home nor made any attempt to meet me.

I still had not made the time to sit down with Lesli and discuss what was going on with her and her alleged pregnancy. Or maybe I was relieved there were always people in the house to create a barrier between me and my now sixteen year- old daughter. I just didn't know how to face this significant crisis without Joyce.

I let the kids stay out of school the first week after the funeral. By the second week I insisted they return to as much of a normal life as possible, considering what we were currently going through. I had to start looking for a job as un-employment just didn't cover it for me. Joyce's car needed some repair work and I needed to attend to that right away, since it was now our only means of transportation. I did receive a small check from Social Security, which helped us over the next few weeks and still had about $5000 in my savings account. I certainly did not have to worry about any food shopping, since my freezers were still over flowing with casseroles of every kind. But I had to get a job, well before I drained what little monies I had left for us to live on.

Offers of loans began to pour in from some of my close friends and family members but I was still on shaky ground after beginning to deal with my lack of parenting skills. I was certainly in no frame of mind to take any hand-outs which would only create further damage to my already low sense of self esteem. My bills were barely being paid. Even though I had not missed any payments yet, I was overwhelmed with all the doctor and hospital bills. After the insurance coverage, my unpaid balances were in the neighborhood of two hundred and fifty thousand dollars. I was determined to take care of all those bills no matter how long it took me to pay them off. I wanted to do this as a last effort in taking care of my responsibilities with Joyce. I certainly didn't want to declare a personal bankruptcy after going through one with my businesses.

The only thing I had left was my home and I was not going to lose it under any condition. We loved our home. It was filled with so many happy memories, so to even think about giving it up was more then I could possibly deal with. Of course I did have to contend with Joyce's aunt and uncle, who now held my second mortgage. It was how I financed the purchase of their dress shops which I recently had to close. Now they were hinting I should take a third mortgage out on my house. They mentioned they would be glad to also finance it, so I could remain in my home. That was never an option I would ever consider.

With all I needed to do, I went into an avoidant mode. For the next two weeks, I didn't think about getting a job, although I desperately needed one. I told myself I wanted to get my house in order and get my children back on somewhat of a schedule. I also still had Lesli's pregnancy to deal with.

"We all have to do our part around the house and so everyone will have responsibilities" I told Lesli and Ian.

They agreed and I started by giving them each one chore. Ian was in charge of the trash barrels being taken out to the front of the house every Thursday and returned back every Friday. In addition, he was to empty all the waste baskets in the home. Lesli's chore was to keep the kitchen clean at all times. They would both be expected to keep their rooms clean and to pick up after themselves or their friends in all parts of our home. They had a 9PM curfew during the week and weekend privileges would be discussed as needed.

This all seemed to be a good plan and worked for about two days. Suddenly, it was the day the trash was to be taken out and Ian began a new game with me, called *debate*. He had as many excuses why the trash was not taken out as there were hours in the day. Here's a few; *As soon as we finish dinner, after this TV show, when I finish my homework, after I take a shower* and always finishing with, *I will set my alarm and get up earlier to take them out before the trash men arrive*. It was a battle of the fittest and somehow he always ended up the victor. The kitchen was always a disaster area and Lesli was never around to debate it with me.

Feeling overwhelmed by the kids resistance, the financial issues hanging over my head and my gut wrenching grief, I often found myself just wanting to runaway from reality.

Instead, I called Rick. He was probably the closest to not facing reality as one could get. He had been badgering me about hanging out with him and I constantly turned down his invitations. Though not intended, Rick soon became my escape hatch. When I spent time with him, I was able to briefly set aside my entire crises which were occurring in my life. He made me feel young and free of responsibilities. It was a surreal lifestyle for me.

I knew I could not possibly keep up with Rick nor did I feel I really wanted to. However, I do know that it was Rick's persuasive personality which allowed me to step out of my funk and into a new beginning. It was almost like learning how to walk or talk all over again. I had lost all feelings of self confidence. I felt very isolated and alone yet Rick had a way of making me feel like there was something out there just waiting for me. I was willing to take that chance and so I accepted his friendship, unconditionally. Thus became a rapid rollercoaster ride with him in the driver's seat.

He recently had scored me a year's free pass to work out at his gym. I found out after my first visit, that the gym where he had a membership was owned by some old friends who I went to High School with. They were so happy they could do this for Rick and for me.

To fully describe Rick would take hours but simply put, he was 32 years old with movie star good looks, fine features which included powder blue eyes, premature curly grey hair, an infectious grin, physically fit with a cocky air about him. Going to the gym with Rick was like hanging out with the most popular kid on the block. He knew everyone and the women constantly tripped over one another just to get close to him. I on the other hand did not have that problem. At the gym, I was painfully aware I was back in the single world and felt completely unprepared. In the midst of the hissing machines and the techno music pumping from the sound system, I found myself terribly missing Joyce. I didn't want to start over. I used the gym as the reprieve it was meant to be and did my best to shake off the stress that was constant in my life.

When I would return home, the house was always a mess. My children were entertaining their friends after school. I was soon to discover a great deal of the entertaining was happening while I was away during the day. As I was looking for work or hanging with Rick, they were supposed to be in school. My kids would have no problem getting up on time and leaving for school but most of that time they were not attending all their classes. They didn't have Joyce to check up on them, like I assumed she did, while I was at work.

I started to get the dreaded phone calls from Ian's teachers at his Junior High and from Lesli's teachers at her High School. The weekly and soon daily conferences with one or more of their teachers became a way of life. I discovered Ian was failing most of his classes which he was already repeating from the previous semester. Why was I just finding all this out now?

"We have had many such meetings with your wife, Mr. Poncher" they would tell me.

Why did Joyce feel it was necessary to hide all this from me? I thought they were both doing fine. I knew that Ian and Lesli had transferred a few times to different schools but Joyce told me it was to keep them from being bussed. I was discovering the price I was now paying for not being involved in my children's lives.

Later on, in therapy sessions, I learned perhaps the reason Joyce wanted to keep so many of the problems she was having with the kids from me, was to keep peace in the house for the last few years that she had left. I guess she didn't want to use her declining time, negotiating big family problems. Joyce wanted the kids to remember her as super mom and they certainly did. She made everything okay, no matter how difficult the problems, including all the school issues that I was now being faced with.

Lesli refused to go to school and was facing being expelled. I finally bargained with her and got her into a continuation school, which seemed to pacify her for a time. Ian was going to school everyday but he was disrupting every one of his classes. He refused to do any work and was fighting with both his teachers and some classmates. Once again, I got him transferred to another school and things seemed to settle down for awhile. What I still wasn't dealing with was Lesli's pregnancy. I did make a few attempts to get her to talk about it but it always ended up with her walking away and soon after, slipping out of the house to meet up with Billy.

Help would come in the form of my sister-in-law Sydney. When I first met Sydney and Joyce's older brother, David, there was instant chemistry between Sydney and myself. She is just a few months older then me and very attractive. She had a fantastic, yet very sarcastic sense of humor which I immediately loved about her. There was always a great deal of laughter when the four of us would get together. I felt a unique closeness with Sydney, more so then any other of Joyce's family members, although I did care a great deal for all of her family. Sydney, however, was my friend first and then my sister-in-law. Since I saw no one from my side of the family except for an infrequent visit from Aunt Beverly and a few phone calls from my brother's sons and ex wives, it was Joyce's family who I considered my immediate family. I think I spoke to Sydney more then Joyce did. Sydney and I could spend an hour on the phone and never run out of things to talk about. I always felt good when I got off the phone, after talking to her. Joyce and I saw David and Sydney socially as well as at all the family functions. We even shared our tenth wedding anniversary with them on a Caribbean Cruise. It was our very first trip away from the kids for more then a weekend and perhaps one of the most memorable trips of our lives.

They had two daughters around the same ages as Lesli and Ian. I always had a great deal of respect for Sydney. She was a knowledgeable resource for just about any topic. I knew that my children felt a closeness to all of Joyce's family and perhaps it was why Lesli felt comfortable in contacting Sydney with her pregnancy dilemma. I understand that Lesli was also in contact with Michel who also suggested a trip to Planned Parenthood.

"Dennis, I know all about Lesli's pregnancy. She has been in contact with me. We have an appointment with Planned Parenthood this Friday for her to have the abortion and some much needed counseling", Sydney calmly explained from her end of the phone.

Planned Parenthood? I had a sick feeling in my gut. Why had Sydney taken it upon herself to make these plans without consulting me? Perhaps we were running out of time and options? Why couldn't Lesli discuss this with me? I am her dad. Was I overly concerned what others would think of her? In her Diary, it was apparent that Billy told her to get rid of her pregnancy. This whole thing was so unreal. How much more was I going to be tested with before I completely fell apart? I had to stay strong for these kids but I was starting to feel I was at the end of my rope. I was in constant mental pain with very little relief.

I thanked Sydney for her help with this situation and then immediately called Michel who also recommended the kids and I seek some type of therapy. I was always under the assumption that therapy was for crazy people. At first, I was unwilling to even consider therapy as a possible solution. It seemed like overnight that my family had gone from normal to what I now thought was the highest form of dysfunction. Michel was right when she said I needed help in opening up the gates of communication between me and the kids. Those gates were padlocked and I didn't have the key. Perhaps the therapist could help me to unlock those gates. The Jewish Community Center offered therapy sessions on a sliding scale and since I was unemployed, we could get to see the therapist at a nominal fee.

When Lesli arrived home on that day, she gave me a few moments of her time, before she was out the door and over to Roxie's; my least favorite of all her friends. This was always a bone of contention between us, although I tried to be tolerant as often as I could. Roxie was into heavy metal and was friends with some heavy metal bands who hung around at her home with little or no supervision from her folks. I guess they trusted Roxie and saw no reason to be concerned. Lesli loved to go over to her house because her parents treated her as an adult. I on the other hand, treated her like a sixteen- year- old teenager. How foolish of me to be so old fashion. They had no problems with the way Roxie or Lesli would dress and the gobs of make-up they would both wear. I swear that if I didn't know these two and I passed them on the street, I would say there goes two hookers. Isn't that nice to be able to say that about your daughter? Lesli loved to dress very provocative with outfits much too small for the size she should be wearing. She was built like a girl much older and knew how to flaunt it. Every time she would walk out the front door, I would feel the embarrassment creeping into my body.

Chains, spikes and even an occasional wheel disc would be worn as the necklace part of her outlandish wardrobe. It crossed my mind on more then one occasion, to install a giant magnet at the front doorway. She'd never be able to leave the house.

Sydney called me tell me that Lesli felt more comfortable talking to her about her pregnancy. I was totally confused. I guess I had my head in the sand and didn't really want to deal with the reality of her pregnancy. I wondered if Joyce knew Lesli was sexually active at fifteen or maybe even younger. So many questions and I so needed Joyce's help. How could she leave me at a time like this? I was so ill-prepared for what the kids were continually handing me.

We managed to have a brief conversation when Lesli told me she was prepared mentally to have the abortion. She said Billy was pretty firm about not wanting to have kids and she didn't want to raise the child by herself. What happened to protection? I was both relieved and sick with this whole situation. This is not how it was supposed to be. Before I could fully explore the life-changing situation with her, she bolted out the door and over to Roxies. As what was true in those days, I let her be and let her do what would keep the peace. I think another word for it might have been, enabling. Maybe I was emulating Joyce after all. But Joyce had an excuse, she was dying. What was mine?

The only break that week was a call from Chad. He was calling to see if I had found a job yet. I lied and said that I had some things in the fire right now and was just trying to decide which one to look into. In reality, nothing was looking up and things were getting to be pretty scary for me. I had already sold some of Joyce's jewelry and also sold our beloved ebony black Spinet piano. I was barely staying on top of the bills. Clearly, my story wasn't very convincing and a concerned Chad asked me to come down to his office the next morning. He and his boss Greg, two of my closest and dearest friends since junior high school as well as former roommates, had something they thought might be of interest to me.

"If it's about a loan or even a hand-out, I'm not interested" I said.

"Don't be so eager to jump to conclusions" he said. "I think we have something to offer you which would benefit all of us"

Who was I kidding? I have no prospects and no means of support and how much more could I sell before I had to go on State Aid. It was a few months now since I had been out of work and I saw no one knocking on my door with offers. My hospitalization coverage had run out and let's face it, I needed a job. I did my best to budget myself but that was a new skill for me. Joyce had always taken care of our finances because I was way to lose with our money. I always lived way above our means. I enjoyed being the big shot and was always first to grab the checks when ever we were out with our friends. I wanted to be wealthy and considered myself getting in practice. Joyce had to hold me back many times from reckless spending but I managed to hide some funds so I could have my own little stash. We always seemed to manage but now things were getting really tight and I was struggling to make ends meet. Chad was the first person that I was willing to listen to, regarding my finances and employment. I agreed to come down to their office that afternoon. They had a very successful paper and plastic catering supply business in the East Los Angeles area.

The receptionist let Greg and Chad know I had arrived. She buzzed me in and told me to head down the hall to that last door on the left. I walked into a beautifully decorated office where Chad and Greg were seated on two leather burgundy chairs in front of a humongous desk of Spanish decor. There was also a velvet couch running along one of the walls and a bar on the opposite side. The walls were paneled in a dark wood and the fixtures were recessed just enough to give a balancing of light.

Chad and Greg both got up and gave me a hug and motioned for me to sit down as Greg moved around to the chair behind his desk. I was suddenly aware of perspiration on the nape of my neck. I don't know why I was so nervous. These were two of my oldest and dearest friends. Chad stood up at my wedding and I was his best man at his. The three of us were roommates along with Michael in a house in the Hollywood Hills for a year of wild parties. What a great time it was and what wonderful memories. We were all just out of the Army and one couldn't ask for a more perfect bachelor pad. It sat on its own hill overlooking a big valley. The living room was huge and was surrounded by floor to ceiling beveled glass windows which allowed a fantastic view from all angles. We eventually retired from our partying ways as each of us moved out and got married. First it was Chad, then me and Michael and Greg followed suit, each a year apart. We all remained very close buddies, although our paths began to take different social directions. There should have been no reason to be nervous around these guys.

I guess part of it was my pride and also my defenses were up. I didn't want to be a charity case but I so needed a job. I was ready to take just about anything short of flipping burgers. As they got down to business, it became evident this wasn't just any job they were offering. I would be their General Manager of both the office and the warehouse. They had a successful catering supply business and they both needed to be on the road, to service their many accounts. They needed someone in charge who they could trust. I was so excited I could hardly contain myself. What could be more perfect then to work with two guys I loved more then my own brother? The salary offered was more then I expected and the benefits were better then I could have hoped for. I felt like I was finally getting a break.

"When can you start?' Greg asked
.

I wanted to say today but then I thought about Lesli's pregnancy issues and I needed to be there for her and take care of that first and foremost. I also wanted to get some therapy under our belts so I asked if it was possible to start in the beginning of February. It would give me several weeks to get it all together.

They really wanted me to start sooner but understood and agreed. We shook hands and then after a big bear hug from each, I made my way back home. For once, I was experiencing tears of joy instead of sadness. I couldn't wait to share this with Lesli and Ian.   As I pulled up to the house, I could see Ian, who was on the front lawn area with a few of the kids from the neighborhood. I wasn't thrilled about him spending any time with any of these scum bags.

"Come on into the house Ian, I have something to tell you" I said with forced cheer.

He took his sweet time coming in and he looked like he was half- asleep. If I didn't know better, I would have sworn he was high. Little did I know then, he probably was? The kitchen was a shambles and there were half-full glasses of milk on the dining room table. The oven was still warm and something was spilled on the floor in front of the refrigerator. But I wasn't going to let this domestic failing ruin my good news.

I told Ian about my new job and received a laid back, "Good for you, Dad" as he made his way out the front door to his friends. All I could do was to shake my head.

I proceeded to clean the kitchen, set the table and answer a few of the many calls which were on the answering machine. Everyone was truly excited about my job. I wished that Joyce was there to share in my excitement. I missed her so much. As I continued up the hallway towards my bedroom, my eyes filled up with tears. I wondered when this spontaneous crying would ease up. I lied down on my bed and just let the tears flow. Just then I heard the front door slam and Lesli came running down the hall into my bedroom. She was very excited to hear about my new job. She hugged me and could see I had been crying.

"Are you thinking about mommy?" she asked.

"I miss her so much. Lesli" I told her.

"So do I Daddy, so do I" she repeated. We hugged each other and sobbed in each others arms. It was the first time since the funeral that I felt like I had my baby daughter back.

Like so many of our moments together, this one was also fleeting and before I knew it, Lesli was asking if she could go over to visit at Roxie's house. I let her go; knowing full well she was probably going to see Billy. By this time, I had lost all control on that issue. I found myself hoping after her experience with Planned Parenthood, she might have second thoughts about her abusive so-called boyfriend.

CHAPTER FOUR

"Not Today, Buddy"

Six weeks ago, I was burying my wife and now I was sitting in the sterile waiting room of Planned Parenthood with my pregnant daughter, burying her childhood. I would have lost everything I owned if I had bet that my life would have never gone down this path. Sydney had picked us up for the appointment and now we all sat in silence as I filled out the necessary paperwork and watched people filter in and out. There were at least a dozen other girls in the waiting room, some accompanied by their parents or grandparents, but a few were alone. They looked no different than my Lesli. If we weren't all in this telling place, you would never guess they were in this life-changing dilemma.

One of the interior doors opened to the waiting room and a young girl, who looked no older than 12, walked out. As she went to release her dark brown hair out of its messy ponytail, I noticed a deep purple hickey on her neck. Two of her girlfriends were waiting for her. "Did they give you the pills?" one of the girls inquired. She nodded yes with a big grin, then looked at the other friend and shouted "Party!" I couldn't help staring at the giddy threesome as they made their way out of the clinic. I was floored. Did they really not see the gravity of this situation? I suspected one or all three would find themselves back here within the year. I wondered where their parents were?

As I looked over at Lesli, who had very little color in her face and was shaking, I pulled her close to me. She seemed to finally get it. She had come to talk to me the previous night and I could tell she had been crying. The reality of the situation had finally come down on her, and she wanted to tell me how she found herself in this bind. Considering how tightlipped she had been over the weeks, she was now a fountain of information and I welcomed her openness.

She and Billy had met at the Troubadour, a Heavy Metal Band Concert Club and bar in West Hollywood where Roxie with her fake id worked as a waitress. Lesli would hang out there often and Billy worked there as a sound engineer. According to her, there was an immediate attraction and Lesli's visits to the club increased to three and four times a week. She also shared that over the months, she had come to really love him and she thought he loved her.

When I asked her why he wasn't going to be here with her to support her, a fresh batch of tears started. Billy had stopped calling her since she told him about the abortion. He didn't want any kids and he just wanted the situation taken care of without any fuss, obligation and without him. Lesli was hurt by his indifference and swore she was done with Billy. I hoped that was true. I wanted it to be true. She was so young; she couldn't see how this decision had the potential of haunting her for the rest of her life.

One by one, girls came and went and then finally it was Lesli's turn. As she got up to go, she turned to her aunt and me; her eyes were filled with tears.

"I'm so sorry I had to put you through this." Her voice cracked under the stress she was feeling. I reached for her hand.

"Don't worry, dolly. This will soon be all behind you, like a bad dream," I assured her. I watched her until the door closed behind her stiff frame. I immediately went outside to have a cigarette and wipe my eyes. After I pulled myself together, I went back inside and waited with Sydney.

We waited for a long time. Finally the door that had swallowed up and spit out a dozen girls while we sat there, released my daughter. She forced a smile as she slowly walked over to us.

"I'm okay," she assured us. She was carrying a list of instructions which she showed to Sydney and a supply of birth control pills which she put into her purse. The deal was done and we would all be changed for it.

Life hummed along for the next couple weeks with no major incidents. But I was becoming increasingly concerned about Ian. He was always a loner but coupled with his consistent school issues, I could feel him pulling away and gravitating toward a set of kids who would lead to nothing but trouble. Christmas was just a couple of weeks away, so like any other desperate father, I used the bribe of great gifts to keep everyone on track. Both Ian and Lesli had supplied me with a healthy list of their gift wants and I convinced Rick into going shopping with me. As I tried to get into the festivity of the season, I could feel an increasing dark cloud starting to form over me. This was my first Christmas without Joyce and I could feel the growing knot which had taken up residence in my stomach months ago.

For all his self-centered antics, Rick could also see my anxiety growing. He invited me out on all his adventures, to keep me occupied and to relieve some of the dread I felt about the kids. He and Michel were going through a rough patch, so he was grateful for my company. Like all the other well-meaning people in my life, he was pushing me to consider dating. He had a ton of single friends and was more than ready to fix me up. Dating was the furthest thing from my mind. A personal life at this time seemed so preposterous. I was content with staying home and having company, spending time with my in-laws and of course running around with Rick and Michel. I was scared to even think about actually going out with a date. I knew that I would have to eventually, but the thought made me sick to my stomach.

I had already attempted the dating scene when I had received an invitation to a surprise birthday party that Chad was throwing for his wife Eva. The envelope was addressed to Dennis Poncher and Guest. It was the first piece of mail that declared my new status in the world. It gave me a real empty feeling. With a pep talk from Michel and Rick, who were also invited to the party, I ended up calling an old high school girlfriend and invited her to be my guest. Renee Greenleaf had been one of those flames that flickered out for no reason, but she was a lovely person and someone I felt I could spend a social evening with. I knew she had been divorced for a couple of years and was into dating several guys. She was surprised to hear from me but seemed pleased when I asked her to go with me to the affair.

The party was high class. The food was wonderful and the entertainment upbeat and glamorous. Renee seemed really impressed. It would have been a perfect situation for a first date but I was distracted and moody and spent most of the evening talking with Michel and Rick. At the end of the night, I took her home and walked her to her door. As I went to shake her hand and thank her for coming to the party, she grabbed my face and gave me a big kiss. It threw me. I responded with another kiss, but with my eyes closed, I imagined it was Joyce on the other end. I thanked her for a special evening and told her I would call her again. I never did. I just wasn't ready.

Before I knew it, Christmas vacation was now upon us and the kids were going to be home. We discussed the rules while they were off from school; however it was only a discussion as far as they were concerned. Ian broke every rule during those two weeks. Lesli didn't have much of a chance to break any rules, since she was hardly ever home. I didn't need to be a rocket scientist to realize Billy was back in the picture and sleepovers at Roxie's were morphing into hanging out with him all night.

We did have the family over for Christmas day. I am sure the promise of gifts helped put my kids on their best behavior. But by the time the loot was divided up and the family gone, it was back to business as usual. Ian locked in his room playing his newest video game and Lesli heading out to hang out with Roxie for the evening, which turned into her being gone for three days.

The first day, I called every one of her friends but no one knew where she was or was willing to tell me if they did. No one had Billy's phone number, including Roxie. She swore she had no idea to the whereabouts of Lesli. I even went down to the Troubadour to see if they were there. Everyone there acted like they had never seen either one of them before.

By day two, I was clearly at my wits end. I surely had no way to actively deal with the situation. Roxie spilled the beans and told me that she had spoken to Lesli and I shouldn't worry. What! My sixteen-year-old had been missing for two days, without a word, and I shouldn't be worried?

According to Roxie, Lesli was feeling overwhelmed with all that had happened over the last few weeks and needed a few days away from everyone. I was enraged that she went back to Billy after all she had just gone through with the abortion. She didn't get to make that kind of decision independent of her father, but she obviously thought she did. I was so angry with her; I wanted to wring her neck.

I took my rage and fear out on her bedroom. I went through everything she owned in hopes of finding a clue to where Billy might live and then go get her. Under all the clutter and disarray, I found nothing, even the diary was gone. As I scanned the room, laughing to myself a bit, because I knew she would have no idea I had been through her stuff since everything was so junky. I realized in many ways she was just a regular teenager; the posters on her wall, the fashion magazines stacked up next to her bed, and piles and piles of clothes everywhere. With each passing day, she was becoming less regular and more in danger of going down a path which I couldn't seem to find the right detour.

On day three, Lesli showed up. The blow up was messy and loud. I threatened and slammed doors. She appeared indifferent to my rage. Whatever she felt for Billy was more important than anything in her life and she willing to pay the price with me and deal with my wrath. I grounded her for a month but as soon as I left the house, she was out the door as well. So I began staying home. It was parent imprisonment. We moved through the house silently, prisoner and guard, she refusing to speak to me and me trying to hold on to what was left of my power. But you

96

don't have much power when you are asleep and that's exactly when she would sneak out of the house.

I would wake up to find her room empty and no idea when she had left. I finally gave up and dropped the grounding, providing she would promise not to stay out overnight unless I knew where and for how long. I knew it was a hollow deal but I had no idea what else to do. I was making no gains on the Ian front either. He had been going to therapy for weeks but I wasn't seeing any changes in his attitude or energy level. He had withdrawn completely. We had very little conversation and he stayed in his room most days.

When the New Year rolled in, I called a family meeting. I suggested that we make some resolutions. I promised not to yell and they promised not to give me any reasons to yell. This lasted about one day. They went back to school and calls from their teachers started almost immediately. Ian was suspended the very first week and Lesli was barely going. I was scheduled to start work in a few weeks and knew I had to get these situations well under control.

I turned to my in-laws. They were sympathetic but ultimately critical. Basically, they believed I had brought this all upon myself because I wasn't an active disciplinarian when Joyce was alive. It was true I had let her do all the heavy lifting and now the kids had no reason to listen to me. It hurt to hear the truth. I had no clue how to rein them in. Lesli had finally agreed to go to therapy but after the first session the therapist pulled me into her office.

"Mr. Poncher, I don't recommend you bring Lesli back."

I was slacked jaw as I sat across from this straight shooting young woman. I had chosen her because she had a teenage son and I thought she would be better equipped to help me. She informed me that Lesli was a master manipulator and it would be a waste of time and money to go through this process at this time. Lesli didn't believe what she was doing was wrong and she had no intention of changing her behavior in any concrete or long-lasting ways. The therapist offered to see me, to help me develop more reliable parenting skills and gain more control over the kids. In order for this to happen, I had to make some serious changes within myself and how I had been reacting.

I saw her for a few sessions until it just became too costly for me and past due bills were really beginning to mount.

On Monday of the second week on my new job, I received a call from Lesli's school asking me to come pick her up. They said she was not attending any classes and just sat in front of the school smoking with some other losers who were also not attending school. Of course she was failing all her classes, mainly because she was not going to them. This made no sense to me at all. She was not a dumb kid. She could do the work if she applied herself.

As I drove to the valley, my mind racing as fast as the car, I wondered what I was doing wrong. This would mean more meetings with the school officials and trying to get her into another school. I couldn't take the time off of a new job? I was so angry. I wanted to pick her up and take her anywhere but home. As I pulled up in front of the school, Lesli was about to get into the dreaded white van of Billy's. She knew I was leaving work to come get her and yet she still was willing to leave, not giving me another thought. I jumped out of the car and headed toward the van. Lesli saw me and the look on my face, and quickly jumped out of the front seat of the van. Billy took off like a rocket leaving about twenty feet of rubber.

"How could you be so inconsiderate of me?" I demanded.

She had no answer. She just gathered up her things and got into the back seat of the car. I stormed into the school building and checked her out at the main office. Lesli's counselor was in the office along with the dean. They were very sympathetic to my situation but would not take her back under any condition. What was I to do? They suggested an IEP meeting, which is an Individualized Education Program offered by the schools, where your child would be evaluated by some professionals. The outcome would determine if your child might need special education or even be placed in a residential program out of state until her completion of high school. But the meeting could take weeks to set up and what was I going to do with her until then?

Lesli did not say anything during the short ride back to our house. As I pulled in the driveway I glanced down the street and I could see Billy's van parked behind another car. I was seething. I yelled at Lesli to go in the house and call her boyfriend and tell him to get the fuck off my street. She looked at me like I was crazy. I informed her that I knew he had a phone in the van and he had ten seconds to leave or I was going to deliver the ass kicking that he had long earned. Furious, Lesli ran into the house. I stood on the porch staring down the van. A few moments later, he squealed from the curb and sped passed our house. I stormed into the house and down the hall to Lesli's room.

"You are not to leave this house until I say so. I am placing a restraining order on Billy and if you think you are going to sneak out and meet up with him, you better think again!" My throat burned from all the yelling. Lesli, who was crying, turned her back to me. I grabbed her door and slammed it as hard as I could. In response, a part of the frame splintered off.

Just then the phone rang. "Mr. Poncher, this is Mr. Johnson, the Principal, at Parkman Junior High School."

Suddenly I had a sick feeling in the pit of my stomach. "Is Ian alright?" I asked.

"We called your office and they said you would be at home. We need you to come to school and pick up your son. He has been expelled for fighting and is in possession of Marijuana." I grabbed onto the wall as my legs tried to give out. I started to shake and tears welled up in my eyes. This could not be happening to me. "We had to notify the police and they are also on their way to the school," he continued.

"I'll be right there," I managed to get out and slowly hung up the phone. Lesli was blasting her stereo as I walked into her pigsty of a room. "Turn that off and get into the car, we are going to get Ian. He has just been expelled for possession of drugs." She didn't look surprised.

"It's about time they caught him. He's been using pot for over a year and I have told him that if he didn't stop, I was going to tell you".

"What?" My head felt fuzzy. I couldn't take in any additional information. Lesli knew about this and never said anything to me. I was more then furious.

As I pulled into the school's parking lot, I could see the police car with its lights flashing, parked in the driveway. I had a white-knuckle grip on the steering wheel. I desperately just wanted to keep going but suddenly had visions of my son being led away in handcuffs. I took Lesli with me to the office since I could not trust her to stay in the car alone. I walked into the principal's office where everyone in attendance looked glum. Ian would not make eye contact with me. Mr. Johnson was very understanding as was Officer Thomas of the West Valley Division. They had decided not to press charges since it was his first offense and suggested that I get help, immediately.

Ian gathered up his things from his locker and returned all his books to the office. He started to cry as he approached me but I was far from being in a sympathetic mood.

"Get in the car with your sister," I barked.

Ian sobbed as Lesli tried to comfort him. As I listened to their conversation in the backseat, I was surprised to hear Lesli express her authentic disdain for drugs. There went my theory that drugs were at the center of her acting out. We pulled into the driveway and I was first to the door.

 "Stay out here." I demanded, as I slammed the door behind me, leaving the kids on the porch. As I paced in the living room, I could see them settle down on the front steps. They looked scared, a fact that made me feel like I had a little bit of power in the situation. But by now, I knew the feeling was a fleeting victory and I was going to be back on this crisis wheel within days.

 I went into the bedroom and sat on the edge of the bed and put my head in my hands. The tears which had been threatening to come all day, finally spilled down my tense face. I was in full despair when the phone rang. "Dennis?" my brother-in-law Howard was on the other end. "What happened? I just called your office and they said you had to go to Lesli's school for some problem."

 I told him the whole story with both kids. I could barely get the words out. My whole body was shaking. As I spoke, I reached into the drawer on Joyce's side of the bed and found her half-full bottle of Valium. I set it on the nightstand as I listened to my brother-in-law. He was not as sympathetic as I would have liked him to be. He finished the conversation by letting me know my kids were out of control because they were spoiled and I had a hand in that. I knew he was right but it was not what I needed to hear at that moment. I mumbled a goodbye and set the phone back on its cradle.

Dejected, I just stared at if for a while. I could feel myself going over the edge. The sum of my life was passing through my head. What was there left to live for? These kids didn't need me. I was a lousy father and didn't know how to parent them. They would be better off living with my in-laws or even in foster homes. I could not take anymore of this. I wanted to be with Joyce. I picked up the bottle of Valium and sat at my desk. The fuzziness in my head got louder and I couldn't stop crying. I pulled a piece of paper off the notepad and grabbed a pen. I neatly printed Ian and Lesli's names at the top of the paper. What do you tell your kids in a suicide note? That you loved them but you could no longer go on being their father? That you had lost all credibility and power and could no longer endure the pain?

I barely finished the first line before the phone rang again. I refused to answer it. Whatever was going on, someone else could take care of it. As I continued to write, the phone continued to ring. The caller never left a message, hanging up when the machine picked up, then calling right back. After the third round of rings, I snatched up the phone. I listened to see who was on the other end before I spoke. I figured if it was anyone I didn't want to hear from, I would just hang it up and then take the phone off the hook. I was hoping it was Billy calling for Lesli so I could have one last chance to threaten him.

"Poncher, are you there? Answer me you dick head," Rick yelled.

I broke my silence. I could barely get out the story of my day. I hinted at the suicide note. I knew he could hear the desperation in my voice.   To this day, I will never forget the story that followed. Rick was in the wholesale manufacturing of maternity outfits for the big chain department stores. His business was very successful, allowing Rick the lifestyle that he was accustomed to. It was around the 10th of February and he was bogged down at the warehouse with huge back orders for a particular cotton pantsuit design for numerous Valentine orders.

"You think you have problems, I was just delivered five hundred bolts of material to do a rush job for Valentine's Day for one of my biggest chains. The fucking factory sent me blue hearts instead of red! What the fuck was I going to do with five hundred bolts of blue hearts?" he yelled.

I couldn't believe my ears, I was pouring out my guts to him, ready to take my life and he was comparing it with blue hearts instead of red. It was the first time I had cracked a smile during this whole mess. He kept me on the phone for a long time. Suddenly, with receiver in hand, I looked up and Rick was standing in the doorway of my bedroom. He had been on his car phone, driving toward my house, the entire time. I started to cry uncontrollably. Shame and relief rushed over me. I was a mess. Rick took the receiver from my hand and hung up the phone.

He picked up the note that I had been writing and began to read what I had started. He crumpled it up tossed it in the wastebasket and said to me, "Not today, buddy."

Michel arrived shortly thereafter with pizza for everyone. Rick had told Lesli to call her and tell her to get over here and bring pizzas. The kids followed closely behind Michel into the house. Eating pizza then was not on my agenda. I knew I had a compelling need to share with Lesli and Ian what had been in my mind before Rick arrived.

I ushered the kids into Ian's room where we all three sat on the floor while I proceeded to tell them what I was about to do before Rick came into my room. They both got hysterical crying and Ian was shaking uncontrollable. I guess I was too. They pleaded with me to give them another chance and made promises to change. They told me how much they loved and needed me and I am sure it was what I needed to hear. Yes, I will have to deal with the many mistakes I have made in the past but will I have any support? Will this journey provide me with a light at the end of the tunnel without it always being a train? I am truly sorry but I cannot change what has happened in the past. I must learn to focus on the future. I need to be strong for Lesli and Ian and yet sensitive to their feelings and needs. I must always be available to them and the real changes must start with me. I must not ever entertain the thought of giving up even though I have found myself giving in many times.

After numerous hugs and kisses and assurance from me that things were going to be okay, we joined Michel and Rick for some pizza. I thanked Rick and Michel for their support that evening and watched from the front porch as they each drove away. I continued to sit there on the steps for what seemed like hours, just listening to the silence. I wanted to disappear into the immense darkness of the sky. I knew that I could not runaway from my responsibilities as a parent but what I didn't know was how long I could endure the stress. The front door opened and Lesli inquired with a concerned tone

"Daddy, are you alright?"

"You and your brother get ready for bed and I will be in, in a few minutes." I softly replied.

She silently shut the door, allowing me a few more moments of self pity before I went into the house to say goodnight to them. I really would have rather got into my car and drove as far away from my life as possible. I wiped away the tears which were already flowing and gathered my composure, as I entered the house.

CHAPTER FIVE

Tough Love

After my emotional break down that evening, Michel had asked me to check out Tough Love; a parent support group she thought might help me and the kids. In doing some research on Tough Love, I found it was created by two Therapists by the name of Phyllis and David York, somewhere in Pennsylvania. They started the group a couple of years ago and it was rapidly growing throughout the country. I had heard about the 12 step programs but this was completely new for me. I was at such a low point at this time in my life that I was open to almost anything. Self-help groups were beginning to pop up all over the country.

Initially, I was reluctant to go. Therapy wasn't working so what would be the point of talking to parents who were having the same issues as me? But after the kids got over the shock of me contemplating suicide, they returned to their shitty behavior. Almost overnight, the hysterical kids who held on to me declaring they loved me and were going to change, went right back to acting out and disobeying the house rules as if nothing had happened. They were selfish and inconsiderate, leading me to believe they really didn't care about me. I was fed up and through with begging their schools to take them back. I was done with roaming the streets looking for Lesli. I was tired of it all.

The day that I called about the Tough Love parent support group was over four months after Joyce had died. I was delighted to hear their meeting was that very same evening. I was feeling so isolated and powerless. The kids were running the show and I was just there to pay the bills.

The meeting was called for 7PM and was in the north end of the valley. I pulled up in front of a large apartment complex and got a parking space right in front. I had never been to this part of the valley before but the area seemed safe and the building well lit. It was only 6:30 PM and I didn't want to go in too early. I was normally not a shy person but this situation seemed totally out of my comfort zone. The meeting was to be held in the recreation room of the organizer's building. I watched as people began to arrive. It seemed as if there were twice as many single people going in and most were women. A few couples also arrived and I was glad to see a few men go in as I didn't want to be the only father there. Around 6:50 PM I ventured out of the car with my little notebook in hand and made it up the sidewalk. As soon as I pressed the buzzer to #204, a deep, harsh voice asked me my name. This was like a low-tech game of I Spy. After giving a satisfactory answer I was buzzed in.

As I opened the door, a young woman hollered for me to hold the door open. "Are you going to the parenting meeting?' she asked. I nodded. "I haven't seen you here before."

"It's my first time" I responded.

"Oh, you are going to love it." She gave me a warm smile.

To look at this woman who didn't seem a day over 30, with her slender figure, friendly hazel eyes and light brown wavy shoulder length hair, you would wonder what she was doing here. She didn't seem to have a care in the world. Very classy and pulled together. She was dressed as if she was just getting home from an executive job. I glanced over to her left hand to see if she was wearing a wedding band and sure enough, there it was. This had become a natural instinct for me in the past few weeks. I began to realize that this was the first time I was checking other women out. Was I looking for a distraction or could I ever be interested in a relationship again, someday?

"First name only," the short brunette woman overseeing the sign-in table instructed.

I gave her a quick smile as I scribbled my name on a name tag and took the information form. I found a seat situated in the center of the room near a few other parents who were also there for the first time. I looked over the form and began filling it out. It asked for the basic identifying information and inquired how I had found out about the group. It then began to ask some questions about my children and what was going on in our lives. I started to check off the various topics I needed to deal with. The list was long and my checkmarks were many. I felt discouraged but not yet defeated.

As I completed the form, the group leader Claire, as her name tag read, a stern-looking blonde woman asked everyone to take their seats. Claire was probably in her mid forties, but her clothing choice was matronly and made her seem a lot older. As the 25 or so parents found their seats, I wondered if any of them were going through the same problems that I was facing. I really hoped this meeting wasn't about parents who couldn't get their kids to make their beds. My challenges were a little more complicated than that.

Surprisingly, the meeting was very structured. They took care of some "housekeeping" items at the very beginning and made a few general announcements. Folks seemed to know exactly what was expected of them. Well, except for us newbie's. After about ten minutes, Claire asked everyone to go to their small groups except for the parents who were there for the first time. Most of the parents got up and took their chairs and proceeded to three of the four corners of the room, forming small circles with their chairs.

I saw my new friend heading towards her small group. She glanced over to me and mouthed "Good luck."

I managed a smile back. Remaining in the chairs around me were four other parents, all who seemed to be around my age. There was one couple, two single moms and myself. Claire, who clearly had a strong personality and seemed to know a lot about troubled teens, was in charge of the new parent orientation. She asked that we take our chairs to the remaining empty corner of the room and form a small circle.

Claire sat down and introduced herself. She shared that this group called Panorama City Parents Support Group practicing Tough Love was an auxiliary of a larger national parent group which had been started by a couple on the east coast. She became involved with the group because of her teenage daughter. She had become hard to manage and her behavior disrupted the family in major ways. I immediately identified with her. Claire was adamant that being a part of this parent support group had saved her life and in turn saved that of her daughters. Ultimately, the way she re-learned to parent, forced her daughter to start making some positive choices. She had been involved with the group for two years. Two years? I had no intention of dealing with my kids' crap for another week, much less two years. I couldn't imagine that.

116

"Why are you here?" Claire asked the plump, sad-looking woman sitting to her right.

The woman started to cry almost immediately. She was a single mother with two children. Her thirteen-year-old son was out of control. He was using drugs, skipping school, and his violent behavior was escalating. He had recently trashed their house and she didn't know what to do. As she poured out her story, I marveled how honest she was with total strangers. Didn't she worry if we were judging her? I know I was worried that I would be judged. I guess, what was the point of that? I was already beginning to feel better. If we were sitting in the group with her, I felt it meant we were in the same boat. Claire handed her a tissue as she sobbed quietly.

As I listened, I began to realize, I am not alone anymore. Next up was the only couple in the group. They seemed oddly mismatched: he red-faced and burly, she mousy and soft spoken. They had four children and were struggling with a son who was a chronic runaway. This time, he had been gone for two weeks and they had no idea where he was. The mother started to cry when her husband shared he was glad that their son was gone because he was tired of all the headaches. I don't know if I believed him when he said he didn't care if his kid ever came back, but I understood the frustration. I felt the same way myself. The mother, on the other hand, was a basket case. She had been searching everywhere and contacted everyone that her son knew. You could see that they were miles apart in their thinking and had trouble communicating with one another. Watching them, I couldn't help wondering how Joyce and I would have been in this group. While I'm a joiner, I think she may have rejected coming to a meeting like this. I suspected she would have rather suffered in silence than find herself in this room of desperate parents, feeling like failures. But I am a desperate parent and I do feel like a failure.

The other single mother was strident in her speech, bubbling over with anger. Her 15-year-old daughter was pregnant and wanted to keep the baby. What was it with these girls racing into adulthood? Why didn't they understand that they were breaking their parents' heart? They were babies themselves. There was no way they were ready to take care of another human being. This young girl was under the delusion that the father of the child was going to marry her and they were going to be a family.

Lesli and I hadn't really talked about her pregnancy but I hoped she wasn't walking around with the same fantasy. I wondered what I would have done if Lesli wanted to keep the baby. I surely wasn't ready to be a grandfather and the thought of raising another child, terrified me.

Claire was a good listener. She was very careful not to offer any solutions and just let each parent tell their story. Allowing us to purge all our frustrations and disappointments seemed to be part of the process. But I could feel my anxiety building. I suspect it was the reason I was more candid than I had planned on being when it was my turn to share. I really did feel like I didn't love my kids anymore. I definitely felt like they didn't love me and didn't care that I was struggling to keep everything afloat. I was surprised to hear myself blaming Joyce for all that was going on. I felt set up. She didn't tell me the kids were out of control. How dare she hide all this from me and then leave me. By the time I was finished, my face was flushed and wet and my stomach was tight with anger. I was there for answers not therapy. I wanted to be told how to fix my kids so I could get out of the hell that I was currently in. Surely I felt as if I was speaking for everyone in the group. I took a couple deeps breaths as the group sat silently.

Claire let the silence hang over us for a bit. When she did speak, she looked at me directly. "I want you all to promise to give this situation you are having with your kids, six weeks of meetings before you throw your hands up." Six weeks! That was an eternity. "In six weeks you will have a better understanding of how to handle your child's behavior. You have lost control and we are going to help you get it back."

The looks on the faces of my fellow parents said they wanted to believe her. I wanted to believe her most of all. I guess if I managed to survive this long, I could hold out a little longer.

"What happens at the end of the six weeks if nothing changes, do you refund my misery?" I asked. I got a few chuckles with that one and I think it relaxed most of the tension we were all witnessing.

By the time the small group session was wrapping up, Claire had given us some concrete action steps to take until the next meeting. I was busily writing everything down in a notepad which I had brought with me. She reminded us how we had been reacting to our children's behavior and we had to start being proactive. She also suggested we all purchase the support group manual and start reading it. I purchased a book for ten dollars which turned out to be one of the best investments I have ever made.

As the other small groups ended, everyone began heading toward the center of the room. A tall skinny woman took my hand and gestured for me to take the hand of the other person standing on the other side of me. Within a few seconds, all 25 parents stood in a large circle. Claire thanked everyone for being there and reminded us what was said in our groups was confidential. It was important we felt safe coming here and what was shared here wouldn't be repeated outside of the meetings. As I looked around the room of parents, I could feel myself relaxing for the first time all evening. These people understood what I was going through. They knew how much I loved my kids and how hard I was trying to make things right. Maybe I could find some real answers here.

Claire began reciting what I would learn was the Serenity Prayer, said in all twelve step programs. Most of the parents joined her. I had never heard the prayer before but as I listened to the words, they really hit home.

"God grant me the serenity to accept the things I cannot change, the courage to change the things I can and the wisdom to know the difference"

The Serenity prayer would be my salvation. I was on the road to recovery and there was finally a dim light at the end of the tunnel that perhaps this time was not a train.

As the parents began filtering out of the recreation room, I found Claire and thanked her for providing a place for us to come to and I promised to be back the following week. She let me know there was another meeting the following evening in Los Angeles, if I felt like I needed additional support before her next meeting. I shook hands with a few of the veterans, as they called themselves, and gave a hug to the mother of the pregnant daughter. She asked me for my phone number in case she needed to talk to someone during the week. I didn't know how much help I could be but I gave her my number. Little did I know then, in just a few weeks I would be opening a new location in the West

Valley and my number would be on everyone's' hot line lists?

As I walked down the path towards the front gate, the good looking brunette who I walked in with again greeted me. "So, how did it go in there?" she inquired.

"It was awesome "I replied.

She told me that her name was Dee and she lived in Canoga Park. We didn't live too far apart so we decided to car pool next week. It felt good to be making such easy connections. I had been feeling so adrift over the last few weeks. She made me promise to call her once during the week just to tell her how things were going. It sounded like a helpful plan as she handed me a card with her phone number. I walked her to her car, thanked her again for her support and went to my car.

It was like someone took a load of bricks I had been carrying on my back and gave each person I spoke with, one of the bricks to help ease my pain and share in my crisis. I felt a complete tone of relief. No, I wasn't walking away with all the answers to my problems. But I was leaving with an element of hope, which I had lost. Here was a group of strangers who seemed honestly sincere in guiding me on a path which appeared to have some solutions, unknown to me at the time. I no longer felt alone in a dark room with no way out. I heard other parents who were suffering with the same or similar problems. The dark place where I was caught became a little brighter with each new sharing. Was God finally granting me some serenity? Could I now be a part of the solution rather then a major part of the problem?

The meeting let out close to ten and by the time I got home, I would need to be up in five hours. It had been a very successful night for me and worth the lost hours of sleep. I quietly opened the front door and proceeded down the hall. The house was still. Ian's room was open and I could see him fast asleep. I continued on down the hall to Lesli's room. Her door was closed so I gently opened it and the hallway light dimly cast a glimmer on her bed. I could see the outline of her body all covered up with the comforter. I let out a long breath as I closed her door. My kids were the most important part of my life and we were going to make it through this crisis.

124

I made my way to my room and started getting ready for bed. As I stood in front of the bathroom mirror brushing my teeth, I realized my stomach was in a tight ball. I had started carrying my stress in my stomach over the last couple months but this tightness felt like a nagging pain. Something just didn't feel right. I put down the toothbrush, walking briskly down the hall and back to Lesli's room. Without a second thought, I turned on the light and when no movement came from the bed, I pulled the comforter back. Three pillows were in the center of the bed where Lesli was supposed to be. Where the hell was she?

As I felt my anger rising up, I took a deep breath. I hadn't expected so soon to use one of the tactics I had heard earlier in the evening, but Lesli was determined to do what she wanted to. I made it back to my room and pulled on my pants. I took another deep breath as I quickly put on my sweater. I had to remember whatever action I took, it had to be a proactive one.

I pulled up in front of the West Valley Police Department and I still couldn't believe I was doing this. I was going to file a runaway report. I was going to hold her accountable for her behavior. As I walked into the waiting area of the station, I was surprised to find it buzzing with activity. It was almost midnight and at least a dozen people were waiting to be seen. Initially, the police officer behind the counter did not want to take the runaway report. She had not been gone the requisite 24 hours and the officer was convinced she was just out with friends and had lost track of time. But I stood my ground and demanded he allowed me to file the report. I was getting good at letting people see my desperation as it related to my kids. As I filled out the report, they informed me she would be detained and brought home; if they found her. I was tempted to tell them to keep her, but I still had some hope in me. Maybe this would shake her up and perhaps this would get her attention. I left a copy of a picture of her and asked for them to call me as soon as they had any word about her status. I could tell the officer felt really bad for me. This was a sad situation.

It was almost 2:00 AM before I made it back home. I would need to be back up in three hours. It seemed silly to get undressed. I kicked off my shoes and I grabbed the support group manual I had purchased earlier in the

126

evening and settled into the chair at my desk. Whatever sage advice they had between these pages, I needed every ounce.

As I continued page by page, I began to see many of my shortcomings as a father. Perhaps these feelings of guilt would prevent me from taking positive actions for the changes needed to make. I desperately needed the support this group seemed to offer. I am prepared to make the changes which will allow them to change. I hope Lesli and Ian will understand I am doing this **because I love them.**

The dark clouds above my head finally had a silver lining with a glimpse of sun shining through. I had entered this new village and could feel the support all around me. I was finally networking with others who I could relate to and I no longer felt the isolation of my crisis situation.

CHAPTER SIX

Consequences?

As I pulled up to my house the following afternoon, I could see the note which I had left Lesli, still pinned on the front door. It was not a good sign. I had written the note before I left the house that morning, explaining to Lesli that I had reported her to the police as a runaway and she needed to go to the station to rescind the report before she could come back into our house. I had also delayed my earlier departure in order to have a locksmith come and change all our door locks.

When I handed Ian his new keys, he looked confused. "Dad, what are you doing?

"Only the people who follow the rules of this house will have keys to it."

"So Lesli can't live here anymore?"

"I'll see you tonight. No one in the house while I'm at work and if your sister calls or comes home, be sure she sees the note I left and do not let her in the house or give her any of her things. If you do, you will suffer similar consequences", I said with some conviction.

I was shocked for the first time on how calm I was in the face of all the shit I was experiencing. What was the point of being in crisis when Lesli was off having a good time and not giving my feelings a second thought? It was almost as if I felt like I was in complete control. I had taken an action instead of reacting. It was the mantra of the support group. I was entertaining the new idea that I didn't have to be the victim

But my early morning calm was giving way to worry; the note lay undisturbed on the front door. As I made my way up on the porch, I noticed that Ian was sitting there with two of the neighborhood scum buckets, as I referred to them.

"Ian, we are leaving in two minutes." I barely gave them a second look.

"Where are we going?"

"Two minutes, Ian, we are leaving for dinner." I went into the house leaving Ian giving his company a shrug of his shoulders, as he got up.

We had finally run out of casseroles and I didn't feel like cooking. Now that I was working, I could afford to take us to dinner. As we sat across from each other at Brent's Deli, Ian expressed how upset he was that I had reported Lesli to the police as a runaway.

"She is probably at Roxie's or with Billy," he said.

"She is out without my permission which is no longer acceptable behavior." Ian was taken aback by my firm tone.

We finished our dinner in silence. When we returned home, the note was *still* hanging on the door. As I made it to my room, Ian went into his and got on his phone. I wondered for a moment if he was calling Lesli to let her know what was going on. It didn't matter; I was not changing my mind.

130

In my room, I got undressed and put on my robe. I wanted to finish reading the literature I had picked up from the information table at the group. My previous late night reading had really opened my eyes. The parent handbook, written by the founders, was clear and direct about my role as the adult in Lesli and Ian's lives. You create the boundaries. You give the consequences. You set the rules. Easier said then done.

As I made my way through the manual, I was embarrassed to recognize how much I hadn't shouldered my share of the parenting duties when Joyce was alive. My family had always been the outward manifestation of my success. I was only interested in the perfect version of us. I left it up to my wife and the nanny to keep the kids in line and deal with the messiness which came with raising them. When the kids were good, I wanted them around. When they were being rotten, I wanted nothing to do with them. But now I didn't have those choices.

Last night, I called Dee from the group to get support about my decision of involving the police and changing the locks. During our hour-long conversation, I couldn't believe I was telling a virtual stranger all the chaos and upheaval I had been dealing with since Joyce died. Dee was a great listener. She didn't judge me and encouraged me to take whatever action that would restore the balance in my home. It felt good to have someone to talk with about all my fears and conflicted feelings. Little did I know at this time, Dee would play a major role in my life with Tough Love and the transition to Because I Love You (B.I.L.Y.). She was very committed to the organization and taught me so much in such a short period of time. Somehow I knew with her as a team player, we would successfully venture in a location closer to our homes. She was wise and compassionate, which drew me and many others into this new web or core group as I called it. We had a great deal in common. We both had two teens out of control. Joyce had died from complications with Juvenile Diabetes and her husband Cary was currently experiencing similar symptoms in his fight with the same dreaded disease.

Dee and I bonded quickly, both through our involvement in the organization and on a social level. Dee and Cary had a vacation home in Lake Arrowhead which was a popular mountain resort about an hours drive from our homes. It soon became a frequent retreat for many of our Tough Love families, skiing in the winter snow and boating on the lake in the summer heat. Taking our kids with us also allowed them to bond with the other teens whose parents were attending the groups. Cary's health issues worsened and it became more difficult for him to make the trips.

I really hadn't thought about opening a new location yet but apparently Dee had this in mind for some time now. In such a short period of time, we formed a core group of close friends who lived in the west end of the valley, where Dee and I resided.

As I flipped through the resource material, taking notes in preparation for next week's meeting, the phone rang. I glanced at the clock on the nightstand. It was almost nine o'clock and I contemplated letting the call go to voice mail. As grateful as I was to the friends who continued to call and check in on us, responding to dozens of messages at the end of a long workday was becoming less appealing and over the last couple weeks it had become a chore.

The phone stopped ringing just as I reached for it. A couple seconds later, Ian knocked at my door.

"Dad, the phone's for you." As I reached over to pick it up, I knew exactly who was going to be on the other end.

"Hi daddy," She cheerfully greeted me. I took a deep breath. At least she was in one piece.

"Lesli, where are you?"

"I'm safe".

"That is not what I asked you. Where are you?" I could feel my calmness slowly slipping away and rage taking its place. This child was as inconsiderate as they came.

"Daddy, I need to think things out. I need a break from…you."

The rage began washing over me like high tide. She was the one creating all the chaos and stress and *she* needed a break? "Tell you what Lesli, when you finish taking your little vacation and before you can come back into my house, make sure you stop by West Valley Police Department and attend to that outstanding runaway report."

134

"What! You called the police on me?"

"That is what you do when you don't know where your sixteen-year-old daughter is and you're pretty sure she is laid up with some creep." My voice was steely and cold.

"This is what I'm talking about! You want to make a big deal about everything!"

I wanted to reach through the phone and strangle her. I took two deep breaths. "If you want to come back to my house, you will have to go to the police station and rescind the report."

"Dad, you already said--"I slammed the phone down before she could finish.

The rage had taken over my body as I stood at the foot of the bed shaking. I reached for the parent manual in hopes it would calm me but I wanted to break something or shred something. I stormed out of my room and down the hall. Ian's door was closed and I pushed it open violently. He was propped up on his bed watching television. I knew I looked like a crazy man by the way his eyes stretched wide at the sight of me.

"You are not to relay anymore messages to your sister. Do you hear me?"

"Dad, I was just—"

"Do you hear me?"

"Yes," Ian meekly replied.

Without another word, I made my way to Lesli's room. The place was a landfill. Clothes piled up in every corner of the room. Her desk buried under paper and shoes and plates. I rummaged through her drawers determined to find a clue where she was. She was not going to come and go as she pleased. I was in charge here. I ripped out each dresser drawer allowing them to fall noisily to the junky floor. How dare she treat her clothes with such disregard? I worked hard to make sure she and her brother had what they needed and this was how they thanked me?

When it was clear that I was not going to find any damning evidence of her whereabouts, I scooped up her clothes off the floor by the armload. I muttered as I made my way to the laundry room. *"I am in charge here."*

It took me two days to wash all her laundry and hang everything up neatly in her closet. I knew I should have left it for her to take care of but I couldn't take the mess and when she returned home I was going to demand she keep her room in the state in which she found it.

The next few days went by without much crisis. Ian mainly stayed in his room, out of my way, convinced I had lost my mind. I imagined it was just a matter of time before he had to call one of his uncles to come get me and take me to the psych. hospital.

When I arrived at the office the next morning, Sal, whose desk was next to mine, was making coffee in the kitchen. He reminded me of a short, thin Jim Belushi from Saturday Night Live. He was a sharp dresser and charmed everyone in the office. I appreciated his humor and compassion. Even though he was a lot younger than me, I found it very easy to talk to him and often found myself unloading my

137

problems on him. Although we were from different cultures, we shared many of he same beliefs. Sal and I had an immediate bonding that would last a lifetime.

With all that was going on in my life. I was grateful for my new job. Not just the paycheck which came with it but also how I felt competent at work. Having a crew that trusted my judgment and depended on my skills was a reprieve from the self-doubt and powerlessness that was a part of my personal life. My in-laws had done a fabulous job of convincing me of my failings as a parent, starting well before I lost Joyce. They had very little sympathy for my current situation.

At 3:30 PM, my phone rang on my desk. I was expecting to hear Ian on the other end reporting he was home from school. It was my only directive he seemed able to follow through with, on a regular basis.

"Daddy can I come home?" a sobbing Lesli was on the other end. I let out a long sigh. "I promise I'll do what you want me to do. "A little laugh escaped my tight throat. "I promise."

138

There was no way I was going to say no. I missed her and wanted her back in our house, where she belonged. "Lesli, I want you back at the house by seven. Not a minute later. We have a lot to talk about."

"I'll be there. I love you, Daddy."

"I love you, too." I let out a long breath as I hung up the phone. I wanted to believe this could be a new beginning for us.

Before I left my office, I called the police to let them know that she was coming back and to cancel the runaway report. I knew it wasn't the Tough Love procedure I had heard at group but I didn't care. I wanted Lesli home. We sat down to dinner together that night and nothing was mentioned about Lesli's whereabouts for the past few days. I told the kids I was attending a parent's support group on Tuesday nights to learn some new skills. There was going to be some major changes around here.

"Is that where you got the idea of reporting me as a runaway?" Lesli asked.

"Yes and this is only the beginning of many changes. It's time for me to get back in control," I replied.

"Well I think it's a stupid idea to go to a bunch of strangers for advice," she added. She was also unhappy that I cleaned up her room. She did not want me snooping around her personal stuff. I told her if she would keep her room neat, I would have no reason to go in there.

"Lesli, I expect that your room stays clean." She responded to my foreign request with a smirk. "If I have to clean it again, there will be consequences."

Consequences, a new word I had heard used quite often at group the previous week. By the time the kids went to sleep that night, Lesli's room already had two or three changes of clothes strewn about her floor. I decided not to make an issue of it. I was going to group the next day and I'm sure the other parents would have plenty of suggestions on how to handle a sloppy daughter. Before I went to bed, I made a quick list of all the issues which had come up over the week and everything I wanted to discuss at group. I couldn't wait to get there. Dee and I had decided to carpool and I was scheduled to pick her up at 6:15PM

My day at work went well with no calls concerning either of the kids which I considered a good day. When I called to check in on them and informed them I was going to my meeting, Ian answered. He was just leaving to go to a friend's house and Lesli was in her room with Roxie. As I listened to him rattle on, I realized I didn't believe half of what he was saying. I had lost all forms of trust.

I got to Dee's house at the prescribed time and she was waiting in front of her home as she promised. During our thirty-minute drive, I discovered we had a lot in common. Her two sons were totally out of control. Until she started coming to the group, she was at her wits end. She was the primary disciplinarian because her husband's illness was so debilitating and he just didn't have the energy to get involved with all the chaos the boys generated in their home. It sounded like he was experiencing a lot of the symptoms Joyce had suffered, towards the end. I wondered if Dee knew she was about to lose him? My heart went out to this nice lady who certainly did not deserve all this pain.

We arrived at the group shortly before seven, just enough time to sign in and have a quick cup of coffee. We found some seats and waited for Claire to get the meeting started.

I was assigned to Sue's group. She was a very nurturing young mom who had been involved with the group for over a year. She had an eleven-year-old son who she was helping to get his life back on track. I took my chair and headed towards Sue's group in one of the corners of the recreation room. I was pleasantly surprised to see Dee heading in the same direction. There were seven other parents sitting in our circle. There was a young couple, another single father, three single moms and one married lady without her husband.

Sue had one ground rule: we were only going to review situations that occurred in the past week. She didn't want us to get bogged down on the family history all the way back to the pabulum days. We were there to develop solutions for current challenges. As the group unfolded, over and over again, each parent shared about the out of control children who had taken over their lives. Home was no longer peaceful. Chaos and pain were what they woke up to every day. She kept the group moving. She didn't get to me until after the break. By that time, I felt well at ease and certainly had no more feelings of isolation. Up until a week ago, I thought I was the only parent in the San Fernando Valley who was having problems. It was a very lonely feeling I wasn't willing to share with my family or my friends, yet here I couldn't wait to talk.

I told Sue and the group about my week. I really wanted to talk about more than the week but she was very good in keeping our topics within the structure. Sue and a couple of the veteran parents commended me on the actions I had taken to manage Ian and Lesli's inappropriate behavior and the "Baby Steps" were the key to getting to the results I wanted to see. The temptation of making sweeping changes would actually cause more damage because both the kids and I would feel overwhelmed by the drastic shift in our homes. The rail thin single father in our small group likened making these changes to the same as having a frog in a pot of warm water on the stove. Let the water get hot slowly so by the time the frog realized what was going on, it would be too late. His graphic example elicited quite a few chuckles.

As Sue ended the group, she offered tailored homework assignments for each parent. I was charged with drafting house rules and posting them on the refrigerator. According to Sue, this was the best place to post anything you wanted your kids to see because it was a place they visited many

143

times during the day. With a laugh, she suggested I make many copies, since the rules have a tendency of disappearing.

One chore needed to be selected which each child had to complete every week and if it was not done, ironclad consequences were to be doled out. Having a plan and being prepared to follow through with it if they did not comply was going to be one of the most important things in our parenting arsenal.

As Dee and I drove home, we laughed at some of the clever suggestions our fellow parents had offered in managing some of the more irritating and chronic behaviors which had our kids pulling at our hair. We agreed that the parent who took all the towels out of their bathrooms, forcing her son to dry off with a wash cloth, until he displayed he understood what it meant to not leave the wet towels on the floor, was definitely the night's winner. Especially when she walked by the bathroom after he had finished showering and he was trying to dry himself with the hairdryer. She heard it through the door and since he had a shaved head, there would be no other reason to have the dryer in use.

When I got home, Lesli was in her room with Roxie, who was planning on sleeping over, even though the rule was no one sleeps over on a school night. Ian was already sleeping. The house was a mess. Some of Lesli's clothes were in the living room and bathroom. There was make-up spilled on the sink and wet towels on the floor. All the lights were on in each room of the house. Closet doors were open. Half-full glasses of milk were left on the dining room table. The kitchen looked like we had just served dinner to a group of twenty. Who knows, maybe they did? The TV was on in the den and the oven was on in the kitchen. My phone was off the hook in the bedroom, so no one would have been able to call me and leave a message. The wastepaper baskets were over flowing and Lesli had managed to have a pile of clothes on the floor of her room. Surprisingly, I was able to keep my cool. I had just the solution for all of this.

I took the Royal Typewriter, prior to computers, from the closet and set it on the desk in my bedroom. I had bought the typewriter during my brief stay in therapy. The therapist had suggested that I keep a journal and record my feelings. I didn't know then, it would become the outline of this book. I kicked off my shoes and settled in to start writing the house rules.

1. No kids in the house when I am not home.
2. Clean up the room before you leave it.
3, Clothes must be hung up or put in hamper, not lying on floor
4. No drugs or alcohol use in or around my house by you or any of your friends.
5, Attend school daily, all classes and maintain passing grades.
6. No verbal or physical abuse to any family members
7. Abide by the curfews
8. No running away.

They didn't seem like hard rules to follow but I anticipated the kids would fight me on every one of them. I retyped three copies and posted one on the refrigerator door. I put one in my group notebook to share next week and one to take to work so I can run off some copies as I am sure they will shortly begin their disappearing act . This was a good start. I couldn't wait for my new favorite word to be used, "Consequences." I was, for the first time, beginning to feel as if I was part of the solution and no longer part of the problem. I can't believe it's been almost five months now since Joyce has been gone. Was I finally getting a handle on things?

I told Lesli about the rules and she and Roxie went to read them. From my room, I could not hear what they were saying but there was a lot of laughter. Enjoy yourself Lesli, I thought, but prepare yourself for some major changes and consequences. I was so hopeful about the idea I could be back in control. I went to my room to type up two more pages: one with Ian's chores and one with Lesli's. I had decided to give them each just one chore and was prepared with a consequence for each if not followed through.

Ian's chore read: Take out the trash every Thursday night by 7 PM and return the barrels to the yard before 3:30 PM on Fridays. Very simply put and to the point with no grey areas. There would be no more need to remind or nag him during the week. For whatever reason, it had become a huge point of contention between Ian and me. His refusal to follow through on the task ended with us in a huge shouting match every Thursday night. I posted this on the refrigerator door went back to write Lesli's. She was in the kitchen at the time and went over to read it.

147

"Good luck," she wisecracked.

"Yours is next," I replied. That got her attention and she sat down at the kitchen table. In a matter of minutes I was back in the kitchen and posted another piece of paper on the refrigerator door. It read: Your room will be inspected every Friday at 7 PM. All clothes must be in drawers or hung in closet. Floor must be clear of any garbage and nothing from the kitchen or bathroom is to be found in your room...

"Or what?" she inquired

"You really don't want to know, so I suggest you comply by just doing the simple required task," I said. I left the room with a big grin on my face which seemed to upset her even more then the posting of the rules. Why? Because kids hate happy parents. A happy parent is a parent in control. They would rather see the popping of the veins in the forehead, the screaming and slamming of doors, the tears and yells which all amount to their being in control . Instead I just would smile and let them know that it no longer works to attempt to push my buttons and manipulate

148

me. It doesn't mean that silently I am not thinking of what I would like to do or what in fact I plan on doing. I just need to stay focused.

The next few days went by without any major mishaps. The trash was beginning to overflow from the various wastebaskets throughout the house and Lesli's room was gathering the usual floor displays as well as towels and used glassware from the kitchen. I found it hard not to say anything but part of my plan was to just ignore it until the appointed time. Pick your battles, I was told by my group.

On Thursday morning, I woke Ian and said nothing about it being trash day. I was also very careful not to remind him when he called me at work that day, as I normally did in the past. Driving home that night, I found myself hoping that he didn't take out the trash because I wanted to test out the consequence. I pulled in front of the house and naturally the barrels were still in the yard. I went into the house with my stack of chore lists and house rules and once again I posted the lists on the refrigerator door for the third time that week. The kids would soon learn that I had an endless supply. I made no mention of the trash to Ian.

149

I made spaghetti for dinner because I needed something that was messy for part of my consequence. After dinner, Lesli said she was going to visit a neighbor. I never knew if it was in our neighborhood or out of state but decided not to question her. I was too involved in my evenings plan with Ian. He went to his room as I began cleaning up the table and doing the dishes. It was my night to do the dishes; actually every night was my night if I wanted them done. I scraped the plates of all the extra pasta and sauce but did not run the garbage disposal. After the dishes and pots were done, I got a large trash bag from under the sink and sat back down to watch the clock

 Ian was in his room or should I say his apartment. He could very easily live there and never come out. He had his own phone, TV, stereo, VCR and other gadgets including black lights and horrifying posters. All I had to do was to shove food under the door daily and he would be very happy.

 The clock finally hit 7PM. I calmly lifted myself off the chair and as I hummed my way throughout the house, I dumped all the overflowing wastepaper baskets into the one large trash liner I was carrying. I went back into the kitchen and took all the remaining garbage from the disposal and dumped it into the waiting bag. Once the bag was at capacity, I made my way to Ian's room. I felt like Santa carrying my bag of goodies. I found Ian on the phone with his Walkman (way before I-Pods) in one ear while he watched TV. It's amazing how they can do so many things at one time, if it pleases them.

Ian glanced my way as I walked over to the bed where he was lying. Our eyes locked for just a moment. Then I turned the bag upside down, dumping all the trash on him and his bed covers. As he jumped up, a clump of spaghetti fell down on his reddening face. A stream of four letter words quickly followed. He never let go of the phone and was repeating what I just did to whomever he was talking to. I left the room with a big grin from ear to ear as he started to throw trash around his room. He got off the phone just long enough to punch a hole in his closet door. He never let up on the cursing and of course it was all directed at me. Normally by this time, I would have been in his room and we would have been in a knock down battle but instead I lay quietly in my room, listening to my son who was in crisis for something he created.

151

A few minutes later, I heard him get back on the phone and in between tears and yelling, he proceeded to call every relative whose phone number he had. He wanted someone to come and get me because, according to him, I clearly needed to be committed. This scene went on for about an hour and then it was quiet in his room. Eventually, I heard him go out the front door and drag the trash barrels out to the front of the house. He went into the garage to do some laundry as he did not want to sleep on garbage soaked sheets and pillow cases. He came back in and slammed the door of his room behind him.

Now it was Lesli's turn. All next day at work, I had been anticipating checking her room. I knew exactly what shape it was in because Lesli had not taken my rules seriously. When I got home and of course Lesli was already out for the evening, I gathered my portable stereo and a few of my favorite tapes to take them into the bathroom Lesli and Ian shared. Around 10 PM, I set the stereo up on the counter then went into the kitchen and got a glass of ice and a bottle of diet Pepsi which I also took to the bathroom. I headed to the garage and found the large shears and filed them down to razor sharp edges. I laid them on the bathroom floor by the pile of clothes.

In Lesli's room, I gathered all the clothes lying about and took them in to the bathroom. Anything of Lesli's which was expensive or worth saving, I put in a trash bag in my closet. The rest was mostly stained tee shirts, midriff tops, tube tops and a few pieces that were not hers, and put them in a big pile in the center of the bathroom floor. I took each piece and carefully began to shred the pile before me. I had no intention of replacing any of the items. As I reached the bottom of the pile, I glanced at my watch and saw that it was almost mid-night. I could depend on my hardheaded daughter violating her curfew, so I knew that I had at least two more hours.

Around 2:00 AM, I turned off the stereo and put it back in my room. I returned the shears back to the garage and the bottle of soda to the kitchen and rinsed out my glass. Back in the bathroom, I made a nice high pile of what were once Lesli and her friend's clothes. I kept the light on in the bathroom so that when she came down the hall towards her room, she would see the colorful pile in the center of the room. It didn't look bright enough so I got a spotlight off one of the pictures in the den and plugged it into the bathroom. Now it looked bright enough. I turned off all the other lights in the hall and living room so that she wouldn't miss the bathroom floor show. Ian fell asleep before I even started the project. I just hope he doesn't wake up to pee before Lesli arrived home.

I went into my bedroom, got undressed and laid down on top of the covers. I surely wasn't going to sleep because I didn't want to miss her reaction. Shortly after 2:30 AM she came sneaking in the house and down the hall. At first I didn't hear anything other then a few quiet four-letter words.

Suddenly she screamed, "Oh Shit!" I knew I would have a visitor in my room very shortly. I quickly got under the covers and pretended to be sleeping.

She stood at the side of my bed probably deciding whether she should wake me or not. The latter won out and she began shaking my bed. I opened one eye and looked at her, willing myself not to burst out laughing.

"How dare you cut up my clothes?" I propped myself up on my elbow. "And not only mine, but Roxie's and Shelby's. What am I going to tell them?" she demanded.

I calmly sat up. "The rule of the house is that any clothes found lying around are subject to being destroyed."

"That is crazy!" she shouted back at me.

I blinked at her, a couple seconds. "Lesli, I need to go to work in the morning so I need to get to get to sleep."

"What am I going to do about Roxie's stuff?" she whined.

"Goodnight, Lesli," I said, as I lay back down. She stormed out the room. "I love you!" I yelled after her. My declaration just inflamed her. Back in her room, she hurled four-letter words to her four walls. I went to sleep.

In the morning, I cleaned up the mess in the bathroom and went out before Lesli was up. I saw Ian and he had already seen the pile of clothes.

"You are really crazy and your group should be banned," he said. I laughed as I left the house. I couldn't wait to tell the group next week.

Both kids ignored me for the remainder of the weekend and also Monday evening. Tuesday night I always stopped by the house to be sure they were home before I left for group. When I pulled up to the front of my home, all three trash barrels were on the curb.

"Ian, why do you have the trash barrels out tonight? They are not due out until Thursday evening" I questioned.

He shot back with, "Because tonight is your Nazi Cult meeting and I am not sure what they will tell you to do next"

I couldn't wait to get to group and share this all with them. It was the hit of the evening.

Driving to work the next morning, I felt a sudden surge of authority. Was I finally getting back into control? I'm not sure yet, but I do feel like I am starting to win the war

CHAPTER SEVEN

I Forgot How Good It Felt

By the time Rick came banging on my door, it had been four weeks since we last hung out. I had been consumed with Lesli and Ian and didn't have time to engage Rick and his antics. But tonight, as he stood in the porch looking spit and polished, he wasn't taking no for an answer. Rick and Michel were on the outs again and he needed to blow off steam and wanted my company. He said, "I've got a surprise for you." With both the kids sleeping over at friends' houses, it seemed like a good weekend night to take off from my duties of "clever dad." As warned by the group veteran, the kids pushed back on every change and rule that I tried to impose. We had gone through nine editions of the house rules and Lesli had sacrificed a couple more outfits to the garage shears. But I was getting their attention, at least Ian's.

I was anxious to share with Rick, how I pulled up to the house on a Tuesday night and found the three trash barrels lined up as if it were Thursday evening. Rick and I had a good laugh together over that.

As I approached the front of the Rolls Royce, I notice a woman was sitting in the passenger seat. I opened the door and a pair of sparkling blue eyes smiled back at me. Her name was Ashley, a perfect 10 who lived in Rick's apartment complex. She had a body that was not to be believed. As I slid into the backseat, I let my hand brush against her golden blonde hair which hung over the head rest. "Our job is to cheer up our little Ashley as she just broke up with her boyfriend."

"Do you mind if I ask you how old you are?" I inquired

"Twenty three "she responded.

"Yeah and her boyfriend was forty-four years old" Rick was quick to add.

"Really", I said and of course Rick responded with

"Maybe there is a chance for your forty-four year old body"
We all laughed.

That fact brought a smile to my lips. The night consisted of us bar hoping at some of Rick's favorite hangs. While he was busy working the rooms at each spot, Ashley and I had plenty of time to get acquainted. She was more mature then I would have expected of a twenty-three year- old. We got along great and I was more than aware at every club we went into, I could feel people watching us. Ashley was undeniably beautiful. The club-goers, men and women, followed her every move. A couple guys gave me the thumbs up after checking her out. Ashley snuggled up to me in one of the banquets as we watched Rick burn up the dance floor. This was the first time I was in an intimate conversation with a women and I forgot how good it felt.

We made our way back to Rick's and enjoyed some wine together. I was expecting him to tell me to take his car home, so he could be free to make his move on Ashley. But Rick went up stairs to his room for what seemed an eternity, leaving Ashley and I to continue where we left off in our conversation. Ashley didn't consider herself a beauty and felt extremely self-conscious if her looks were pointed out to her. She modeled so that she could pay her tuition. She was attending law school and was living at home with her parents to try and save some money so that she could move out on her own someday.

When Rick finally came downstairs, we were busy talking so he just lay down in front of the fireplace and immediately fell asleep. Rick started to snore, which we took as a cue to walk over to Ashley's place. I grabbed his house keys off the coffee table so I could get back in and we quietly slipped out the front door.

Ashley offered her phone number and asked if I would call her. She said she really enjoyed talking with me and to seal my trip to *Fantasy Island*, she took my face into her hands and gave me a kiss on the lips. I stood there in semi shock as she went inside and closed the door behind her. I thought I didn't know if I could really call her. I still felt as if I was with Joyce. When I got back to Rick's, he was still knocked out. I decided to leave him there, grabbing his car keys and my jacket and making my way home across the valley.

At six the next morning, I was ripped out of my delicious sleep by a wide awake Rick. "Bring my car back and we'll go get breakfast," he demanded.

"Are you crazy? It's barely dawn, and I am still in my pj's" Rick does not take no for an answer and rather then have a crazy conversation, I told him I would be there in twenty minutes and to be out in front. I was surprised to see so many people as we walked into Fromins Deli. The popular little deli was another one of Rick's hangouts. The food wasn't spectacular but Rick was a creature of habit and he liked that everyone knew him there. While we waited for our breakfast, I gingerly brought up the issue of Ashley. Rick was completely nonchalant. He almost acted like he didn't recognize how gorgeous Ashley was. It was clear he was not interested in her and only had eyes for Michel. However conflicted I felt about dating so soon after Joyce's death, I was happy to hear that Rick was not a competitor for Ashley's affection.

I waited a week before I felt comfortable in calling her. I thought a lot about Ashley. She seemed genuinely excited to hear from me. Ashley was fun and full of energy. We started to see each other. It was a rush to walk into a club with her on my arm. I could feel the stares. It was certainly great for my ego. It felt good that I could attract someone like Ashley. She was all over me and it felt great to be desired.

I started to notice that the more time I spent with Ashley, the more I wanted to talk about Joyce and the more depressed I became. The numbness I had been dragging around was giving way to a series of confusing feelings. In any moment, I would endure grief, rage or longing. The woman I was holding in my arms wasn't the one I wanted. I was not fulfilled. It was irrational but I felt like I was cheating on Joyce, betraying her. The reality was that the last five years of our life together, there was very little intimacy. Joyce was physically failing and she was seldom out of pain. The few times that we did make love; I knew she was doing it to make me happy and every time I felt guilty when it was over.

My family and friends had no confidence this relationship with Ashley would last, so they were standoffish with her. I even brought her to my friend Molly's home for a Passover dinner and you should have seen the looks we both got from the crowd. It took lots of willpower not to break up laughing, especially when the guys could not take their eyes off of her. I was getting accustomed to those looks whenever I took her clubbing.

We continued to date for a few weeks, when I was invited to a neighborhood party with the kids. Ashley thought it would be a good time to meet Lesli and Ian, so I brought her along. When I showed up with Ashley, Ian was pleasantly surprised and so were all his scum bag friends. Lesli thought it was disgusting that I was dating a girl who was so close to her age. She made no attempt to come over to meet her and left the party shortly after we arrived.

Then a month later, our relationship was to come to an end. My brother-in-law, working up into a full froth, called me at my office just before one o'clock. He insisted that I go to a newsstand and pick up the latest copy of *Penthouse*. He refused to tell me why, demanding that I call him back as soon as I had it in hand. I hurried off the phone and rushed to the newsstand to pick up a copy of the current Penthouse.

As I settled in my car, casually flipping through the racy magazine, nothing prepared me for what I found on page 53. I blinked a few times giving myself a couple moments to adjust to the overly made up blonde posed in what looked like an uncomfortable position. It was Ashley. She was the centerfold. From the glossy page she and her shaved vagina stared back at me. I frantically flipped through the five-page spread, each picture more graphic than the next. I was dumbstruck. I almost thought I should hurry back to the newsstand and buy all the remaining copies but really, what good would it do. My hands were perspiring. I wiped the left one on my slacks as I read the article that accompanied the pictures. *Ashley loves to dance, is attending law school and is dating an older man who she is very fond of.* I am sure that was her old boyfriend as this had to be shot before we began our brief relationship.

When I made it back to the office, a couple of the guys from the warehouse grabbed the copy of the magazine and began passing around the office while giving me a few atta boy looks. I was a reluctant hero as I wondered why she hadn't told me she was going to do this spread in such a tacky magazine.

After work, I drove over to see Ashley. She came down to my car and got in the front seat next to me. I said" Why didn't you tell me about Penthouse?" I felt like such a fool.

She reminded me she had told me she was doing some modeling and had no idea as to what pictures they were going to use. She also didn't realize they would look so graphic.

"You never even mentioned that you posed for Penthouse" I responded.

She told me how sorry she was and she really cared about me and my feelings. I reflected on how much Joyce cared about me and yet chose to hold back all the serious problems that she was having with our children. I wondered now why another woman who I was close to, wouldn't be completely honest and open with me. Was there something wrong with me that prevented me from hearing the complete truth? Sadly with tears in her eyes, Ashley reached for the door and slowly got out of my car. She never turned back as I drove off. That was the last time I saw Ashley.

CHAPTER EIGHT

The Beginning of
Because I Love You, Parent Support Group

I'm not sure why I was surprised, as I flipped through my desk calendar, that it had been six weeks since I embarked on the journey of getting control of my kids. As Claire, the group coordinator promised six weeks into the process, I had seen significant changes mostly in myself. I was attending two meetings a week. The shift in me had put the kids on edge and over the weeks, we experienced the growing pains that go with forced change. When I was being honest with myself, Ian was the one who I felt I could really reach. Lesli was still fighting me, still pushing against the rules, waiting to see if I would give up the silly notion of putting restrictions on her freedom.

Right after the holidays, we had a flare up over her social calendar. It did not include asking my permission if she could go to a concert which required she spend the night at a friend's house who I did not know. My sixteen-year-old believed she could come and go as she wanted. She had made up her mind I had no clout and she was not going to respect my authority. I was letting her run wild. There were times I felt completely demoralized in the face of this reality. I was grateful to have the group to go back to and receive the support I found so essential, especially when I felt like giving up.

The group was also allowing me to share my leadership skills which had come to me naturally over my life. New parents had started using me as their hotline connection and consistently commented on my ability to come up with clever solutions to some problematic teen issues. How ridiculous was this. I can't even keep my own kids in line and yet I am advising other parents.

By my third meeting, I was asked to step in as a group leader because Claire was out sick. I initially begged off, believing I didn't have the formal experience to lead a group of desperate parents looking for real answers. I ended up running a robust and informative group that night. I ran two more groups and when Claire came back she asked me to sit in on the parent orientations with her so that I could take over while she was on a month long vacation. When I asked her why she had selected me to substitute for her, she said I was one of the more vocal parents there and my sense of humor helped the parents deal with the hard things needed to be shared. I was flattered.

With my increased involvement in the group I should have seen the next step coming. Sometime in late February, Dee, the good looking brunette and our group leader Sue, approached me with the idea we open another chapter of Tough Love on the west end of the valley. There were about eight families already coming from our area. I was immediately concerned we could be encroaching on Claire's group. Dee suggested that we have the meeting on Monday nights so parents would have a choice of nights or even attend more than one meeting a week if they were in heavy crisis. Sue promised we would co-facilitate the group and Dee would do the parent orientation.

I approached Claire with our idea. I didn't want any bad feelings. She was open and grateful we had chosen a different night for meetings. She believed the more choices the parents in the valley had the more support we would be able to offer everyone.

In March of 1982, we opened Canoga Park Parents Support Group practicing Tough Love at a church in Canoga Park. Eventually we dropped the Canoga Park part of the name and I suggested Because I Love You Parent Support Group practicing Tough Love. We could not call ourselves Tough Love, since it was considered a philosophy not a group name by the founders. David and Phyllis York were very adamant about any group listing themselves as Tough Love. It really made no sense to me but I wasn't going to break any rules… at least not yet.

I loved the new name. I can't even count how many times that was an answer to why I was acting instead of reacting with my kids. It was so much easier to have one name for all the groups that I soon started to open. We began to call it B.I.L.Y. for short. Can you imagine me using the name BILY when I preached to my kids that I never wanted to hear the name Billy in my home. Oh well, the spelling was different. As promised, we scheduled them for Monday evenings. We made up flyers and sent them around to the local schools. I made some public speaking engagements at various clubs and organizations alerting them about the group. The church also gave us some press in their monthly newsletter.

They were also nice enough to give us a number of rooms so each group could meet separately during the small group sessions. I did not like the way Tough Love meetings were always in one large meeting room. I felt that while one small group was sharing some major crisis it was very distracting if another group was laughing about a comical consequence that one of their parents succeeded with the prior week. I changed the format, lengthening small group from one hour to two and reduced the large group meeting to thirty minutes at the end.

Eight parents showed up for our first meeting. We were in business. Soon enough, word spread and week after week, attendance grew. It was affirming to hear parents share they had been looking for a support group for months. They were at the end of their rope and finding us was nothing short of a miracle. I did have to learn not every parent was ready to embrace our philosophy and tackle the issues in their homes. We experienced more than a few who only came to one meeting and every week we made sure our doors were open to help in any way possible.

My number was on top of the hotline list. My phone rang off the hook twenty-four hours a day. When I got home from work, there were no less then twenty calls, either with a parent in crisis or someone seeking information on our group. Parents came from all walks of life. We had the young parents with pre-teens and the older parents with young adult children. The rooms filled up with single parents, parents of adopted children, stepparents and widowed parents. We were even inundated with grandparents. The problems ran the gambit from attitude to drug abuse, from school truancy to runaways, from pregnancy to physical abuse, we dealt with it all. Low-income parents sat in the same group with high income professional from various fields. We had parents dealing with children as young as 2 years- old and all the way up to a 54 years- old child.

Within three months, the east valley group closed. Claire was burnt out and didn't have the energy to keep it going in light of the consistently low attendance. We absorbed the parents from the east valley group and continued to attract folks from all over Southern California. We began to get some media coverage, now under the name of Because I Love You. In no time at all, Dee and I continued to grow our core group of friends. One of her sons also appeared with me on a Geraldo Rivera show and Dee was on several talk shows with me. I was so fortunate to have her on the team in our continuing growth once we moved to the west valley location.

With all that was going on with establishing the group and managing its quick popularity, it was hard to ignore the fact of as much as I was helping other parents, Ian and Lesli were reverting back to their problematic behavior. I especially didn't want to deal with the idea Ian was smoking marijuana. I soon learned from the group all the signs were there i.e., disrespect for family rules, withdrawn and reluctant to participate in family activities, hiding out in his room, poor hygiene and complete disinterest in school. He was simply stoned, which allowed him not to deal with his feelings regarding his mother's death. I had attempted to broach the subject with him as we were approaching the one-year anniversary. He just shut me out. I couldn't get through to him.

For Lesli's part, Billy was her drug of choice. She was no longer attending school and was brazenly having Billy pick her up at the house. He brought her home at all hours and sometimes days later. She no longer listened to anything I said. Finally after her being gone for a few days, I changed the locks again and left a note on the door telling her she was no longer welcome at the house. I wasn't running a motel. I told Ian if he let her in, he would suffer serious consequences. Lesli didn't seem to mind moving out and went somewhere in Simi Valley to be with her beloved Billy. I knew she would burn out soon and return. In many ways her absence selfishly gave me a breather, allowing me to focus my energies on Ian. I explained to Ian that Lesli has chosen not to live with us by her negative actions. I needed to get a handle on his drug use before it escalated into something more dangerous.

Ian and I began to communicate much more and I began to feel a greater closeness to him. I continued to work with him to improve his school work, yet was still unable to talk about his mother to him. I was told by various therapists I was not to push it and he would open up when he was ready. Perhaps he was using the pot as an escape from the pain of his loss. Right now, I just needed to be close and available. He had a great fear that I too was going to leave him, especially with the scare when I almost followed through with my suicide attempt. This explains why he continued to track me down each time I left the home, whether it was for a short period of time or for an evening out. Ian had a fear of abandonment as he watched the demise of our family. With the loss of his mother and now his sister leaving our home, I can't say I blame him for his frightening thoughts. Whatever I had to do, I was not going to lose my son.

CHAPTER NINE

A Youth Group with Bobby the Bear

My little family was down to two. It was just Ian and me.
Lesli was out in the world doing what she wanted. We
missed her but we had come to appreciate the calm and
order which her absence afforded us. She did call to check
in but I refused to interact with her in the casual way she
requested. I was not going to pretend it was okay for my
sixteen-year-old living with some creep and she was just
calling to chat. Our phone calls pretty much went the same
way, every time.

"Did you call me because you want to discuss the
possibility of coming back home?" She would avoid
answering so I would hang up the phone. It was very
difficult to do this at first, as her calls kept coming more

frequent. I wanted her home and missed her terribly but I wasn't going to give in. She told me she wanted to come home with no restrictions, no school and no curfews, which was totally out of the question.

Joyce's family did not agree with my tactics and had never ending suggestions on how I could do better, so my daughter would stop running away. They constantly reminded me how Joyce would not approve of the way I was handling things. I remember telling my sister-in-law Jo Ellen that I would be happy to move Lesli into her home and let her raise Lesli since she seemed to feel she had all the answers. Her reply came back that Lesli was my responsibility, not hers. I agreed and followed with, "Then stay out of it". I tried not to discuss Lesli with them, whenever possible. I was grateful I could now turn to the group to give me the strength to carry on with my expectation that someday Lesli would come home. My relationship with Joyce's family became strained.

When it came to Ian, Lesli's absence gave me the energy to have the difficult conversations I had been avoiding for months. After coming home from a rather enlightening group meeting, I heard Ian's television blaring from behind his closed bedroom door. He didn't hear me when I pushed the door open. I watched him as he flipped through a magazine. Although he had just turned fifteen, he was completely immature. He was really a very handsome guy. His hair was light brown and bushy. He was 5'5" and weighed about 140 pounds. He looked like a typical teen of that day. I watched him for a little while longer before I walked in and sat on his bed. He barely wanted to peel his eyes off the magazine.

"Ian, can you turn the television off, I need to talk to you."

He looked up at me with suspicion as he hit the off button. I took the magazine from his lap and folded it closed. "Dad, what?" Ian questioned. I looked at him fully.

"How long have you been smoking marijuana?"

His raised eyebrows made it clear, he didn't see this coming. He shuffled around on his bed doing his best to avoid eye contact with me. "I started smoking right before mo" He didn't want to finish the sentence as he chocked up and tears welled in his eye.

177

"Why," I asked.   He shrugged.

Ian had said he had been smoking weed since he was twelve. That fact made me queasy to hear. How did we not recognize the signs before this?   The elephant in the middle of the living room had finally been pointed out. Where was I when this was going on? Was I so preoccupied with Joyce's illness? I had a son living under our roof using drugs and now three years later; he was finally able to admit it.

"Do you think you have a problem?" He responded with another shrug. "Well I think you do and I'm going to get you some help."

He refused to look at me but he did not protest. Maybe he felt if he didn't agree with me, I would tell him that he had to move out. That consequence would never cross my mind, although I do remember times when I told him he should try running away with Lesli. Maybe he would like the time off; I know I certainly would have.

I wasn't going to let his drug use go unchecked. Getting Ian to attend a twelve-step program was surprisingly easy.

In many ways he seemed relieved I had confronted him and went about addressing his addiction in a serious and consistent manner. Working through this made us closer every day and we relied on each other to face the frustrations and upsets.

Between my time with Ian and running B.I.L.Y., it left me no social life, a fact that didn't sit well with Rick. He still came over but we were not running around together as before. I was not about to exchange my time with Ian for him. My priorities had shifted.
I still found some times to have a meal or coffee with Michel and Rick but not on a regular basis. Michel and I spoke often during the evenings, if I wasn't at a meeting or helping out a parent in crisis.

On Monday night we had standing room only at large group, so it was obvious that word of mouth was taking hold. Parents were showing up at the church in droves. It was clear to me when I was facing almost 80 parents; we had to add another meeting night to the week. One of the parents, coming every week for several months, was a stepfather by the name of Jimmy. He was a chunky man with a thick lumberjack beard. He had come to the meetings to support his soon to be ex- wife who was dealing with a chronic runaway daughter from a previous marriage. He needed some help in how to deal with one of his step daughters He was quick and affable and I sensed he would be around for a while. I admired that even when they decided to divorce, he continued to come to the meetings as he maintained his relationship with his step daughters.

When I had to identify someone to take over the new meeting night, I approached Jimmy. He was shocked at my suggestion that he had the skills to become a group leader. I suspect it was how I looked when Claire made the same observation about me. The church made another evening available.

We moved some of the small group leaders to Wednesday night and Jimmy took charge of that evening. Of course I was still there each Wednesday to help out either doing orientation or leading a group. I also needed to put in my two cents in large group. I knew I had become the driving force why parents kept coming back each week. They called me the guru of B.I.L.Y. The reality was, it was easier for me to solve other people's problems, especially when you could convince them that *Pain was Inevitable, Suffering was Optional.*

Even with the second night, we were averaging sixty to seventy people at each meeting. Many parents were coming from the city and Orange County as well as Ventura County. We were becoming very well known throughout the valley. Because we were the only *free* parent support group in the area and our success rates were extremely high, it helped to increase our referrals from the courts, legal departments, school officials, the medical field as well as the media. The idea to start a youth group surprisingly came from Ian. He often complained that he was the youngest person at his twelve-step program and a youth group would be more comfortable for him and the other kids who had the same or similar issues.

The church where we were meeting had a youth group which met on Tuesday nights and was run by a guy the kids called Bobby the Bear. He was a young man in his mid-twenties, a former drug abuser who had turned his life around and found religion again. His personal mission was to give back to the community because he felt his life had been saved through the church. Jimmy and I approached him with the idea of running a youth group for B.I.L.Y. We were coming to understand that giving the kids the opportunity to meet was a way to support their family more fully. With only the parents tackling the issues, it made for a lopsided equation taking longer to solve. What we were all facing were family problems and they should be dealt with accordingly

The parents, including the other group leaders, thought the idea was a solid one agreeing our success rate would go up if the kids were a part of the solution from the very beginning. The rules for attending the youth group were simple enough. The youth had to be at least thirteen-years-old. They could not come to the group high or carrying drugs and they had to maintain the strict expectation of confidentiality. Their parents had to be attending B.I.L.Y.. Bear agreed and in a short period of time, I wrote a youth group program. Once the church gave us Thursday night for the meetings, we met to strategize how to get the kids to attend the group.

Developmentally, teens don't excel at identifying how their problematic behavior might be causing significant and long-lasting consequences for their parents and themselves.

182

We initially contemplated bribing them to attend but we eventually left it up to their parents to get them to the meeting. Thirty days later we opened "B.I.L.Y. Too" the Youth Group and to my surprise the parents were able to persuade their kids to attend, dropping them off by the carloads.

The structure was similar to the adult sessions. They broke up in small groups then met in large group. In small group, I added the element of "parent notes." The kids had notes to read from their parents disclosing the issues that needed to be worked on for that week. I initially thought that the kids would not challenge each other on their bullshit and be permissive in their feedback, but interestingly enough they were actually really hard on each other. As it was with adults, the kids could see their peer's issues better than they could see their own. Their feedback was often thoughtful and clear and they worked hard to hold each other accountable from week to week. I attended the youth group infrequently, because they needed confidentiality, just like their parent groups had. When I did sit in, I always walked away being impressed with their intriguing insights.

In their large group, Bear usually did some type of a workshop. One night he had them all write a letter to their best friends who had revealed they wanted to commit suicide. The note was to tell their friends why they did not want them to die. There wasn't a dry eye in the house, including mine. The irony was not lost that I was making ways for parents to recover their children while one of mine was almost totally cut off from me.

Lesli was completely out of control. The progress I was seeing in Ian was based very much on the fact that he was a homebody and responded positively to my time and attention. But no matter what I did with Lesli, she refused to be parented and I felt powerless with her. Maybe it was why I was so deeply involved in growing B.I.L.Y. In those groups, I had control and they made me feel I was not a complete failure as a father. Like the thoughtful peers in the youth group, I could see other people's issues better than I could see my own. When a parent succeeded in reconnecting with their child, it afforded me some level of hope for what was in store in my relationship with Lesli.

The call I was hoping for but on some level was not anxious to receive, finally arrived. Lesli wanted to come back home again. On the verge of tears, she made all the right promises and swore that once again she was over Billy. The temptation to say no was palatable. Things were going well in my house with very little crisis. Ian was doing his best to follow the rules.

"Lesli, I can't talk to you about this right now" I managed to respond.

"Oh, okay." The disappointment in her voice was apparent.

I hung up without another word. What was I doing? Of course I wanted my child home. But I couldn't stay on this emotional roller coaster with her. I picked up the phone and called Sue, who was now the co-coordinator in another of our new groups. I dispensed with greetings and launched in, "Lesli called and she wants to come home."

Sue let out a long sigh. "Are you ready for that?"

"No." I felt shitty saying it aloud.

"Okay." Sue's tone lacked any judgment.

"She says she's ready to follow the rules. I miss her." My emotions were all over the place.

Sue and I processed a plan for over an hour. When Lesli called back, I explained to her why she needed to call Sue, a B.I.L.Y. parent, so that she could stay with her for a few days until we could schedule a parent/child contract conference. It was going to be necessary for Lesli to sign a written agreement with a non-negotiable set of rules before she could come back to the house. I took a deep breath

"Write down this number, Lesli." After I gave her Sue's number she inquired why she couldn't just come home. I let her know that we were doing things differently this time

"This is Bull Shit" Lesli shouted.

She was reluctant but promised to call Sue. I didn't have the faith that she would but I had to show she couldn't keep doing this on her terms.

I paced most of the evening waiting for Sue to call and say she had Lesli in her possession. When I finally heard from her, my heart sank. Lesli never called. Sue told me not to worry. I gave Lesli the option and it was in her court now. I walked around in a daze for the next few days wondering if I had done the right thing by not taking her straight home. It was easy to give the advice to others but when it came to your own it was a lot harder to follow through. Not hearing from Lesli, I was sure that she was back with Billy

A week went by and finally Lesli showed up at Sue's. We agreed to meet at the church on Wednesday night. Jimmy was going to do the contract and Meloney, one of the teens from the youth group, would be there to support Lesli. I went over the contract with my small group on Monday night. Most of the rules were the same. I knew I couldn't control who she saw outside of my home and I shouldn't spin my wheels in that area. I had to deal with her where I had the most control.

On Wednesday, Sue pulled into the lot and I could see Lesli sitting in the passenger seat. I wanted to run over and give her a big hug. I hadn't seen her in almost a month. My eyes welled up with tears. Jimmy put his arm around me and reminded me I needed to be strong.

187

We used one of the small offices to meet in. Sue walked in first. Then Lesli followed behind. She had on very little makeup and she was wearing an oversized sweatshirt. Her jeans were torn at both knees and her hair was pulled back into a ponytail. She seemed paler and thinner than I remembered. I wanted so badly to reach out and hug her but I remained in my seat and waited for Jimmy's direction.

"Hi daddy," she said.

"Hi dolly." I called her, a nickname her mother always used. For a moment I felt a million miles away from the life I used to have with Joyce and the kids. Lesli sat next to me and put her hand in mine. I could feel her shaking and it reminded me of the time we sat together in the limo at Joyce's funeral.

Jimmy explained why we were having this meeting and if she or Meloney, her teen support, thought there were any rules they felt were unfair, they should speak up. He read the rules and neither teen said a word. Lesli was so anxious to get home; I think she would have signed anything. Part of the contract was she had to attend the B.I.L.Y. Too

188

meetings which didn't go over too well with her. She was unconvinced even when I let her know her brother had started attending the meetings. However, either she agreed or she needed to find somewhere else to live. She finally relented and signed the contract.

When we got home, Ian was waiting like an expectant pup. He and Lesli gave each other a huge hug. As I watched their tearful reunion I wondered how two children who were so different, had such a tight bond. We sat around and talked for a while and then they went to bed. Closing up the house, I realized I never gave Lesli a hug. When I walked into her room, she was asleep. I sat on the floor near her bed and watched her. All the defiance and chaos was nowhere to be found in her quiet face. She slowly opened her eyes.

"Hi daddy, is everything okay?"

"I just wanted to give you a hug," I offered. She sat up in bed and stretched her arms out for me. I sat down next to her, pulling her to me. We held each other for a long time.

The next morning, I dropped Lesli at Canoga High School, where they were going to give her another chance.

189

As she got out of the car, I reminded her of the first youth meeting which was that evening. She gave me a sour look but promised to be ready when I came back for her. I went to work feeling really good.

Ian was the first one I spotted when the kids spilled out from the youth meeting. He was in high spirits. As a kid who kept his emotions close to the vest, it was good to see him smiling and cheerful. Half dozen kids came over to him to say goodnight. He really had acquired a lot of nice friends. Even knowing that many of them had been in trouble in a way Ian never had, I knew they had parents who cared and were doing something to make positive changes. One of his new friends was Darian. He was one of my favorites. His parents were small group leaders on Monday night. We had become close friends and now our sons were good buddies. Darian came over to the car to say hello. He was a foot taller than Ian, a good-looking kid with blond hair, blue eyes and a great smile. To look at him, you would never think he was an addict. His drug use had played havoc on his family and he had all but failed out of school. After an especially verbally abusive incident, his parents finally put him into a rehab program. The inpatient program had referred him to our youth program. Now his transformation was almost complete.

Lesli exited the building a few moments later. She was walking with Bear and Jackie, one of the newer girls in group. According to Bear, Jackie was turning the corner. Her parents had brought her to us because of her drug abuse and bouts of depression. I would be pleased if Lesli and Jackie became friends. The trio was engrossed in their conversation as they approached the car.

"Dennis, she did really well," Bear reported.

Lesli beamed. "Good." I responded. When was the last time I was proud of her?

"Give her a month and she will be a group leader," he said, as he patted her on the back. It didn't come as a surprise to me.

"I need her to first get a handle of her issues," I said. Lesli stuck her tongue out at me.

I knew it was premature but I was elated to see this happening. They were finally on the right road and soon I would be able to get back to some of the unfinished business in my life, mainly grieving the loss of my wife. With all the problems that were occurring with my kids, I felt like I had not given my loss of Joyce, the proper attention. So many days went by when I would forget that Joyce was gone, reaching over for the phone to call her and tell her something funny which had happened at work. I should have been missing Joyce every waking hour of every day but all my time had been filled with the stress and pain of raising two teenagers, who I was unable to communicate with.

Lesli was very talkative on the way home and it seemed as if she really liked the group. She said Bear and the other kids were easy to talk to and it hadn't been as bad as she envisioned.

For weeks, Lesli seemed on course. She was going to school on a regular basis, meeting her curfew and seeking out the B.I.L.Y. kids to hang out with on the weekends. She seemed serious about making changes. But little by little, I started getting calls from her school inquiring about her whereabouts. As soon as I heard this, I knew she was back with that Ass Hole Billy again. When I confronted her, she denied seeing him and tried to bullshit me again by saying it was some sort of mix up in the attendance office. She was seventeen and just one semester from graduating. I just wanted to get her to the finish line. She assured me she was going to graduate. Even after all we'd been through, I wanted to believe her. She continued to go to group and was training to be a group leader.

After a youth group meeting one evening, Bear approached me to pitch the idea of taking some of the B.I.L.Y kids on a church retreat to the San Bernardino Mountains. At first I was reluctant because our group was primarily secular and I didn't want religion being forced down their throats. Bear said there was very little religion at the retreat. They focused mostly on feelings, trust, and personal responsibility. The price was reasonable, so I alerted the support group parents of the opportunity. I was surprised how eager Lesli was to attend. Ian was not interested. We took Lesli to the church on the Friday night of the weekend camp. There were five busloads of kids. They were laughing and bouncing from seat to seat. Lesli

193

boarded the bus with Meloney and two other B.I.L.Y Too kids. We sat by our cars and watched them take off.

"Sure hope this works," one of the B.I.L.Y parents remarked.

I didn't know what to expect, so I didn't have any great expectations. Ian and I spent most of the weekend together and on Sunday night we went to the church to pick up Lesli. I was in a state of shock when she got off the bus. She was hugging everyone and crying. She especially clung to one of the counselors, a good-looking kid by the name of Rod. She brought him over and introduced him to us. He was a real gentleman with some class. Not anything like Lesli had ever been attracted to. He had to be at least eighteen or nineteen years old. He told me that Lesli did very well on the retreat and would I let her go again in three months as a junior counselor. I told him Lesli and I would talk about it and let him know. He gave Lesli a big whopping kiss right in front of me and then thanked me again for having such a wonderful daughter. If he had asked me for Lesli's hand at that moment, I would have probably said yes.

Lesli didn't stop raving all the way home and then we talked about it until midnight. Rod called Lesli Monday and he promised to go to her group on Thursday to see her. This was all too good to be true. He told her to buckle down because she had to graduate. I saw a big change come over Lesli. Rod was a regular at group every Thursday and she started seeing him on the weekends. Billy was still calling the house everyday but she seemed pre-occupied. Roxie was still coming over, but not as much.

The next youth retreat was approaching and this time we could send as many of our kids as we wanted. I told Ian he was going to attend. He wasn't thrilled but because Darian and a few of the other guys from the B.I.L.Y. Too youth group were going, he agreed. They both left on Friday night. Lesli was in seventh heaven. She knew about half the kids before she even got on the bus. Of course Rod was there.

The real test was going to be Ian. It didn't matter where you sent Lesli, she could have a good time and she was very open with her feelings, but Ian was a totally different story. Lesli had shared about one of the workshop she attended at the last retreat was dealing with loss. She

195

had talked about the death of her mother. I knew this wasn't going to go over well with Ian. Two years had passed and Ian still had a very difficult time accepting the loss of Joyce.

Sunday night, I was very anxious for buses to arrive back at the church. You could have blown me over with a feather when I saw Ian. He got off the bus and ran over to me. There were tears in his eyes. "I loved it, dad!"

A couple kids came over that I didn't recognize and gave him a big hug. He exchanged phone numbers with them and continued chatting with them until Lesli arrived on the second bus. She got off the bus all grins, holding Rod's hand. I didn't have to ask if she had a good time. My kids were happy and I was ecstatic.

A few days later as I hustled out the door for work, I realized I had left my wallet on my dresser. Walking past Lesli's room, I noted that it was shut all the way. She never shut her door all the way. I went to open the door to check on her and to make sure she was there. She had been known to climb out of her bedroom window on numerous occasions in the past.

196

The door was locked. My gut immediately told me something wasn't right. I'd gotten good at listening to my gut. I knocked softly. No response. I began banging. "Open the door, Lesli" I demanded.

"Daddy, I'm not feeling well so I am staying in bed and not going to school," she answered.

"Open the door, Lesli!" She refused. So I broke down the door. A shocked Lesli sprung to her feet. In her bed was the legendary Billy, with eyes the size of saucers.

I became a madman as all the suppressed rage in me erupted. I grabbed him by the throat and dragged him from the bed. He was naked as a jaybird. He fought back but I was determined to squeeze the life out of him. A hysterical Lesli clawed at me and tried to pull me off of him. My fury shot into my hands as they tightened around his throat. I finally let him go just before he passed out.

"Put some pants on and get the hell out of my house before I call the Police or kill you" I demanded "and wait in your Van for Lesli because she will be out as soon as she gathers some of her belongings" He scrambled into his jeans, scooping up his shirt, socks and shoes, as he ran out the front door. I stormed back to Lesli's room where she was rapidly dressing.

"How could you do that?" she whined." You could have killed him" I grabbed a small suitcase from the hall closet and threw it at her.

"You have five minutes to pack what you can carry. I'm sure your boyfriend can give you a ride where ever you want to go."

She said nothing and started going through her drawers, throwing a few things in the suitcase, and then going into the bathroom to fill the remaining space in her bag with toiletries. She returned to her bedroom and took the big picture of her and Joyce off the wall then headed down the hallway. Ian was sitting up in his bed and she waved goodbye to him. He started to cry as she slammed the door. I went into my room and lay down on the bed and also started to cry. I could feel my blood pressure boiling and was just waiting for the migraine, which was soon to appear.

I couldn't miss anymore work, but I sure didn't feel like going. I managed to get myself together and went in to talk to Ian. He was visibly shaken so I spent a few minutes trying to explain why I had to do what I did. I think he understood. I don't remember if I told him I was changing the locks again and not to let her in under any circumstance. However I knew that I had no intentions of discouraging a relationship between them.

When I returned from work, I packed up all the remaining clothes in Lesli's closet and drawers and put them in the garage. Anything else of hers she left in the bathroom or her bedroom was also packed and stored away. I was still very angry and needed to get to group as soon as possible. I used my hotline and spoke to some of the parents in the group who I was very close with. Everyone assured me that I took the right action. The reassurance made me feel a little better, but not much. Here I thought everything was going so well. Lesli only had a few more months until graduation and she was seeing Rod and going to group and camp and following the rules. What happened? There was no answer, it just happened and I had to take the action I took. I didn't have a clue at that time how long she would be out of my life.

"Hi this is Dennis. Ian and I can't come to the phone right now, so please leave a message and one of us will get back to you. If you are calling for Lesli, she no longer lives in this house. I don't know where she is nor do I care". That was our new answering machine message. I was filled with anger and disappointment. I really thought I had a handle on things with her. Now I had to focus in on where I did have some control which was with Ian and growing B.I.L.Y. I was now entering a new chapter of my life and it was tearing me apart, bit by bit. I lost my wife and now I gave up my daughter. God, how much longer will you be testing me?

CHAPTER TEN

PHASES Teen Disco

Over the next few weeks, group leaders and parents were reporting about a teenage disco in Canoga Park called Phases. It was open until 5:00 AM on weekends, with no age restrictions. Kids as young as eleven-years-old were found to be hanging out in the club. Southern California had no age or time restrictions for teen clubs as long as alcohol was not served. But alcohol was not the issue at this club.

Eventually we would hear from a parent who had first hand experience with the illegal activities that were happening in the club. She had a son who was in rehab as a result of going to Phases. According to the boy, on his first visit to the club, he was given Cocaine by the management. On his second visit, he was picked up at the club around midnight in a limo and driven to a house in Hollywood were he received his second blast of Cocaine. When he came back for a third time, he was again taken in the limo to the same location, only he was told he was going to be put out on the streets of West Hollywood to do some male hustling for them before any more drugs could be given out.

By this time, the fifteen-year-old was hooked on cocaine and was willing to sell his body for the drugs. She ended up having to hospitalize her son at a local rehab. I asked the parent if she would come with me to the West Valley Police Station where we could file charges. She was unwilling as she did not want to disclose this to her family and especially drag her son into any additional crisis.

Initially I thought the mother was overstating the situation so I decided to do a little bit of investigation and check in with a couple of people to see what was really going on. First, I asked Ian if he knew anything about the club. I was told Roxie and Lesli used to go there frequently and it was a real haven for druggies and their suppliers. He'd gone there once but didn't like it and didn't return. According to him, the manager was gay and he would let most of the boys into the club, free of charge. When I checked it with Sandy, a parent whose son had been going to the club for over a year, she confirmed that it was a hang out for both gay and straight kids. When I dug a little deeper, I discovered that the clubs owners also ran an adult club in Hollywood known as the Odyssey and that is where the limos were coming from.

There seemed to be enough to be concerned about so I went to the police to issue a complaint. They listened but determined there were no ordinances being violated and their hands were tied unless the parent was willing to file charges. When I went to our district councilperson, she was equally resistant to take a stand on the issue. She said it was just a sign of the times. These clubs were opening everywhere.

When I brought my findings back to the parents with the local authorities' unwillingness to address this potentially dangerous situation, Sandy suggested we form a committee and visit the club a few times on our own.

It was a late June evening on our first visit to Phases. Eleven B.I.L.Y. parents came along for the disco-dancing stake out. From the street, the club was somewhat invisible, with a tiny sign and no front entrance. We had to enter the club through an alleyway door. Internally there was a small entrance area where the manager collected our admission and directed us through a nondescript door. Immediately the kids were alerted to our presence in the club and they were none too happy. The management played it very low key.

On the surface, it looked safe inside. The kids milled around in one room where they watched television and played pool. The dance floor was bathed in flashing blue and orange lights, where about fifty kids gyrated. Boys were dancing with other boys and the same was true for the handful of girls. There were no other adults in the club, except us. We sat up in the area by the bar, which was serving cold drinks for a dollar a can. From our perch, we noted the bathrooms at the back of the club had a high traffic pattern. Additional visits to the club would alert us to the use of the bathrooms as a drug marketplace.

The kids were primarily between the ages of thirteen and sixteen, although we did notice a few older kids now and then. As the evening progressed, we noticed that some of the kids were nodding off and lying on the floor in the pool hall. One of the boys looked about ten years old. I asked the manager why he was allowing the kids to come in and sleep on the floor. He felt it was safer for them to sleep at the club than on the streets. When I pushed regarding the kids' potential runaway status, he snapped back he didn't get into all that. It really pissed me off. A handful of kids blatantly came up to us and asked if we would like to dance with them and others not so politely asked us to leave them and their club alone and not to make any trouble for them.

I went back to the police with our findings but they still saw no laws being broken. They did promise to patrol the area more frequently and pick up any stragglers. More reports of drugs and prostitution were filtering into group and after a shooting outside of one of the other teen clubs in the valley; I decided that the media needed to be informed of the happenings inside Phases. Perhaps this was a sample of what was also going on in the other teen clubs.

I called a few of the local papers and spoke to some of the storywriters but it wasn't news worthy enough. Even the shooting was only on the third page of the second section of the Valley News. We had to do something to attract their attention. A crowd of parents picketing the club perhaps would get us some attention.

When I presented it to the groups, the response was very favorable. They believed our actions should have a two-prong approach to move us toward creating ordinances for teen nightclubs. The new ordinance would restrict the clubs from admitting kids under sixteen and after midnight, only eighteen and older. The picket would bring public attention to the situations at hand.

Plans were made to send Sandy to Sacramento, with some of the funds we had in our treasury, to lobby for a bill. Sandy, along with two parents who were attorneys, worked on a plan to lobby for a California Teen Nightclub Ordinance. Armed with a letter of introduction from our local assemblyperson to our representative in Sacramento, a petition supporting a need for the ordinance, and letters from parents who had first hand negative experiences with the club, she headed off to Sacramento.

For my part, I contacted every newspaper editor and television station to alert them of the mass picket planned for the club. I went to the youth group to elicit their support. While some of the kids were receptive and agreed to join in, most of them told us to butt out including my son.

With permit in hand, we met at 9:00 PM in the parking lot behind the church. I expected about fifty parents and youth but was pleasantly surprised to see well over one hundred parents and some of our youth show up. Even Michel added her support by joining our picket line. Jimmy walked through the buzzing crowd checking everyone's signs to be sure there wasn't anything slanderous on them. Folks had spent a lot of time on the signs and many of them were very creative. We had already obtained a permit, however the police were standing by in case of any trouble.

I hopped up on the roof of my car.   "Alright folks are you ready!"

The crowd gave a weak "yes."

"Let's try this again. Are you ready?"

"Yes!" the crowd responded.

"I want to be clear what this protest is about. This is about letting these vultures know they can not endanger our kids for their personal gain! Right?" I repeated.

"Right!" The crowd's energy level was escalating.

"These are our kids and we are going to do whatever it takes to save their lives!"

"Yes, yes, yes!" The crowd was jumping and screaming yes in unison.

The pumped- up crowd started marching toward the club. They were parents with purpose. I did not see any media but there were a couple TV trucks from MTV parked in the rear of the club. I did not call MTV but I guess someone had notified them of the picket. On the second go around, as we were passing the back entrance door, out came the TV cameras, lights and a few reporters from MTV, the 24hour music station. Fifty or more kids followed them along with a handful of parents from the club carrying their own signs declaring: *This is a safe club*; *Teens need a place to be off the streets...* Later we would find out that the youth at Phases had been tipped off by some of our kids from the youth group who were against us picketing Phases. The club kids circled the opposite way around the club yelling, "Parents go home" and "Leave our club alone"

On the third go around, I was approached by one of the newscasters from MTV to come out of line and be interviewed on live TV. I was introduced as the leader of a radical pack of parents in Canoga Park who wanted to stop teens from dancing. I couldn't help but laugh and imagined myself as the Reverend from Footloose. They were obviously on the kids' side.

Then a reporter from the Daily News showed up with a photographer, fortunately being much more receptive to our plight. He began to ask some questions and hearing my responses, the MTV reporter left my side and began to interview some of the club kids and management. Sixty minutes later, the picket was over and everyone was loaded back in their cars.

The interview and picture showed up on the first page of the second section of the newspaper. It was a great article and hundreds of letters started to arrive into our office. The first batches were in favor of the club and they were all about the exact content with just different names which lead me to believe the same person or persons sent them all. The second batch was a more important mail and we were delighted to discover that we had the public behind us. I gathered up the supportive letters and dumped them on our councilperson's desk. She finally got off the fence and gave us her support, as did the local police.

* * * * *

You don't tick off dangerous people and not expect to experience some of their fury. I began receiving hate mail at my house and numerous phone threats.

"I guess you bastards don't know who you are fucking with," I hollered into the phone

Once they threatened to burn down my house, I packed up Ian and sent him to my brother-in-law and sister-in – laws house for a couple of weeks. They were happy to have Ian but they made it clear that they were very angry with me for putting my son's life in danger, for an issue they didn't believe was worth all the exposure. Because of my

210

involvement in B.I.L.Y., they thought I was not only endangering Ian but I was driving Lesli further away. They wanted me to back down, but there was not a chance.

I also received push back from some of the parents in the group who agreed maybe we had bitten off more than we could chew. I wasn't going to let anyone scare me away. I believed someone had to help protect our youth from these drug dealers and perverts. The police did increase their patrol of the church and my street, which quieted some of the concerns with my neighbors.

"How about increasing your patrol around the club and what happed to our curfew law?" I shouted out at the patrol cars as they passed my house.

Our picket attracted more parents to our group and our attendance went way up. We also had visits from most of the local network news affiliates in town. Reporters from KNBC, KABC and KNXT were begging to come out and talk to us.

The group and I were becoming famous. Many of our families were doing interviews and the press kept coming. In addition to all which was going on, I still had a full time job and I needed to make that my priority as well. Sandy returned with the good news that the proposal for the ordinance would be placed on the fall ballot allowing for the public to vote on the issue.

Eventually the hate mail stopped and the calls became less frequent. The introducing of the new Teen Ordinance and favorable passing caused many of the Teen Clubs to close their doors for good. The fight was far from over as we were now being faced with many of the teens who attended the club in the valley, had now obtained phony ID and were going to the club in Hollywood, owned by the same people. It was also rumored the owners were affiliated with the mafia.

I decided to check out Club Odyssey and see how our underage kids were getting into the club. As I approached the Odyssey, I could hear the pounding music coming from the glass and silver structure. It was a beautiful building that attracted an older and classier-looking clientele.

There was a beefy guard at the door checking ID but obviously not very well. It was clear some of the

212

people going in were under the mandated 18 years old. After a couple weeks, I was recognized by some of the kids and was pointed out to the management. An 8x10 photograph of me was posted by the doorway with some copies of the newspaper articles on my work in getting Phases closed. There was even a caption under my photo quoting MTV's interview with me. It read ***here's the guy who wants to stop teens from dancing.*** They tried to intimidate me by making my stay very uncomfortable so I started observing the club from my car. It was surprising to see how many of our youth group kids showed up each night. Not one of them was denied entrance.

One night when we observed about twenty underage teens enter the club, we called the "We Tip" police line. Within sixty minutes, the West Hollywood police raided the club, checking IDs. A number of the kids jumped over the stone wall on the outdoor patios to avoid being discovered. After the second raid, the threats began again. The frequency and viciousness of the calls prompted me to record all of them and take them to the police. They weren't able to trace the calls but once again increased the frequency of their patrols around my home and the B.I.L.Y. meetings.

After the Teen Night Club ordinance passed, a local TV talk show invited me to appear with Sandy to talk about our concerns with Club Odyssey. The ordinance had effectively shut down many of the teen clubs because the age and curfew limitations, causing financial loss for the owners. What I didn't know was the show had also invited one of owners to confront me and deny all my claims. Carlo Nasini was a thin version of Al Pacino with a receding hairline and a wicked smile. Nasini mostly laughed off our accusations of underage drinking, male prostitution and drug trafficking. He said we were ridiculous and our concerns unfounded. He demanded we stop interrupting his business and calling the police with baseless claims. I was grateful Sandy was there because I wanted to smack the smug look off his face. We made a good team, as her cleverness and level-headedness balanced out my inclination to be explosive, which would have been a perfect way to lose all credibility.

Once again, we had the community on our side, which forced the club to be more diligent about checking IDs in a meaningful way and turning away the kids that were attempting to sneak into the club. The surrounding residential neighbors were also up in arms as some of the

214

club clientele were urinating on their front lawns and blasting car radios all hours of the night on their streets.

Our last major interaction with the club went down like an episode of *Mission Impossible.* One of our parents had a daughter, who was a chronic runaway. She was heavily into the drug scene, still frequenting the club and they wanted our assistant in getting her into rehab. A bed was waiting for her at Pasadena Hospital; we just had to get her there.

Three carloads of parents and a couple of the older youth from B.I.L.Y Too, including my son, showed up at the club. I wasn't thrilled about taking Ian with us but he pleaded with me to come along, claiming he knew the girl very well and she might listen to him, before any of us. I suspect his desire to tag along was due to the fact he had been away from the house for three weeks, since the increase of the threatening phone calls, and he missed being with me. I guess a "sting" was a perfect way to reconnect.

Our excited crew unloaded on the side of the club which was decked out in holiday lights. Bundled up to protect us from the cold evening, we quickly executed our plan. We sent the older kids, who were eighteen, into the club. Other then Ian, our other youth having never met Willow, had a picture to help them identify her. Willow was only sixteen and should not have been admitted into the club. We wanted to get her out without causing a scene but kids inside the club got wind of our plan. They alerted the girl that two guys were looking for her.

We waited outside of the club for over thirty minutes. It seemed that she had found a way to get out of the club. As Ian and the two other teens walked around the building, they saw her creeping down a flight of stairs. They grabbed her before she knew she had been spotted. She didn't go without a struggle, screaming and cursing at the kids. The car with her parents and older sister pulled in front of the club. Ian and I tossed her into the car and scrambled in behind her.

"You're a fucking traitor, Ian!" Willow shouted at him.

Ian just kept repeating "We are going to get you some help Willow, and you will thank us later"

Not accepting that, she began on me. "Why don't you stay out of other peoples business!" she shouted. "Fuck

B.I.L.Y. and Tough Love!" Getting no reaction she turned on her parents. "I hate you! I am never going to forgive you for doing this!" Her mother began to cry but no one lost their resolve to get her to the hospital.

When we pulled into the parking lot of the hospital, Willow's rage was on full tilt. The other two car loads of youth and parents surrounded the car to be sure she didn't dart out while someone rang for the admittance personnel.

Two big techs came out into the parking lot and extracted her from the car, without much effort. She continued to kick and scream but there was no chance of her escaping. Her relieved parents followed behind, as they ushered her through the doors of admitting that locked behind them.

About two weeks after our sting, I heard on the news that the Club Odyssey had burned to the ground and arson was suspected.

I got a call in my office that morning from Paul Dandridge, a newscaster on KABC. "Any knowledge on who might be responsible for the burning of the club?" he inquired.

The way he stated his questions, it appeared that he believed I might possibly have some additional information on the crime. By noon, it was clear that he wasn't the only reporter in town who held the same belief. My phone rang off the hook and our parking lot at my office filled up with news trucks from all the major stations. I think all the celebrity attention was what stopped me from being offended. Dennis Poncher, an arsonist. It was laughable but I guess the idea again of the "Footloose Reverend" burning down a club sold copy. The case was never solved.

A few months later, for my 50th Birthday, I took Michel to the Palm Restaurant in West Hollywood. As we were just finishing splitting some dessert, the waiter approached our table with a bucket containing a bottle of Dom Perignon Champagne. I looked over at Michel.

"Don't look at me, that's way too expensive for my budget."

I looked back at the waiter. "I think you have the wrong table."

"He sent it over." The waiter was pointing over at a gentleman on the end of the bar. I looked over to acknowledge the extravagant gift. There on a bar stool was Carlo Nasini, the old owner of Phases and The Odyssey, smiling and waving in our direction. I was not about to refuse this, even though Michel was now anxious to leave. I didn't want to give Carlo the satisfaction of thinking he had rattled me so I had the waiter uncork the bottle. We took a few sips. It was really good stuff.

As we exit the dining room he shouted out "No hard feelings!"

Hard feelings? Are you kidding? I had great feelings of relief and accomplishments. Perhaps many lives will be saved now that there is some valid restrictions put on all these nightclubs. I turned to Nasini with a big smile on my face as Michel and I proceeded out of the restaurant to retrieve my car from the valet parking.

CHAPTER ELEVEN

Let's Go Meet the Yorks

We had more parents attending our B.I.L.Y. groups than all the other Southern California Tough Love Chapters combined. In fact many of the smaller chapters were closing, due to low attendance. This fact enabled us to start a new chapter in Santa Monica, our first city venture. We were confident that we could attract as many parents as we had attending the Valley meetings. With all the activities going on and the expansion of membership, it was easy to forget that we were still affiliated with the national group who oversaw the administrative operation of each chapter. The York's did not experience the same amnesia. They were requiring now that we charge attendance and in addition, a monthly dues from each location in order to belong to Tough Love. Of course I just ignored it since we were purchasing dozens of their books and other products every week. We had always advertised us as a Free no-profit service and I was not about to change that.

The notoriety of the B.I.L.Y. support groups had finally reached fever pitch and the founders felt that we needed to be brought in to explain ourselves under the guise of mandatory attendance at the National Convention of Tough Love Support Groups. The invitation didn't come with the willingness to pay for our plane tickets, so our group took on the expense and came up with the money to cover our trip.

Jimmy and I arrived at the Doylestown, Pa. Holiday Inn, fully expecting a dressing down for all the attention our chapters had been receiving. I was prepared to take full responsibility for the ways I had morphed the program and my philosophies differed from them, in many ways. I was also prepared to point out of the four years we had been affiliated with the national organization; we had tremendous success stories which numbered in the hundreds. B.I.L.Y. groups were bringing in more money in book sales than all other California groups combined and had been faithful and excited about the cause. We had definitely put their names on the map, especially with all the media coverage we were receiving.

The convention was somewhat like a pep rally. The founders acknowledged that membership had been falling off except in the California B.I.L.Y. groups and we had to be more aggressive about attracting parents and selling the sanctioned material. Jimmy and I networked with the other support group coordinators and exchanged ideas which could make their groups more effective. Everyone was interested in hearing our secret to attracting so many parents and holding on to them. We avoided the mention of any monetary issues. For us, it came down to growing the groups in a way that parents saw it as a valuable resource and we were available to them outside the weekly meetings. Also, our addition to adding youth groups to our program drew a lot of interest and inquiries from both the various coordinators as well as the York's.

For years other then the B.I.L.Y. groups, the Tough Love programs did not have a youth group. I had no problems in letting them know how we ran our youth groups. It was no big secret. It would probably even be easier for them to start their youth groups since they had paid employees and would probably have an easier time in finding affordable counselors. We were fortunate to have the volunteer counselors who allowed us keep our youth group alive. Remember, we were still a major part of Tough Love and as long as they weren't bothering us or attempting to control us in any way, I was certainly willing to share our reasons for our growth.

During a networking night David York pulled me aside. I steeled myself for the expected tongue-lashing. "We would like you to be our west coast chapter coordinator."

"Excuse me?" I questioned what I just heard.

"We like your energy and drive. We would like for you to oversee our Arizona, Washington State, Oregon and, of course, California chapters." David leaned back in his chair.

"I'm not sure what to say." My brain was still catching up with what was going on. It would require traveling back and forth to all the locations in the four states.

"Of course this is a paid position and we would cover your travel and expenses."

I took a deep breath. There was nothing to think about. "I'm flattered but I'm not interested in doing this fulltime." Actually I probably would have loved to take this on had it been offered once Ian was well on his own but I was not about to leave Ian for any length of time on a regular basis.

"What?" David leaned forward, the smile fading from his lips.

"I volunteer to do this because the group was critical in helping me get a handle on my kids, but I never considered this to be a career. I can't fly around the country and spend anytime away from my son."

Once it was clear I was not going to be swayed, he ended our meeting and I was left to return to the seminar. The York's actively ignored us for the remainder of the convention. However, I was continually approached by many of the different out of state leaders and many asked if they could call me once I returned back home. They wanted to further discuss our format and how it differed from their

Tough Love training. They were also very interested in our B.I.L.Y. Too Youth Group but I let them know that it was not yet available outside of California. I knew that the addition of youth groups would be of interest and that is why I had the program copy written before making this trip. I put it under Because I Love You without mentioning Tough Love. I wouldn't have any problem with families from other Tough Love groups out of state who wanted to learn about how we ran the youth groups and why I felt it helped to increased our parents attendance.

Soon after we returned from our east coast trip, I had a charged conversation with David about the use of a particular physician that had been instrumental in getting our kids into rehab. Dr. Dave, the founder of the ASAP inpatient rehab programs, had set aside two free beds for B.I.L.Y. youth. We were then able to assist parents who could not afford the full price of placing their child at the facility nor had any insurance coverage for inpatient. The York's discovered our arrangements and demanded they have the opportunity to inspect the facility before *they* would approve B.I.L.Y. kids using the program in the future. Our doctor was caught off guard. He had extended himself because he believed in our work but he did not like

225

the way the York's had approached him. They were expecting his facility should cover their first class travel cost and luxury hotel stay.

The York's interpreted his reluctance to cover their travel and open his facility to inspection, as a sign that he and I were doing something underhanded. They were under the impression that I was getting some type of kick back for every youth who we were placing in Dr. Dave's programs. I guess you could say it was partially true, only the kick backs were free beds. I was instructed by a formal letter from the York's attorneys, not to use the Dr. Dave's facility. I refused to comply and forwarded all communications to Dr. Dave and his attorney. In the end, Dr. Dave's attorney sent the York's a letter threatening to sue them if they did not retract any and all slander activities they accused us of being involved in. The situation seemed to go away.

However, David York did not go away. On a random Thursday night, while I was coordinating one of our valley locations, David York was sitting in our Santa Monica parent orientation as if he was a new parent to the group. The coordinator reported that he sat in the back of the room and observed the evening's proceedings. Once he was called upon in orientation, he then told the lady doing orientation that he was the founder of Tough Love and asked her if he could say a few words in large group that evening. She was so excited to have David York at her meeting but was very surprised that I had not prepared her ahead of time of his visit. How could I when I had no idea he was planning on attending one of our meetings or even knowledge he was in California.

At the end of the meeting, in the large group, David stood up in front of the parents and group leaders, and with little fanfare announced all Because I Love You locations as well as Dennis Poncher were no longer affiliated with Tough Love. Confusion rippled through the room. When he was asked why he was taking this drastic action, he declared he did not need to explain his reasons other then we were not practicing the Tough Love philosophy.

My Santa Monica coordinator called me as soon as she returned from her meeting, late that evening, to inform me of our being tossed out of Tough Love. How dare he do this, especially in front of all our parents in the group? I immediately called his exchange. I got the answering machine but it didn't stop me from leaving my message

"David, it's Dennis Poncher from your California Tough Love Groups or should I say, who used to be from those groups. How dare you go behind my back and make those insinuations and toss us from the National Group without even discussing this with me. You had a problem with me; tell it to my face like a gentleman would do. It's your loss, Fuck You" and then I hung up the phone and called Jimmy and woke him up with the events of the evening.

He was thrilled and said "Now we can just be called Because I Love You"

Within days, we received a cease and decease letter from the York's' attorney. We could no longer use any of their training materials, banners, or attach their name to any of our recruitment information. We had two choices: fold up or go out on our own.

I invited our core group of 25 parents including all my coordinators of our various locations, to a special meeting at my home. We formed a Board of Directors the night after we were thrown out and stayed up until 6 AM the following morning, establishing the bylaws and operating principles of our "new organization. With the assistance of one of our parents who was an attorney, we submitted our paperwork to become an incorporated non-profit organization. We reworked our handbook and supporting paperwork, eliminating all mention of the national organization. I had to create our Ten Steps to Success which was basically my philosophies. It took many months of hard work and reams of paper but we emerged as a separate and successful parent support group, offering help to families in crisis. For several years, we still got calls from people thinking we were Tough Love.

The media continued to call and refer our numbers. I was thrilled with the coverage and just said to everyone that we were called Because I Love You, the parent support groups. Our name was trade marked and I also created a logo that we also trade marked. I then got busy and wrote the program book with the help of one of our parents who had a computer to correct all my spelling errors and malapropism.

Still, so much work was in front of us. Most of us had full time jobs and it was difficult to give the organization the time that it needed to grow. We had to have someone out there, full time. Then Jimmy offered to become our only paid employee. It was the perfect solution. He was committed to the organization and was a perfect set of ears and eyes in keeping the organization growing. We agreed on a salary we could afford and Jimmy began the footwork. The Board mapped out a schedule and Jimmy used his apartment as our office. Little by little, we acquired some donated office equipment, including a copy machine and a computer.

We were able to get one of our parents, who lived near the office, to give us some volunteer hours each day to take care of the mail and the phones. This soon became a full time job for her and she loved it. It gave Jimmy the freedom to go out and scout around for new locations as well as booking me for speaking engagements and personal appearances. Everything was falling into place and we began growing in leaps and bounds. By 1986 we opened our seventh location, so it seemed as if being kicked out by the national group was the best thing which could have happened to the families of Southern California. We were averaging at that time, a total of over 600 parents attending our weekly meetings and about 90 youth who were involved in B.I.L.Y. Too Youth Groups.

I wanted to do something big which would bring all the parents and youth together at one venue. Perhaps a BILY convention might be what I was after. I spoke to Vanessa, one of our BILY parents who worked at the Police Academy, to see if we could use their facility. They had a huge gymnasium which I thought would work out well for the event. Vanessa was able to obtain the place for a Sunday in April, from 9.A.M. until noon for no cost.

So now that I have the place, I need a committee to work on the program. Naturally, the first person always to come to mind was Dee and she suggested a few others to help us. We had a meeting at my home and it was suggested I call Dr. Dave to see if he would not only be a guest speaker, but perhaps he could bring someone from his program who would be a draw, to entice our youth to attend.

I called Dr Dave and asked him if he could get us a celebrity to join him on the dais. "How about if I bring Drew Barrymore?" he responded.

I was very excited to hear his suggestion and even more when he called back to confirm her appearance. Yes, it was a few years since her performance in E.T., but I was sure she would be a big draw for the youth and I was right. Not only for the youth, but we packed the house with over 700 current and past alumni from B.I.L.Y... We had a couple of families share about their past experiences in BILY and where they were today because of their involvement in our support groups.

After I introduced our BILY speakers, I brought Jimmy to the podium to introduce our guest speakers. Dr. Dave spoke first and then brought on Drew. You could have heard a pin drop when this 17 year old spoke about her involvement in drugs and alcohol. Drew received a thunderous applause as well as a standing ovation. She even hung around for pictures with some of the youth and signed autographs. It was a very successful event and I was extremely pleased to see the socializing of parents and youth from all over the valley and the city. Some of the youth who were there that day had been saved by Dr. Dave's in patient program. It was a thrill to see the emotional bonding that occurred. As I looked around the huge gymnasium which was filled to capacity, I was excited to see Ian mixing with not only the youth but also with the parents. He was finally coming out of the shell he had been in since his mother's death. Of course my thoughts and prayers on that day as in everyday were also about Lesli.   I was so sorry that she wasn't there because I know she would have loved to be a part of this and I know she would have been very proud of her dad and his accomplishments in B.I.L.Y...

CHAPTER TWELVE

"I Don't Have Anywhere to Go"

Letting go is one of the most painful acts that a parent often experiences. I was trying to let go with my burden of sorrow in losing my wife for the past years and it was now being mixed with the letting go of a rebellious daughter. Was I ever going to learn how to live with this heartache?

In sharing with other parents, I realized in letting go, I was also going to let Ian grow, which at this point was where I was with him. Even though I found myself giving in many times, I was convinced that I would never give up on Ian. Perhaps I could not change Lesli or Ian and if I could, I realized first I must continue to change myself. I was the living example of the definition of the meaning of Insanity. That is, ***Doing the same things over and over and expecting different results***. I had to stop sharing in their crisis but I never wanted to stop loving them. I had to bring some element of structure back into our home. I needed to be consistent with my actions rather then reactions. I

234

needed to get them on the right path and must not forget to also give the positive strokes which had been missing lately. Perhaps I had been sending out too many negative messages.

After so many nights of working with Ian, trying to get him on board to do his own homework assignments and my continuing trips to various teachers for the teacher/ parent conferences, I would learn what I already knew. Ian was not motivated and the teachers felt they could not get through to him. His refusal to do the work was interpreted by me as he was just a stubborn, out of control teen who expressed his defiance of any authority. I certainly related to it since I was having the same issues with him as far as responsibilities in the home.

My meetings with the teachers became so frustrating that I would look for ways to blame the teachers. I remember his math teacher repeatedly calling me for one of our conferences. It went like this. Phone rang on a weeknight about 6PM.

"Dennis, this is Mark Jordan, Ian's Math Teacher (I was on first name basis with many of his 9th grade teachers since there were so many calls, back and forth) I need you to come into my office in the morning to discuss more problems and possible solutions regarding the behavior of Ian in my classroom" I wanted to ask his teachers if they would come to my office and help me with my work, since they were continuously asking me to come to their office to help them with theirs.

The meetings continued through the 9th grade and although Ian did not graduate or was even held back an additional semester; they passed him through to High School. Of course there were no pomp and circumstances and I did not get to see him graduate but not completely cheated of a graduation because Joyce and I had seen Lesli graduate her Junior High. Little did I know then, it would be the last graduation for either of my kids? Ian entered Taft High School in Woodland Hills and in a matter of a few weeks, calls from various teachers once again started to arrive. Yes, he was making attempts to follow some of the posted rules in our home and attending meetings to control and eventually refrain from any drug use. He just could not

236

get his act together in school. He could not seem to get caught up nor did he seem to want to.

I knew I had to give him some options. This was something I was teaching other parents to do and my philosophy was for a parent to give their child some ownership so the child has full responsibilities of the outcome. Now, what were the choices I was going to offer this 16 year old regarding his school situation? He wanted to drop out of school. His recent progress report contained all fails. Clean and sober or totally stoned, I learned he was just a bad student. I'm not sure why I was surprised. We could never crack the code as it related to his school performance. He could not maintain his grades and was consistently frustrated with his schoolwork. He was no longer the cute nine-year-old that melted his parents and teachers' hearts, letting him smile his way into passing grades. I worked with him for months trying to help him get a handle on things but he had lost all his confidence and just did not want to do the work.

I gave Ian three choices "Get yourself back on track in school and maintain passing grades, is your first choice" I started.

"What are the next choices?" Ian followed with.

"Quit school and get a 40 hour a week job or pack a bag and leave this house" I finished.

Now that he was sixteen, he felt that his time would be better served getting a job and earning money. I was extremely frustrated and disappointed knowing I could not win this battle. Education had always been very important to my family and now I was faced with the fact I had two children who were not even going to finish high school. Was I selfishly concentrating on my wants and desires for my children or theirs? Was I worried about what others would think?

Their failure had become mine. I wrestled with a sense of loss. I was not going to have the opportunity to experience a graduation. There would be no prom pictures. I would not get to worry while they were off on their senior trip or debate on how much to pay for class rings. There would be no year book to look back on or show their kids someday. I was being cheated of all this because my kids insisted on hanging out with losers and did not have the discipline to follow through. They were spoiled. They never had to work for anything. His choice was to quit and I walked around brimming with anger for most of the week. I resented my kids. Was I selfish because I felt cheated?

I wanted children from the very first day that I knew Joyce and I were going to get married. I told her on our honeymoon that she no longer had to use any protection .I was hoping that she conceived our first night in Hawaii. I couldn't wait each month for the possibilities that she would be late with her period and she continually took the pregnancy tests. I remember so many times rushing home from work with glee because Joyce would call me and tell me she was ovulating. I wanted kids and even told Joyce I would like to have a big family. That was of course before she went through the turmoil of the first pregnancy.   We spent so much time with our kids in their early years, especially because our large groups of friends were having children around the same times. Even Joyce's Brothers' and Sister in- laws were also having kids shortly after Lesli was born and my nephews and nieces and our kids grew up together. We were a very close-knit family. Joyce and I always felt so much richer in our lives then any one else.

I was very proud of the kids as they were growing up. I remember pulling out all the old videos and photo albums of all our trips and birthday parties and picnics and so many of the fun times we shared as a family.

Lesli was very talented and it appeared as though she wanted to be in show business. She had a great singing voice and we gave her many private lessons followed by numerous recitals and various performances. This led us to believe that Lesli would most likely choose a career in musical theater. She seemed to love singing and the attention which surrounded her. However, she lost interest around the age of eight and we never forced her to continue. Ian was into some sports and Lesli enjoyed cheerleading. We supported the many games they were enrolled in at our local parks.

As I was coming home from work and pulled into the driveway, I saw Ian walking up the street with one of the no-goods from the neighborhood. I sat in the cool silence of the car watching him joke and horseplay. I felt the resentment bubbling up in me. How dare he be so carefree? He and his sister had been such trouble and they never gave a second thought how I suffered under all the responsibility of making a life for them. As I sat gripping the steering wheel, I once again turned my resentment toward Joyce. She died and left me with all these crises. She had hidden all the problems which the kids were having. She knew she was dying and it never occurred to her to let me in on our family dysfunctions. How did she think I was supposed to handle all their problems, with my hands tied behind my back? I was surprised to find tears dripping on to my shirt. I wanted to bolt. I didn't want to do this any longer but I knew I didn't have a choice.

I told Ian that he would have to get a fulltime job and pay rent.

"I'm not paying rent to live in my own house." Ian shot back.

I laughed. "This is my house and now that you have made the decision to quit school, you are going to take on the full burden of that choice."

He was not happy but he accepted this as the price of being freed from the self-esteem draining obligation of school. He understood the contract to read he had to pay twenty-five dollars a week and I was able to convince him to take a night class at the occupational school, a couple blocks from the house. Ian was good with his hands and to avoid being stuck in fast food dead end jobs; he needed to develop a trade. We agreed and he signed the contract. Ian found work in no time at all and began to pay rent almost immediately.

Unfortunately, he could not seem to hold down any job for any length of time. I think Bekins could have delivered his W-2 forms for the first year, since the stack was enormous. But he was working and making his commitments. Finally it seemed like I had some control here, unlike that of his sister when she was at home. I wondered how she was and if I would ever hear from her again. It was still a sore spot for me.

Lesli's call for help came when I was not feeling generous in any way. It had almost been a year since I had heard her voice. She was now almost 19 years old. I knew she stayed in contact with Ian and occasionally I would get a letter raving about her fulltime job or how great she and Billy were doing. She still thought I overreacted to finding Billy in her bed and was no closer to taking responsibility for her behavior. Somehow, the hysterical version of Lesli, calling

242

at two in the morning, didn't sound so carefree nor did she seem to be in control of her emotions

"Daddy, Billy threw me out!"

I sat quietly in bed, the room lit only by the light on the porch.

"Daddy?" She sounded small and frightened.

"Lesli, I can't keep going through this." I said, as I swung my legs off the bed.

"I don't have anywhere to go."

I turned on the lamp by the nightstand and took a deep breath. "You can't keep coming home when it's convenient for you." Lesli was openly sobbing.

"Your brother and I have been making a life here and ..." I didn't want to tell her that we were doing fine without her, but it was true. "Lesli, you need help and I can't give it to you." I didn't want to let her back in to disrupt our lives.

"I'll do whatever you want, Daddy." I almost wanted to believe her.

"Lesli, if you want to come home, you will have to do thirty days at the Buena Park Hospital program."

There was silence from the other end. Because I had no expectations, the disappointment she didn't want to help herself barely registered. I prepared to get off the phone. "Okay…but I don't do drugs," she offered.

"Lesli", I began, "Dr Dave's program at Buena Park Hospital works on more then just drug addiction. Things like obsessions and abusive relationships and other health issues", I informed her. "Billy is your drug and until you face it, you will keep making the same negative choices over and over again." I could hear her taking a pull off her cigarette.

"Okay." she agreed.

"Can you find a ride to the hospital?" I asked,

"Yes" she replied, "My friend, whose house I am at in Simi, will take me there"

244

I had chosen the Buena Park program because it was far enough away from Billy, hoping the thirty days would help her look at why she was making these choices and messing up her life. Lesli made arrangements to get to the hospital that night and I contacted Dr. Dave who helped to get me a free bed for her. Unfortunately, my insurance coverage would not pay for Lesli's hospital visit and a 30 day program was in no way going to fit into my budget. I was still working hard to pay off Joyce's doctors and hospital bills. Because of B.I.L.Y.'s relationship with Dr. Dave and the ASAP programs, I was able to get Lesli into one of their in patient 30 day hospital programs.

It was 4 AM when I arrived at the hospital. I slipped a note and a twenty dollar bill in the bag of toiletries and a change of clothing that I had picked up for her plus a hard copy of *"Women who loved too much"*. In the written note I let Lesli know how thrilled I was she had finally come to her senses and was going to accept help. I wasn't able to see her when I arrived on the wing of the hospital so I handed over the package to the staff on duty and promised to call later in the day.

It was too late to go back home so I went to
Denny's to wait out the 90 minutes before I needed to get
on the road to work. As I sat there nursing a cup of coffee, I
wrestled with why Lesli had taken this path. She was adrift
with no direction. She had been such a confident and
engaging little girl. As the first grandchild, she was well
loved and the center of attention. What did she need from
Billy she wasn't getting from her family? Did she really
want to live this half-life? What were her life aspirations at
this point? I wanted to believe she was going through a
phase and she would pull it together, before it was too late.

I called the hospital later in the day to check in on
Lesli. Each time I called, I was informed she was in session
and I was encouraged to leave a message, which I did each
time I called. After my fifth call, a member of Dr Dave's
staff invited me to come out on Sunday for a family
session. She explained the first few days the kids were in
the hospital, it was best they focused on their program and
their first meeting with our family be in a structured setting.
I found myself seething at the suggestion I was just another
father with a lost child in his care. Didn't they know how
many families I had helped get into their program? I knew
how this was supposed to work.

Ian and I got up early on Sunday morning to get to the hospital in time for the family session. We planned to have lunch with Lesli after the meeting. Normally her hospitalization would have cost me a great deal of money, but with the help of Dr. Dave, I had thirty free bed days to reach my child.

We arrived at the hospital at 10am with a care package of onion bagels and a pint of sour cream herring, Lesli's favorite, from Brent's Deli. I was hoping that we could visit with Lesli before the family session. We went up to the receptionist desk and announced we were here to see Lesli. As she looked up the charts, I glanced around the lobby. A few other parents were seated in the waiting area anticipating a reunion with their teenagers. Long ago, I used to believe parents who had problems with their kids were because they weren't paying attention or letting their kids run wild. The reality was at a certain point, kids exercise their free will and parents are left to watch them work out their choices, good or bad.

"Lesli checked herself out early this morning," the receptionist said. I could feel my entire body tense up.

"There must be some mistake," I said. She got on the phone and called for one of the techs from the unit. A few moments later a young man in his mid-twenties came through the double doors of the unit and asked me to follow him into a small office off to the right of the receptionist desk. A silent Ian followed as we entered the office and sat down on the two chairs in front of the desk. Terry, his name was printed on a nametag on his shirt, sat behind the desk.

"Mr. Poncher, we tried to get you on the phone this morning but you must have left early" he began. "Lesli was doing fine in all her sessions yesterday and we really felt she was sincere," he continued. I was feeling myself getting very angry and defensive.

"Who picked her up?" I asked, already knowing the answer. He told me she had called Billy. I set myself up again for this and I had nobody to blame but myself.

"Mr. Poncher, she is pregnant again." The tech seemed reluctant to deliver the news. "She said she had to leave so she could have an abortion. This will be her fourth.

I turned to Ian, "Did you know your sister was pregnant again?"

248

Reluctantly, Ian nodded. "Dad, you said you didn't want to know about her pregnancies, but I didn't know she was leaving the hospital."

That was no consolation. I thanked Terry for his time and left the small office. As I made my way to the bank of elevators, I dropped the care package in a trash can. The pint of sour cream herring made a thud sound at the bottom of the empty bin. I wondered how long it would be before the herring started to smell up the waiting room.

Ian could see how upset I was and thought it better not to try and defend her as he had done so many times in the past. But he did offer that Lesli was feeling desperate when Billy put her out of their place because she had gotten pregnant again. This information increased my irritation. In order for Billy to come get her from the hospital she had to have called him. She never returned one of my calls over the weekend. Why did she keep using me, hurting me?

Once again Lesli had put me into a crisis and I was playing the role of the victim. Pulling up into the driveway, I made up my mind then and there that this would never happen again. I began to feel the gnawing pains in my abdomen. I am sure I have or at the least was developing an ulcer from all of this aggravation. I knew stress can cause many diseases too. I have to stay strong for Ian. He still needs me and I need him too. That's not to say that I don't need or want Lesli in my life, it's just I cannot continue to take the failing path of rescuing her. The next time I would allow Lesli back into my life was after she had gotten help and was rid of Billy, for a least a year. This whole situation was ripping my guts out.

In my bedroom, I sat at my desk to write her a letter. The first draft was harsh and angry. I told her I had written her off and she was a huge disappointment. I continued on to let her know she no longer existed in my life and not to contact me anymore. I didn't care what kind of crisis she found herself in, I was not a resource to get her out of it. As I read over the letter, I could feel the sadness washing over me. It was a horrible letter. Is this what I really wanted to say to her? Didn't she need to know how frustrating her behavior had been? She was being selfish and unfair in her actions and I was out of control when it came to dealing with Lesli and her issues. I loved Lesli so much and missed her terribly but I couldn't go through this torture any longer. I ripped up the letter. I re-wrote a shorter version and mailed it to the only address I had for her which was in Simi Valley. I told her I was extremely disappointed in her choices and I trusted she would not attempt to contact me again until she had her life together and Billy out of it.

CHAPTER THIRTEEN

Open Your Heart, Communication Camp

I walked around in a numbing haze for a couple weeks. I had disowned my first-born child and knew in my heart it meant I didn't want to see her again, as long as she was living the life she had embraced. I felt like a fraud. Yes, this was a stance I would have told any one my B.I.L.Y. parents to take with their own kids but I felt I should have been a better example to them by having my family intact and functioning at a higher level. I was concerned that the B.I.L.Y. parents would question why they should listen to me and take my suggestions, while in reality; I was still struggling with my own two kids.

When someone asked some B.I.L.Y parents about this, here were some responses;

"Dennis could easily be in charge of the groups while he was struggling with his own kids because he knew first hand what to do and not to do. He was someone the parents could relate to. He was human and overwhelmed, just like

us. As parents, we needed to hear real situations and analogies. Dennis has an innate wisdom of how to approach the situations and how to offer choices and solutions" said Heidi, a mom who had been attending B.I.L.Y. for a few years.

Brett, a B.I.L.Y. dad, also replied to the same inquiry with *"When someone cares about something bigger then he, it is easy to listen to him. Not only to listen but to take him into your confidence, bare yourself and trust that whatever he offers comes from the most sincere of places within his soul. What he offers comes with no strings attached, is mostly innately accurate and to those who have allowed him to lend some guidance, better lives has been built.*

That desire to provide a resource for families (and maybe give them a chance which I had lost) led me to developing a family communication camp. The church had been generous about providing slots for the B.I.L.Y. TOO kids to attend their church camps but I wanted to provide a camp experience for the entire families. After all, one of the major problems with most of the families who were attending B.I.L.Y. was a lack of communication. I contacted Elizabeth, the church's Minister, about my idea and as always, she was supportive. She outlined how they ran their camp and the workshops they provided for the attendees. Some would work for the whole family and some would not. I decided to write my own camp program and would incorporate some of what Elizabeth does at her retreat. I spent the next few weeks working on writing the workshops and the structure of a weekend while Jimmy scouted around for local camp sites. He found us a great place in the Malibu Mountains at a very reasonable cost.

I hadn't told the group about the camp yet but I knew I could sell it to them. I would bring Ian and a few of the other kids in to large group to help persuade the parents to sign up. The kids also worked on the B.I.L.Y Too group to get their parents to sign up for the camp. Elizabeth got together with Jimmy and me to go over everything before I presented it to our parents. The camp was going to be called" Open Your Heart- Communication Camp." I wondered if I was biting off too much. With all we were doing at B.I.L.Y., would the parents feel like this was overkill?

254

We had to guarantee the camp with at least eighty people in order to break even. There were close to six hundred and fifty people attending our six locations. If only twenty percent went with their spouses and at least one youth, we were home free. We would pick our committee and facilitators after we saw who signed up. On Monday night, I spoke in large group about the camp. Because I had built up such trust from all my parents, I felt the idea of spending a positive weekend with their families and offering them a loving and rewarding experience was a gift they could give to one another. When our presentation was over, I asked how many people would be interested in attending. Almost every hand went up.

On the following Sunday, we met with the camp coordinator for a tour. The name of the facility was Camp Hess Kramer in the Malibu Mountains. It was a very serene setting nestled high above the Pacific Ocean, loaded with winding trails ,running brooks, a huge dinning hall as well as two other large auditorium style halls. The cabins were located beyond the halls and past those was a cozy fire pit. We decided to hold the number of participants at 104 because for the times we would be in a large circle, the room would only hold that amount.

Jimmy and I made up camp registration forms and handed them out on the next meeting nights. We told everyone it was up to them to get their deposits in as soon as possible because we had to close it at a certain number. Each parent/parents had to take at least one child who had to be at least thirteen years-old. We anticipated some of the workshops would be quite emotional which would not work for the younger kids.

Some parents wrote us the deposit checks and filled out the forms on the first night we offered the registration slips. In a matter of two weeks, we had the camp filled and started a waiting list. I continued to question whether I knew what I was doing, with all these families relying on me. We picked six strong parents to be facilitators plus Jimmy and me. I decided to break the camp up into eight camp families. Everyone would be assigned a camp family and this would be with whom they shared each workshop.

We had a few meetings at my house to go over the workshops with the facilitators and they were very receptive to all I had presented. I felt confident I could pull this off especially with the support I was receiving from all the groups. A committee of four was put in charge of the ancillary administrative duties for the camp. Our list of things to do ran the gambit from money to make change for the vending machines all the way to developing a menu for the seven cycles of meals needed to be provided over the course of the camp.

I had a blank space in the schedule which needed to be filled. Sandy, one of the parents who co- chaired our efforts with the whole Phases episodes and who lobbied in Sacramento, was going to camp with her son. She was a comedy writer and a previous regular on a popular TV series. She suggested we have a talent show during the open time frame. As with everything about the camp endeavor, the talent show took on a life of its own. I sat down and wrote about twenty song parodies for both parents and youth. We had a casting call and had rehearsals at my house. Of course I made all the facilitators perform in the show. We got some guitar and banjo players, singers, actors and folks willing to be clowns.

A week before camp we had a couple of cancellation but the waiting list filled the slots and we found ourselves with an almost flawless planning process. Now it was time for execution. It was finally the day of our

257

first communication camp. The committee, with our kids who we were bringing to share this experience, all arrived early that day to get everything set up. Dinner was to be served at 7 PM and registration arrivals were to start at 5:30 PM. Cars began to arrive and security directed them to the parking areas. Families brought their sleeping gear and personal items to the small cabin outside of the parking spaces where Dee had set up registration with a few of her committee members.

Everyone received a button with the color of their camp family, the cabin number and the table where they would have all their meals. They unloaded in their assigned cabins and then went to the dining room to have coffee and punch while waiting for us to start dinner servings. As expected, many of the kids did not look too excited to be there. Some we even had to coax out of their cars. There were those that had that nasty look or attitude but I felt certain it would change as the weekend progressed. At least, I hoped it would.

One such story I will never forget. We had a single father in our Pasadena location who shared how much he wanted desperately to take his sixteen year old daughter to the camp. She of course refused. I suggested a bribe and he proceeded to offer her $50 if she would go to the Camp. She accepted the bribe and they arrived early Friday evening. I saw the distressed Dad exit his car and approach me.

"She refuses to get out of the car and says she will just stay in the car for the whole weekend unless I upped the ante" he sadly claimed.

I told him to let me handle it. I went over to the car and she would not look at me. I offered her $100 if she would join us; however, I told her I would give it to her on Sunday afternoon only if she would tell me she hated the weekend and would never go again. Of course she was out the door in a split second. Still had an attitude but I informed some of the B.I.L.Y. Too girls to take over and introduced them to her. I was so busy all that weekend that I failed to notice how she was doing. However, after the Talent Show on Saturday evening and the emotional workshop that followed, she approached me and asked me if I would take the $100 of our bargain and apply it to the next camp. She loved it. The father was blown away and so was I. The kids who attended the B.I.L.Y. Too youth group were more relaxed as they had been prepped by Bear for weeks and they also did not arrive without knowing others It was the kids who were there the first time who had the problems, but kids have a way of sensing it and soon all the youth were hanging out together at the fire pit. It was the only place on the camp grounds where you could smoke.

At 7 PM, everyone found their seats and almost everyone had arrived on time. After Jimmy and I welcomed the families, we introduced the committee. Elizabeth was also a trained nurse who filled in if we needed her. Then after introducing the security, we all sat down for a surprisingly very good and filling dinner. After dinner and a short break, we proceeded to the first of our workshops in a large hall about 150 yards down a path from the dining area to the large hall where the workshops were being held. After a few exercises by Elizabeth, we sat down in our camp family circles and we were given our first work sheet to complete with about 30 different questions or directives which needed to be completed and we had to walk around asking questions or doing some silly things like London bridges i.e., finding someone born the same month. This worked as a great ice breaker although there are always those few not ready to join in.

We then were instructed to sit back in our groups and the facilitators took over. First a song was played and then some questions were read and each person wrote down the question and their answers. Once all the questions were answered, the facilitator would call on each person to share what they had written. We made the questions very simple and easy for the first session just to get members of each group to begin to feel comfortable and not judged.

After the workshop, we were instructed to proceed to the fire pit which was a good hike past our cabins. We tell everyone to sit with their immediate families. A song is played and it is usually a theme to that workshop such as a salute to mothers or fathers and a letter is read from a youth whose mom or dad is no longer in their lives. Of course I wanted to have Ian do this workshop but there was no way he was going to participate, so we had one of our youth from the group who recently lost her mom, read a letter to her on how she wished she was there sharing this experience. It always gets emotional but no one else is required to share. I, however after the reading of the letter, play another song and then tell everyone it was a time for open sharing. If you are having a positive feeling now, please share it with us. We also had a few shills in the group who we can always count on to get the sharing started. This usually goes on until midnight and then we play a closing song and hike back to the cabins where lights out is at 1 AM.

Saturday morning I had security wake Jimmy and me up at 6AM. We are in a small cabin for the two of us which is also known as the Crisis Center. In case of any issues over the weekend, it is where we discuss and work on them. We shower and get dressed. Jimmy heads down to the dining hall to see that breakfast is being readied while I have the lovely job of going from cabin to cabin with a very large boom box playing very loud music which we began with "Good Morning Viet Nam": from the movie. We used it for a few camps until we had our first experience with one of the fathers, a Viet Nam Veteran who went ballistic when he heard that played. Elizabeth

262

had to calm him down. It's the last time I used that tape, but found some other equally annoying disco themed tapes that seemed to work to get everyone out of bed and down to the dining hall.

After a great breakfast, we made our way to the hall where we did our morning workshops. The questions became a bit heavier and emotions began to flow in some if not all the camp family circles. Each circle had its own two large boxes of Kleenex and this is when some started to be used. After the second semi heavy workshop, we were directed to head out to the amphitheater where we had a guest speaker. Following an hour presentation, we went to lunch which again turned out to be very good. Brenda really did a great job with the cooks in selecting good meals. After lunch and a short break, we headed on down to the afternoon sessions and then there was a two hour break for naps, sports or rehearsals for the talent show. Many of the parents were so exhausted they welcomed a couple of hours of sleep before the big evening. They were also told that it would be a late night, so the rest was mandatory. The kids are gifted with an abundance of energies and so it was the courts for them with basketball, volleyball and the likes.

We had a very filling dinner and then went down to the hall which had now been set up with all the chairs facing the stage. Sandy was ready with her performances and the show was very well received. We had guitar players, dance numbers, skits, and many singers and of course our chorus with the many songs I had written. The talent shows continued to get better, every year. Sandy did some great production numbers. One that sticks in my mind at our 4th or 5th camp was the closing number from A Chorus Line, complete with top hats and canes. After the show, there was a short break while facilitators set up their circles for the final workshop of the evening.

I won't tell you anything about this workshop other then it is a self esteem workshop generally runs into the wee small hours of the morning. Perhaps someday, you, the reader, or someone that you know, will have the opportunity to attend one of our family camps. I see no reason to spoil it for you by disclosing all the goodies now.

So now it is 5:30AM and I have had about 1 ½ hours sleep when I am awakened and I have the horrible task of getting the troops up now so they can clean their cabins, pack their bags and load their cars. Once they have loaded their cars, they proceed to breakfast. The cabin area is then off limits. Security does a final sweep and after breakfast, we hike up a small hill to a different hall where Jimmy, security and I already set the room up in one giant circle. Under each chair is a candle and holder. In the center of the room is a big candle in the shape of a heart and two lighters. In the dining room after breakfast, the final workshop begins.

The workbooks are passed out to each person chair and needless to say, they pretty much get used up. I can only tell you that this becomes the most emotional workshop and of the hundreds of parents and youth who have participated during the past 30 years, I can count on one hand, the ones that did not get something out of this experience. The lack of sleep adds to the vulnerability of the participants in their sharing in this particular workshop.

Usually we finish about 1PM and then down to the dining hall for a final buffet lunch and goodbye ceremony. Everyone except for Jimmy, Ian & I are gone by 2:30PM. I do a final sweep, pick up the signs and anything else that was left and then head on down Pacific Coast Hwy and home for a complete collapse.

I always take Monday off work because it takes me a good day to catch up with the loss of sleep and the draining of emotions. Not only what Ian share but to also witness first in my camp family through out the weekend and then in that large circle of Sunday watching the families who have experienced a unique and highly emotional weekend. Rarely are there any mishaps except getting the kids to go to bed usually on the Friday evenings and getting them up in the morning. We also have had a few of the youth hike down in the middle of the night to the beach. Of course, when they returned, their sleeping gear was confiscated and they had to sleep on empty bunks until the morning. Boy, were they pissed.

One of the highlights after a camp is the sharing in large group at our meetings, the following meeting nights for those parents who were unable to attend the weekend. It was never hard to book a camp until the last few years, when the economy went into the cellar and then we could not book a weekend because of the expense. I therefore wrote a one day communication workshop and added a few new sessions and of course eliminated others such as the talent show and a meditation workshop. So far they have been a success and I look forward to the day when we can once again do weekends.

For me personally, it was mind boggling. To hear Ian share how much he loved me and how important I was to him and so much more, was worth the world to me. Prior to our first experience, Ian would always use one tool to totally destroy me. When he got really mad at me he would tell me" I wish you had died instead of mom"

This would always result in my going into my bedroom and falling apart. However, after all he shared in the various workshops, I packed those sharing's up in my heart and when the occasion arrived a few weeks after our first camp and he said those words, I just looked at him with a big smile and said" That doesn't work any more because I know how important I am in your life and how much you love and need me" He never said it again. We also tell each other all the time, especially in the evenings after a phone conversation, "I Love You."

This was surely a milestone in our relationship. Hearing "I Love You" from my children usually meant they either wanted something from me or they did something I would not be happy to hear about. I rarely told my children as they were growing up, that I loved them. I thought they would figure it out by themselves. I knew I loved them and certainly validated that with Joyce. When they were very young, I would always tell them I loved them but I guess I forgot to continue it as they grew into the formative years. I regret it now but after several camp experiences, I feel the warmth of telling Ian and look forward to catching up someday with Lesli

CHAPTER FOURTEEN

Looking down the Barrel of a Magnum 45

The success of the family camp lulled me into the false belief that once a family attended, they would be changed and wouldn't have to revisit the same issues which brought them to the camp. A call in the middle of the night disabused me of that notion quickly.

"Richard just got home and he is stoned," a shrill voice came through the receiver. It was Maggie Brown.

She and her sixteen-year-old son had attended camp a couple of years ago and experienced some really profound moments between them. Prior to the camp they had been struggling through his chronic running away, school disruption and increasing drug use. Maggie's husband had abandoned the family years ago and she was left to raise an angry, hurt son. Richard took out the anger he felt for this father on his poor mother. Maggie was one of the lucky parents who had insurance covering rehab and she could access at least 30 days for her son. The problem was Richard refused to go. She needed our help to get him to the hospital.

I called Stan, one of our support parents who was an ex-cop, to go along with me. He brought a pair of handcuffs with him just in case. We arrived at the home and found a frantic Maggie. She reported that Richard was packing a bag and planning to runaway. Stan suggested we go to the bedroom and talk with him. I felt only one of us should go in so not to overwhelm him.

I went down the long hallway toward his bedroom while Stan and Maggie waited in the living room. As I entered his room I could see Richard standing in front of a dresser with his back to me. He was about six-foot-two and built like a halfback. He turned around just as I crossed the threshold of his room.

"What the fuck do you want?" he growled. I kept my distance.

"Richard, you are in trouble and I am here to help you."

"I don't need any help, now get the fuck out of my room," he shot back.

I knew I was not talking to Richard. I was talking to the drugs. His eyes were glossy and he was having difficulty standing in one place. Richard was extremely agitated and I realized I only had one chance to connect and bring him off the ledge. As I slowly made it from the doorway to the have a seat on his bed, I told him his mother was extremely upset and wondered what had triggered him because he had been doing so well since they attended the camp. His room was filled with posters of heavy metal bands, some looked familiar as I am sure I had seen them hanging in Lesli's room over the years. A pile of dishes were stacked on his nightstand and the requisite piles of clothes sprung up from various areas of the room.

As I sat down on the side of the bed, a sweaty Richard reached into the top drawer of his dresser.

"I told you to get the fuck out!" and I knew he meant every word of it when pointed directly at me was a Magnum 45.

"Richard, I need you to relax. I am just here to help." I wasn't sure if the gun was loaded but I was sure he was and in his condition there was no telling how quickly this situation could escalate. I was very aware of the droplets of perspiration collecting along my temples but I acted as if I wasn't moved by his action. This upset him even more.

"This is loaded and I will have no problem shooting you if you don't leave."

I believed him yet something kept me on the bed. "Richard"I began, "I am not here to make trouble for you and I know this is not what you want." I kept my voice low and held his gaze.

His statue was wobbly yet he never took the pointed gun off me. There was no point telling him that his mother loved him and was worried about his downward spiral. The drugs were a perfect muffler and I didn't need to agitate him any further. I looked over at the half packed duffle bag.

"Richard, where are you going?" I asked. He blinked his eyes rapidly, seemingly caught off guard by my question.

"I just need to get away for awhile."

"I could give you are ride," I offered.

"Nah, that's alright. I have a friend picking me up." He answered with a much calmer response.

"We could talk and figure out what to do after you came back." I took the risk of slowly rising from the bed and taking a step to the left. Richard continued to point the gun at the spot I had once been sitting.

"I don't have a drug problem. My mom is just wigging' out about a couple of joints." I nodded sympathetically. Again, I offered to take him to his friend's house, thinking if I could get him out into the living room Stan could handcuff him and we could take him to the hospital. "You are really going to give me a ride?" he questioned.

"I would be happy to take you where ever you want to go if you let me have the gun." He looked down at the pistol in

273

his hand, seemingly disconnected from the malice he was wheeling. To my astonishment he handed me the gun. "I have a friend in the other room who is going to ride along with us." I said.

"No. I only want you to drive me." His anger sprang back up.

"Okay. That's fine." Since he was willing and had handed over the gun I didn't want to complicate things by insisting Stan go along.

I offered to give him some privacy so he could continue packing and told him I would wait for him in the living room. He seemed agreeable and I left the room with the gun in my hand. It felt heavy and dangerous. I approached the living room where Stan and Maggie were sitting on the couch. Stan jumped up and asked if everything was okay. I handed him the gun in response. Maggie gasped and started to cry as Stan took the gun from me. "Look at my hands," I said, as I held my shaking hands in front of me.

"It's loaded, but jammed," Stan reported.

I finally let my legs buckle under me and plopped down on the couch. What the fuck was I thinking, standing in a room with a drugged out boy waving around a loaded gun? I guess I was to busy just being in the zone to analyze it. These kids were upping the ante.

"Where is he?" Maggie asked.

I told them Richard had agreed to go to his friend's house for a few nights to think things out and then we would talk again. Maggie was prepared to protest but I shook my head and put my finger to my mouth to convey it was not what was going to happen. Stan pulled out his handcuffs.

"He is a big kid," I whispered. Stan gestured he could handled him and not to worry. We sat for a few minutes. Eventually, Maggie called out to Richard to hurry up. There was no reply. We waited for a few minutes longer. Something was up. I decided to go back down the hall to see what was going on. This time, Stan and Maggie were right behind me. As we got to the room a blast of cold air came at us from the large window over his bed. Richard and his duffle bag were gone.

Why didn't I anticipate he was going to hop out the window? We searched the area and then took Maggie over to the police station to make a report. We didn't tell the officer that Richard had pointed the gun at me but we surrendered it to him declaring it was best that it was not in the home.

After reporting Richard missing, we took Maggie back home. She was still upset about what had happened and didn't want to stay at the house by herself for the remainder of the evening, so we stayed with her while she waited for a friend to come pick her up and give her a break from the heaviness of the night.

The following evening, we told the group what had happened at Maggie's house. One of the parents, who was an attorney, advised us we should discontinue transporting kids to the hospital. We were putting ourselves in harms way and at some point someone was going to get hurt and B.I.L.Y. could not survive a liability suit. I was not open to leaving parents without a way to transport their kids to the hospital when they were being uncooperative and refused to get into the family car.

The next morning, Stan called with a brainstorm. He and his wife wanted to open a teen hospital shuttle service and were willing to give the B.I.L.Y. parents a deep discount. Within a few weeks, they were fully insured and bonded and the parents had a formal service to call for transportation assistance. Just as we resolved that issue, we started hearing rumblings of insurance companies lessening their coverage for the kids going to the inpatient rehab programs. Dr. Dave also had to reduce the number of free beds he could offer to our parents as his hospital complained about the money they were losing as a result of his generosity.

The drug problems were increasing just as our parents resources were shrinking. It made no sense. There were in-patient programs available, but they were not locked facilities and the kids would leave as soon as they were registered. This made them an ineffective service, as far as we were concerned. According to Bear, at least 80 percent of the kids in B.I.L.Y. TOO were involved in drugs on some level. They had all tried marijuana and alcohol and some were moving toward harder drugs. He wasn't clear what was causing the increase but he was sure that it wasn't going to slow down anytime soon. The increase of drug use by youth of the day was brought to my attention by Bear.

One of the problems I was dealing with was so many of my parents in group were Baby Boomers who, although they did not condone the use of Pot, also did not see it as a big problem. After all, they smoked it as a teen and they survived. I would remind them that B.I.L.Y. does not support any drug use by youth or parents and if they did not see a problem in the drug use, I simply suggested that they find another group such as AlAnon for some support. I continued to invite guest speakers from various local rehabs and out of state who were there to inform our groups of the ever increasing problems in our communities.

The idea that our kids were drowning under the disease of substance abuse came barreling home a few weeks later. I appeared on the Roberta Weintraub TV Show. It was a talk show dealing with current issues and problems of teens in our society. She was President of the Los Angeles Unified School District Board of Education at that time and also did not believe in some of the philosophies of B.I.L.Y... She was a feisty young mom who I adored, even though we continuously bumped heads over many school

278

issues and rules, until she retired. Roberta was a dynamic lady who I had nothing but the greatest respect even though we seldom saw eye to eye. I had several run -ins with the Board especially on my continuing disagreement on school suspensions. We spent the entire show debating the hard line stance that B.I.L.Y. took with our kids and the idea that kids were capable of some really destructive behavior once they were out of their parent's supervision.

She could not believe that parents did not know where their kids were when they left the house. She assured me anytime her son, who was seventeen at the time, left the house; she knew where he was going and who he was hanging out with. She did not worry about his involvement in drugs and alcohol because she had made her self clear about the consequences if he chose to involve himself in those activities.

Her smug attitude infuriated me. "Come on Roberta, you are in denial" I argued.

"No I'm not" she kept repeating over and over again.

"Are you telling me that just because your son is telling you that he is going to the movies with one of his squeaky clean friends, that he is telling you the truth?"

"Yes "again was her reply, and once again I called her on it.

She was insistent that she had control of her son and she didn't have sympathy for parents that didn't make the effort to have control over theirs.

The show was taped two weeks in advance. It was a good show for us and I was excited we were going to get more exposure. About two days before the show was to air, Jimmy called me at work insisting that I turn on the news. I hung up the phone and switched my radio from the background music that played all day to KFWB, the all news station. Within moments of changing the station, the news item that Jimmy wanted me to hear, cued up. Two young men had been killed in a car accident. They were on the 405 freeway and opened beer cans were found in their car. The announcer offered his condolences to Ms. Weintraub. Her son had been killed in a drunk driving accident. I was in shock.

I immediately called the television station and asked to speak to the producer who had been in charge of the show I had taped ten days earlier. He was not available and I left word for him to call me back. I waited a couple of days but didn't hear back from him. This time when I called I got him on the phone. I started to let him know I didn't expect my episode to air but he cut me off. Roberta had insisted the show air and she had taped a short message which would be shown before the episode. She advised parents not to be in denial like she had been.

Everyone who saw the show was moved by her message. I sent her a long letter and visited her at her home a couple weeks later. She was a dynamic woman and it was horrible to see her in so much pain. There can't be anything worse in the world than a parent losing a child. We spoke about her son and I also shared about the struggles I was having with Lesli and the loss of Joyce. I told her how much I respected her decision to run the show when I was her guest. She was a brave and highly respected person who I now considered a dear friend and colleague in a quest to help our youth.

After the show was aired, we had another huge surge of parents coming through our doors. It was becoming more difficult to find locations to run the meetings. Most places wanted to charge us a lot of money. The costs were really squeezing us. But I couldn't imagine turning a single parent away.

Once we were able to secure our first school to allow us free of charge to hold our meetings, the next schools seem to fall into place. Probably there would be a few issues I had to deal with such as, I needed a certain amount of classrooms as well as one major room which was a drawback because not all the schools would open in the evenings for us. Once the word got out from some of the schools where we were successfully meeting, we were no longer looking for them; they were calling and asking us to open a group in their schools. The problem was no longer the location as much as it was in getting someone to run them. I was going four times a week and trying at one time to visit fourteen locations.

Then we had the schools like Beverly Hills High School who did not want to put a group like ours in their school because they did not feel they had the kind of problems we were dealing with. They had no drug problems in their school. I almost burst out laughing when the principal told that to me. "You must be kidding" I said, "Your kids have the bucks to buy the best". Still he was afraid it would send out the wrong message to his parents.

As we got into the schools, we began to receive dozens of calls from the various PTAs to speak to their parents. They wanted what we had to offer and wanted to get a handle on their kids. We quickly learned my attending some of the PTA meetings in the inner cities was a waste of time. I would go to a meeting of a school that had up to three thousand students and less then twelve parents would show up. This was after two bulletins were sent home by mail. When we asked why more people weren't at the meeting, we were told it was hard to get parents to leave their homes at night. The crimes in their communities were a barrier to them getting help for their kids. We weren't sure how to get around those barriers and realized mostly middle class parents had been accessing B.I.L.Y. up to that point. But this was not going to be laid to rest by any means. I wanted to spread B.I.L.Y. in all communities.

Several months later, I had the opportunity to once again connect with Roberta Weintraub. This time I was able to obtain a time slot in front of the Los Angeles Board of Education where Roberta still resided as President. I had a big issue with school suspensions or as I referred to them, vacation days for our kids. I knew the schools were only paid for the students who attended classes and not the ones who were sent home for a day or two of suspensions. How stupid was this, to send a youth home to an empty house where both parents were at work. Where do you think this child will end up that day: the beach, the mall, dealing drugs or worse?

Ian would pre-plan a day with a couple of his scum bag friends at school, to disrupt a class and get suspended. This usually occurred on a warm beach weather day. He would cause enough of a problem resulting in his being sent home for a day or two. I was called and I would ask them to hold him in the office until the school day was over, but was told, such a service was not available. So off he went to our home to entertain his friends.

I suggested schools should develop on campus suspensions where a supervised room would be provided they would have to stay all day and just do homework or class projects or even community service. There would be a teacher or aid or both to oversee them. The response from the Board was negative as they claimed they could not afford to hire an additional teacher and aid.

I responded back with, "You can't afford not to." Especially after I now had the availability of the records of the number of suspensions in the past three months at several schools.

A motion was made by one of the members to have a trial run of my suggested program and Crenshaw High School in the inter city became the guinea pig. From what I understood, it was a success and eventually it was introduced to many of the other schools. Unfortunately it did not stop most of the schools from continuing the suspensions but I suggested to our B.I.L.Y. parents to continue fighting the system by refusing to leave the home or workplace, to pick up their youth.

One of our new sets of parents, Marv and Rikki, had a sixteen-year-old daughter who was a runaway missing for

285

the past three weeks and in an abusive relationship with an older boyfriend. I could definitely relate. Marv was in his mid to late thirties, over six feet in height and very slender. He had reddish brown hair and a full beard. Rikki was younger, maybe in her early thirties. She was about 5'4", great figure with shoulder length blonde hair and pretty blue eyes.

The next week, they were placed in my small group. They were extremely upset about their daughter Ann's disappearance and came to the group to get tools on how to deal with her self-destructive behavior. They made up their mind they were going to put her in rehab the next time she showed up. Marv had good coverage on his insurance policy and was prepared to access all their resources to get her the help their daughter needed. They also had two younger daughters who were doing well but they of course were concerned and knew that Ann's sisters were watching all of this and it was starting to affect the atmosphere in their home. The girls were crying out for attention and beginning to feel the way to get it was to act up since all the attention was being directed by her parents to Ann and her crisis.

Marv and Rikki had been coming to group about six weeks when Ann finally surfaced. They immediately swooped in and placed her in the ASAP in-patient drug program. She had been belligerent and resistant during the intake process, but they didn't care because they had her back in their possession. She was scheduled to be in the program for at least thirty days.

While Ann was in the ASAP program, our small group came together to provide a concrete action plan which Marv and Rikki could execute once she returned home. One condition of the contract was she had to attend the B.I.L.Y. Too meeting every week. During a coffee get together after group, Marv shared a picture of Ann. We all had been working hard to make sure she would succeed when she returned home but we had no idea what she looked like. The snap shot was of her at a birthday party. She was a very pretty girl. If I didn't know her back-story, she looked like any other high school sophomore.

In the next week I introduced Ian to Marv and Rikki as they were in need of someone to rewire their home for surround sound to accommodate their new stereo system. That was Ian's line of work then so I thought it would be a chance for him to earn some extra money on the side. Also it wouldn't hurt for them to get to know Ian and what a good kid he was.

Marv and Rikki's daughter Ann was released from the hospital as summer was approaching. Her first night at the B.I.L.Y. Too group she was very quiet and rather shy. Ian immediately felt an attraction to Ann but it appeared her interest in him was strictly just a platonic friendship. By this time Ian had already created a bond with Marv and Rikki and was beginning to stop by their home with the made up excuses of checking on their stereo system and how it was working.

* * * * *

Even though Ian had struck out with Ann, I was extremely grateful to have her parents as small group leaders. Rikki was especially skilled in providing support and a sense of hope to frazzled parents. Her great sense of humor served as lubricant while she suggested radical action plans for their out of control kids.

One night, a minister and his wife came to group complaining of their sixteen-year-old son who had a very foul mouth. They were afraid to have any company over to their home because of his bad language. He didn't direct it to anyone in particular but didn't seem able to complete a sentence without dropping the F-bomb. Nothing they did had any impact on his behavior.

The group sent the couple home one evening with an action plan they thought would get the kid's attention and yield immediate results. When the parents got home, their son was watching television on the couch in the den. When the father walked into the room to say hello, he was greeted with a random F-bomb. The father very quietly but firmly walked over to his son and planted a big kiss on his lips.

"What was that for?" the startled child yell.

With a big smile on his face, his father calmly explained, "Every time you say that four letter word in my presence, I am going to give you a big kiss, even if it is in front of your friends."

The mortified kid stormed out the room. A few days went by with great success but on the third night the father overheard his son on the phone talking to one of his friends.

289

Historically his coarse language popped up most frequently with his friends. His father listened carefully. As predicted he rattled off a string of offensive words within minutes. As promised, his father made his way to his son's room. The moment his son saw him, he slammed down the phone and attempted to bolt from the room. Not to be thwarted, his father chased after him.

With a bit of a playful wrestling, his father finally hit the mark. Once he saw that his father was going to follow through on this method of stopping him from cursing in their home, he became hyper vigilant regarding his language. Within two weeks, his parents reported the cursing had completely disappeared.

Rikki and Marv were also good with parents of chronic runaways and the kids who complained they didn't like living in their homes. Marv suggested that the parents take home flyers from our resource tables that highlighted the various placement centers which were available for them to go live in. Many times these veiled threats were enough to stop the kid from their threats. Parents also posted Room for Rent signs in the windows of the runaways' rooms or even posted them on the front lawns. When they returned from their latest adventures, they found the sign and decorating books. When they inquired what was going on, they were informed that their room would be rented out and if their youth was a boy, what did he think of pink drapes to liven up the soon to be rented out space. Almost across the board, they were shocked that their parents would take such drastic action and this realization brought down our runaway threat rates significantly.

For the more chronic runners, we encouraged the parents to take more dramatic action, like changing the locks. This was always hard for many parents to do, emotionally and physically. They would allow their child to come and go until some random straw broke the camel's back and they agreed to change the locks. Anger and frustration was always the driving emotions in their change of heart. They were desperate to get some level of control back in their lives. They were tired of their child running the show.

For the parents who couldn't afford a locksmith, a handy parent would volunteer to come over and lend a hand. We even had monthly lock exchanges so parents would not have to go out and purchase new locks. Once the kids realized they could not do what they wanted, it opened up a line of communication so the family could get to the bottom of what was going on.

So much of what I was experiencing, along with many other families, was the lack of communication. I had to find a new method to open those doors that were shut in my family. I needed to validate and refrain from so much judging. I began to dig deeper into this new path, trying to find some solutions. Perhaps we could do more then one communication camp each year. And so we did increase the number to sometimes as many as three camps in one year, After all, we had about 1200 parents meeting weekly at all our B.I.L.Y. locations.

CHAPTER FIFTEEN

Letting Go

On Ian's eighteenth birthday, he was the first in line at the Department of Motor Vehicles. I had refused to sign off on a driver's license because he quit school, but now he didn't need my permission. He returned home with a big smile and a California issued license. It was one of the first tests Ian had passed in years.

I had mixed emotions about Ian driving but I had promised him he would get a car as soon as he passed his test. He had the choice of a used car or saving some money which I would match so he could get a new car. Of course I knew what his choice would be. Saving money was against his better judgment. We took the money from his savings account which was an accumulation of birthday monies and savings bonds over the years, and purchased a low mileage 1980 Honda Accord 2dr. Burgundy in color, which was in good shape from a private party. I paid to have the car checked out by a mechanic and agreed to pay for Ian's first year of insurance. The car was in his name.

He kept the car for almost six months but then decided he would get some extra cash by selling his car and getting an older model. He said the Honda was an old man's car so he bought an older VW bug which fell apart in no time at all. With the help of some friends, he managed to get it in to good enough shape to sell it and then bought an even older car. I couldn't believe what he was doing but I stayed out of it since he wasn't going to listen to me and as long as it didn't cost me any money. At this rate, he will end up with a bicycle.

One evening when I got home, Ian was waiting up for me. We often chatted now after a B.I.L.Y. Too meeting. Ian had finally started dating and was seeing an adorable little gal from the neighborhood. But since it wasn't serious, I asked him how things were progressing with him and Ann and expressed my opinion on how cute she was. Ian already had his sights set on Ann but told me he didn't need my opinions or suggestions on who he should be dating.

"Hey, I have good taste, remember how beautiful your Mom was" I responded.

"Yea, I do Dad" Ian admitted.

It was still fun fantasizing on how it would be if Ian started dating a nice girl from a good family. This was something that passed me by with my daughter. I never got to go to the front door and welcome in her date and remind him to bring her home by her curfew. Or to take her shopping for new clothes and gets her hair done and take lots of pictures. I was cheated out of all these fond memories.

Ian told me that Lesli was pregnant again. I took the same attitude of staying out of it. Was this the fourth or fifth time? She had been sexually active since she was fifteen and since then had decided how she was going to treat her body. As long as she was ok, that's all I cared about. I was not ready to hear that this time she was keeping this pregnancy to full term. Her doctor had told her if she ever planned to have a baby someday, she would need to stop having abortions. Her uterus had taken a beating over the years and she was jeopardizing her chances of carrying a baby to term. Billy was adamant again in his responses as far as wanting a baby and he convinced Lesli to see an attorney about giving up the baby for adoption. Lesli had finally agreed and once she delivered the baby, they would be given ten thousand dollars by the adoptive parents.

A week before Lesli was due to deliver the baby, Billy took a gig on the road and so she wanted Ian to be in the delivery room with her. I felt sad for Lesli. Whatever her reasons, she was going to keep chasing after a man who didn't think enough of her to at least support her during the birth of their child. Lesli didn't know I knew all this. Ian had long given up being the bridge between us but felt I needed to know about this important milestone in my daughter's life. I found out much later that my in-laws and also Michel were in contact with Lesli and well aware of her pending short term motherhood.

The day Lesli went into labor was April 8th 1987. She called the adoptive parents who then called Ian. He rushed to Tarzana Medical Center and to the Maternity Ward where he found Lesli and the adoptive parents trying to make her as comfortable as possible. When Ian and Ann, his now girlfriend from B.I.L.Y. arrived, the adoptive parents went to the cafeteria to get a bite. Ian and Ann sat at Lesli's bedside with a washcloth, wiping Lesli's brow and trying to keep her calm. Lesli was scared and began crying and Ian called for the nurse. She was going into Hard Labor, prepped and taken to the Delivery room. Ian and Ann joined the adoptive parents in the waiting room and within an hour, Lori was born. They waited to see the baby and went into the Recovery room to be sure that Lesli was okay, before leaving the hospital.

I didn't know Lesli went to the hospital or that Ian and Ann also went shortly after, until a few days later when I heard it from Ian. When he started to tell me about his experience, I cut him short.

"Just tell me that your sister is not in any danger and that the baby is fine and no more" I explained.

I told him it was too painful for me to hear any more of the details. This was not supposed to be the way I wanted to hear about Lesli's first born and I was both angry and

297

sad. I remember crying most of the night. As a father of a daughter, I wanted to see her walk down the aisle in a beautiful wedding gown with all our family and close friends around. I wanted to be in the delivery room when she gave birth to my first grandchild and hold her child in my arms. I wanted to share the special day with my son and all those close to me. All my wants and desires but obviously not hers.

This was not how it was supposed to be. I wanted to wipe this day away from my memory forever. I was sure I would never again mention this child or want to hear anything about her. She deserved much more then my daughter and her asshole boyfriend could have possibly provided for her. I was glad at least they did agree on giving the child up for adoption. This was all just a bad dream that became way too real. Although there were moments when I wanted to sneak into the hospital to catch a glimpse of the child, I was so fearful it would make me so emotional and not able to handle it. I just wanted to be sure Lesli was physically okay. Emotionally she had to be a basket case. I know how much she loved kids and always talked about having children someday but not like this....

After the baby was given to the adoptive parents, Billy managed to pop back up in time to collect the money. Lesli saw very little of it. He bought a car in his name and doled out the money to Lesli like he was the one who had delivered the baby

Ian, now 20, was unmotivated and did not understand responsibilities of adulthood. No idea on how to budget himself, how to stay employed, how to take care of himself and relied on me to do all these things for him. He needed to grow up and learn to be on his own. He needed to be forced to deal with life's reality and to be able to take care of himself. He needed the first lesson in survival and it was time for me to cut the apron strings.

I knew the hardest day for me would be the day he had to move out. I was willing to help him in any way, I just needed him to get started and give it a try. He knew of this move for months but I don't think he ever believed I would follow through. I don't think when push came to shove, I would have locked him out and not let him back in. Ian was not street smart nor could he survive living on the streets. I loved Ian more then I ever thought I could and knew I would miss him at least as much as I hoped he would miss me but I wasn't planning on cutting him out of my life like I did with Lesli. I wanted this to be a positive move for him and a growing experience. It just didn't go that way.

He was not the first of many B.I.L.Y. kids who left the nest. I witnessed many B.I.L.Y. kids from the ages of 18-21 who when they had to leave their homes and could not find a place to stay, were taken into my home until they were able to move out on there own. This meant they needed to have a good paying job and be able to meet their responsibilities. I wanted Ian to experience the same and there were friends out there who were willing to take him in for a short period of time and adjustment. He was just too comfortable in my home and it was time to have him move into the next phase.

Another family camp was approaching and I was harboring significant expectations I would be able to get through to Ian and have him open up. I felt the pent up feelings he had been suppressing for the past six years was one of the major stumbling blocks in his young life. I also thought camp would help us talk about my decision for Ian to move out and start a life on his own. He couldn't hold a job longer than three months. He did earn just enough to pay his weekly rent and keep gas in his car. Ian was not into dating much although he was spending more time at Ann's on the weekends. During the week, he stayed close to the house and always called me wherever I went, to find out when I was coming home. He was too comfortable in my house and he was going nowhere

Ian of course did not agree with my decision and things had been growing more tense between us. By the time we got to camp, he was barely speaking to me. I was not expecting the letter he shared while we were in one of our communication workshops.

Dear Dad,

There has been many times when I almost left our house. I'm glad I didn't because we were not on good terms. Now I am leaving for good and on good terms. Thank God they are good because there are too many memories I don't want to forget. Dad, I couldn't have asked for a better father then you. You are a very special person to me. You have helped me through so many problems. I can't thank you enough for the relationship that we have had together. I always wondered if things would be different if mom were alive. I never thought I would have to grow up with no mom around. It was and still is very hard. I had a very close relationship with mom and when she died I was lost and didn't know where to go or who to turn to. It was hard for me to turn to you with my problems. I didn't think that you cared, but boy was I wrong. You did everything for me. I'll never forget my Bar Mitzvah for it was the last time we were all together and happy, before mom died. I know that I have depended on you for everything but I have to grow up and only depend on myself. The only way I can do this is by breaking my relationship with you completely. I know that this is the best thing for me and I hope that you won't be hurt by it. I have to start my life all over again by myself. I will never forget the fun that we have had. I will pray for the day when Lesli, you and I can be together again as a family but until then may you continue to make miracles for all the families that have come to B.I.L.Y... I love you very much, your son, Ian

There was not a dry eye in the place after he finished reading this letter, least of all, mine. We hugged for what seemed like an hour and cried in each other's arms. I thanked God and this camp, for Ian's growth and the beginning stages of him dealing with his mom's death.

By now, I had learned attending group and camp had a way of bringing up issues to the surface which often played themselves out in disruptive ways when we returned to our every day lives.

Ian's anxiety began to escalate as it became clear I was not going to change my mind and the date of his moving out was fast approaching. I even posted a huge calendar on the refrigerator and circled the date he was to move out. I watched as he did nothing to prepare for his move and I resisted the urge to intervene other than to offer a few suggestions of where he might rent a room or friends he might stay with.

On Sunday evening, the night before he was to move out, I helped him pack some clothes and other things. I told him he didn't have to take everything right away. He could store some of his things in the garage. He was crying most of the night and kept saying he had no place to go. I was heart broken but was determined not to back down.

On Monday morning I went into his room to give him a kiss good-bye and he pulled the covers over his head.

"Get away from me," he cried. "I hate you for throwing me out of my house".

I knew it was best to not engage him and just went to work with a heavy heart. Edgy and distracted, I had a miserable day. By the time I got to group, I was in crisis and needed the support of the other parents. Sue greeted me in the parking lot. Ian had just left after confronting my small group. He cried and yelled and accused them of supporting my decision to throw him out of the house. They were good with him but didn't back down and tried to show him how this was the best move for both of us. In the end, Vanessa, one of the parents in the group, suggested he move in with her and her son Evan who Ian knew from B.I.L.Y. Too. He would be renting out her other son's room, who was in placement for at least another year.

Vanessa was a very attractive lady, mid to late thirties, single mom of two teenage boys. She had been attending BILY for a few years and was a member of our Board, serving as secretary. She worked at the Police Academy which had become a venue for many of our events. She was also a small group leader and eventually became the coordinator of one of our valley groups. She lived in a three bedroom apartment near by and had a spare room she was willing to have Ian stay in until he got ready to move on from there. She told him he would have to pay her the same as he was paying me so that it would not be an additional burden on him. Vanessa was a very caring mom and I felt comfortable with the fact that Ian would be there with her and feel again the nurturing of a mother image which I knew he greatly missed.

Since it was my teachings that adult children needed to get out into the world and survive on their own as soon as possible, I needed to practice what I was preaching. So many of the youth who were floating through my home, turned their lives around and took charge of adulthood. I wanted the same for my son. I never considered it a punishment. I wanted to see this as a growing experience for Ian. I would never do anything to harm him. He was the most important person in my life and I thought what I was doing at the time was for his benefit. I knew I would miss him as much or more then he would miss me. I am sure I cried as much or more when he left and my nights were certainly much lonelier at first then his. Ian was always my sunshine or as I often referred to him as my son-shine. My home was a little less bright now.

He moved in with a family and I was now alone. I was as scared as he was, if not more. After the first few days, I wanted to call him and tell him that I missed him too much and I needed him to come back home. But somehow I knew this is what was best for both of us. He needed to grow as an adult and I needed to start the mourning process with out company. I needed to move on. I had no idea how I was going to do that but I knew it was time to start thinking about what it was going to be like, living alone with just the ghosts of Joyce, Lesli and now Ian.

I attempted to keep myself busy in my brief moments of solitude within my home. I decided that it was a good time to clean out some of my cabinets and closets. When I got to my linen closet, I noticed on the top shelve was the large ornate wooden case where we kept our Sterling Silver place settings, service for eighteen. This was one of the wedding gifts that we received from Joyce's grandmother.

I can remember the many times when Joyce would take down the case and spend hours polishing the silverware prior to many plush dinner parties at our home. As I reached for the case, I was immediately aware of the lightness of its weight. There was no surprise when I found that the case was empty. With my children now out of the house, there was no point in making a big issue of this discovery. Obviously, someone had stolen all this Sterling Silver and found a place to sell it. I continued my exploration of the home and realized much of my Sterling Silver serving pieces including a huge tea set, were also history. For some reason, I was not angry. It was material things I no longer had any use for. I am sure, sometime in the future; perhaps there would be a discussion on the missing items. But for now, I returned to my chores of cleaning.

It was a time when I had no B.I.L.Y. kids living with me and I promised myself that I wouldn't let anyone move in until I had some alone time. My house was quiet for the first time in years and I really welcomed the serenity. I took some time to reflect back over the few years since B.I.L.Y. began.

307

I thought of all the visits to various rehabs, the hospital waiting rooms with life threatening overdoses, sitting in so many court cases with abused parents, searching the streets of skid row for a runaway and the many threats on my life; and these were not even involving my own kids. Have I taken on more then I can handle? Of course these thoughts didn't last long. Like many B.I.L.Y. parents, my house was an intermediate stop-over for kids who were having difficulties at home. For those who needed to be away from home for an extended period of time, I rented them rooms and provided structure. My house was also used for all committee meetings and various training sessions. We had mixer parties so parents from different group meetings could meet each other and expand their support network. In many ways my house was the B.I.L.Y. clubhouse.

Dating at that time was really group related. We would all go out as a group. There were always single parents available but I could not find myself getting attracted to moms in the group who had troubled kids. I did not want to take a chance of getting close to those types of problems, other then what I was willing to offer as a supporting parent from group. I must admit, I was hit on many times and even had a short affair with a beautiful parent who had been a cheerleader at a rival high school back in the days when I was also in high school. I didn't know her then but she came into the group one night in Santa Monica and I was immediately attracted to her. She was divorced with one child who was Autistic. Perhaps it was the reason why I pulled away from her. I was sure that I was not in a good place to be able to add her issues to my plate. We had a few passionate experiences but I felt her pressuring me for a commitment which scared me away.

I also dated Brandi, a girl I met at work and I carried on with her for a couple of years Brandi was a real trip. She was twenty years younger then me and a bit of a scatter brain but I found her very attractive and stimulating.

She did want to have children and I kiddingly told her, "You can have mine" But she was inferring to us having a child together and I was offering her Lesli and Ian.

There was no B.I.L.Y. connection between us which was both difficult and refreshing for me. I kept her away from most of my B.I.L.Y. friends. I needed some space and time for a personal life. We did see Marv and Rikki together and of course Rick and Michel but most of my time with Brandi

309

was either alone or with my kids, who loved her probably because she was closer to their age then mine. She spent a lot of time at my house even when I was not there. I even had her stay in my home and take care of the kids when I took a trip to France for two weeks to visit my ex- sister-in- law who was then married to the Mayor of Nice, France. I believe that Brandi even taught my kids how to drive.

When I returned home is when I discovered that Brandi was addicted to Cocaine. This was the end of our dating relationship as that certainly did not fit into my profile of a potential mate. We continued our friendship over the years but dating was no longer an option.

CHAPTER SIXTEEN

So Much for Home Serenity

Could I really enjoy the serenity in my home now? I found myself missing the constant turmoil, but not for long. It was 3 AM Thursday morning when I was abruptly awakened by my doorbell ringing over and over again. At first I thought I was dreaming but when the pounding at the front door followed the bell ringing, I grabbed a robe and ran down the hallway to my front door. Not even looking through the peep hole or asking who was there, I quickly swung open the door. In front of me, clad in bright red and white stripped pj's, a red knit cap and barefooted, stood Terry. He was a Twenty-three- year- old druggie whose mom used to attend B.I.L.Y... She was a prime example of an enabler. She loved her son and helped him to get into many rehab programs but he never completed any stays for more then a few days and then hit the streets again. Sometimes he could go for months without some re-occurrences.

"What the hell are you doing here at 3AM in the morning?" I hollered at Terry as I ushered him into the living Room.

He was not very coherent as he began his wild tale about the demons who were following him here to my house and they were waiting at the curb to capture him and take him to their planet. He spoke of their plans to annihilate the world and he wanted me to take him to the police station. "I have to let the police know of their plans" he pleaded with me as I led him to my bedroom so that I could get dressed.

I informed him that I had to call his mom to let her know we were going to the police. He didn't seem to fight the call and told me to be sure and tell her he was going to let the police know so he could save our world. Terry was not going to get into my car and insisted he drive his own truck to the police station which was about six blocks from my home. There was no way I could convince him to not drive but insisted he follow right behind me at a slow pace. We parked next to one another in the lot adjacent to the station.

We entered the semi- crowded lobby at the West Valley Police Station and I had Terry sit down in one of the chairs near the desk as we waited our turn. Right before we were called to the desk, Terry's Mom Shirley, rushed through the door. "He needs to be in the hospital" I told Shirley as I met her in the waiting area.

She told me he was covered by Kaiser and I suggested we at least get him into a 72 hour hold. I was called to the desk and began to tell the officer about Terry when he jumped up and started screaming "They are going to kill us all"

The officer asked me what drugs he had taken. I was sure that it was Meth as it had been his drug of choice. I asked them if they could arrest him and put him into a 72 hour hold, while Shirley tried to quiet Terry down. The officer told us we needed to take him to the hospital and this was not their problem. We told Terry we had to take him to the hospital and the police would follow us there and take down all his information about the demons and their plans, once he was in a safe place at the hospital.

I was not happy with the police's responses until I told them he wanted to drive his truck to the hospital. They told him if he got into his truck instead of going in the car with us, they would have to arrest him. That seemed to calm down his frantic mode and he went semi-quietly with us to Kaiser under the assumption the police would be there also.

Now the next step was to get him admitted. I kept him busy just outside the emergency room listening again to his tales while Shirley went in to fill out the required forms. A male nurse soon came out the door and having been told what went on at the police station, he continued to be a part of the sting. He took Terry willingly to get him admitted and told him they would wait for the police inside.

I sat with Shirley in the waiting room and tried to comfort her as best I could. She was a mess. "He needs long term rehab, not just the few days like he has been doing for the last couple of years." I pleaded with Shirley. She knew I was right but he is an adult and she cannot make him stay in any program. I suggested an intervention with the family and she seemed responsive but I know Shirley's pattern. When Terry is released, he will make his usual promises to attend his meetings and this will satisfy her until the next crisis. The door swung open and the nurse came out to let us know that Terry was admitted and he was in good hands and seemed responsive. Shirley and I left the hospital at 5AM. I dropped her back at the police station. Terry's truck was gone and she told me she had her husband pick it up and hide it somewhere.

I went home, showered and headed on to work. At 7:30 A.M. I got the call from Shirley at my office. Terry had taken off from the hospital and was spotted on the 101 Freeway, trying to hitch a ride. Shirley called her cousin who lived a few blocks from where Terry was last seen and he immediately got into his car to see if he could find Terry. He did find him and managed to talk Terry into going back to rehab.

Terry did stay once again for less then a week and checked himself out. This time however Shirley and Paul, her husband, had finally reached their bottom. They told Terry, as I had suggested so many times, "Do not call us again until you have at least 6 months of sobriety under your belt and can prove it". They also told him that his truck, which by the way was still under their name, had been sold. I heard, Terry was back in rehab and hopefully this time, it will work and it did. For an update, Terry has been clean and sober for two years and is holding down a respectable job while maintaining his own home and attending 12 step meetings 3-4 evenings a week.

Ian refused to have contact with me for about three months. It was ok with me because I saw Vanessa at group every week for an update. According to her, Ian was still working, paying his rent on time and had become more social. I also heard that he was attending B.I.L.Y. Too every week so things were moving along just fine.

As our stalemate entered into the fourth month, I decided to drop by the B.I.L.Y. Too group one Thursday evening in hopes of seeing him. There were about thirty kids in attendance as I made my way into the classroom where the group was being held. Ian sat near the front door talking with Evan. He looked surprised to see me but made a great show of ignoring me as I spoke to the new head facilitator. Bear had moved on to another opportunity and Kirk had taken over the group. He was a gregarious tech from the ASAP program and the kids really seemed to like him. Kirk and I spoke a few moments. I wanted him to assist with a family meeting. He left his assistant in charge of the group and ushered Ian and I into another room.

A reluctant Ian didn't look at me for the first few minutes until Kirk put us on two chairs facing one another. It was similar to a workshop that we did at camp. When I first saw Ian, I realized he was no longer that little boy that I let go of. He looked well fit, dressed sportily with khakis and a white dress shirt. His hair was well trimmed and he even had a bit of a tan. He looked as though he may have put on a few needed pounds and I felt he had been taking good care of himself. He looked so good, all I wanted to do was to just grab him and hold on to him and not let go. I had to go along with the way Kirk was letting this reunion happen.

When he looked up at me, his eyes filled with tears. "I miss you, Ian" I managed to say.

"I miss you too, Dad," he answered, as tears rolled down his cheek.

I gave him a big hug and he got up and went back to his group. I stayed a few minutes to talk to Kirk and then waved good-bye to Ian. On his way home from group, he stopped by the house to pick up a few things and it was the beginning of a new and very positive relationship between us.

By late October, Ian asked Ann to be his date at the annual B.I.L.Y. Halloween party. She said yes. He was so ecstatic that he even allowed Rikki and Ann to pick out his costume for the party. They had an attic full of costumes for the girls.

The night of the party, it was unseasonably warm. I was sweating buckets in my rented gorilla costume. The party was well attended and the evening extremely festive. As expected, Rikki had her home decorated to the nines. Nothing was left out of the Halloween theme.

For the first hour, no one knew who I was. When Ann and Ian made their grand entrance, I was extremely grateful for the anonymity. Ann looked adorable in her mini skirt with a white pirate blouse and tall black boots plus a plastic sword hanging from a wide black belt. She had a pirate's hat and even wore a patch over one eye.

Ian was self confident as he made his way into the crowd. Oh my God, he was dressed as Minnie Mouse, of all things. His short back skirt and white tights highlighted his scrawny legs. He fidgeted with the black ball perched on his nose. Although I wanted to shoot him for letting them talk him into the ridiculous getup, I had to chuckle at his willingness to embarrass himself for Ann.

Ian and Ann's courtship moved very slowly. He was hanging out at her house even on the nights when Ann was going out on a date with someone else. I prayed he wouldn't be hurt as he waited for Ann to succumb to his charm and date him exclusively.

CHAPTER SEVENTEEN

Spreading B.I.L.Y.'s Wings

Lesli was heavy on my mind as I made my way home. I vacillated between wanting to be free of all her trouble and wanting to save her from her decisions. Checking my answering machine I hoped to hear her voice on the other end. That unrealistic prayer was not answered, but I did receive an unexpected request.

A Tough Love affiliated group, located in Arizona, was reaching out to us in hopes that they could come under the *Because I Love You* umbrella. They had been unceremoniously booted from the national organization. They left their name and phone number and asked that I call them back as soon as possible, no matter what the time.

I got the group coordinators, Jane and Lyle, on the phone. They sounded desperate. I could certainly relate to their feelings as I went through the same situation, The

Tough Love group in Arizona was booted out because of the politics; very similar to why we had left.

They did not agree with the money which was expected to be sent to the main office and questioned their use of non-profit as opposed to a for-profit organization. They felt there was very little support from the York's and they were very disenchanted with the whole organization. Jane and Lyle were rebels and wanted to expand using tools very similar to ours. They were as shocked when they were thrown out, as much as we were when it happened to us. The York's had given them no warning and used the same method as they pulled on us. Jane and Lyle were devastated. They began looking up various groups on the internet and found us. When they read my bio and realized B.I.L.Y. was once a Tough Love group, they immediately placed the call to me. We had instant chemistry, even just on the phone and I couldn't wait to get there and meet them in person.

At the end of our hour-long conversation, they were more adamant about wanting to become an affiliate of

B.I.L.Y... I told them I would have to speak to the board and get back to them in a day or so.

Wow, a B.I.L.Y. group in Arizona. I flipped over the idea of having a group in another state. My mind raced as I tried to decide what to have for dinner. Maybe this would be the beginning of spreading B.I.L.Y. all over the country. Why not? We had worked hard to help hundreds of Southern California parents save their kids. We could do the same for the parents in Arizona. My bubbling excitement made me abort my dinner prep and call Jimmy.

He was a little more reserved in his reaction. He was rightfully concerned about liability and our dwindling treasury, but I didn't want to hear any of the negatives. He suggested we call a special board meeting to see what everyone else had to say about this opportunity. We met at my home on Friday night to talk about the pros and cons of taking on an affiliate. At the special Board Meeting, there was little or no resistance to opening B.I.L.Y. groups in other states. We just needed to do it legally and fortunate for us, we had our own built in Attorney Lawrence, who helped us draw up a contract for affiliates and we were on our way to expansion in other states. As President, my vote was only available in the event of a tie. But you must know I was so convincing whenever I wanted anything in the way of a change or event or even structure. I always seemed to know how to win over the Board and get my way.

We spent the week establishing a format and guidelines for the affiliate group. To protect us from any liability, we would insist they apply for their own tax identification and non-profit status. We came up with a package price and a binding contract, drafted by our attorney, which would be signed if they agreed to our terms. We shipped off the contract, training manual, and letter of expectation to Jane and Lyle and waited to hear their feedback.

Three days later, I received an enthusiastic go ahead from Jane and Lyle. They thought B.I.L.Y. and their newly dubbed TALK (Tender and Loving Kare) was a perfect match. They invited Jimmy and me out to Phoenix to attend a big open house seminar they planned for the following month. Their excitement was contagious. I remember what it felt like to go out on our own with B.I.L.Y., the independence and sense we were going to save the world. As I hung up with Jane and Lyle, I was grateful for the reminder of the excitement. I had gotten bogged down with the daily administrative responsibilities of B.I.L.Y. and stopped marveling at the network of support and respite we offered parents and their kids. Our villages were expanding.

We were the bridge between parents and the world their kids were desperate to keep from them. In between the escalating and problematic behaviors, there were times when we were there to give simple lessons on botany. Last month, a mother brought in a plant to the group to verify her suspicions. Her son was away for a week and had asked her to water his plants for a science project. She hadn't had any problems with him prior to this (she attended the group to manage her daughter who was a chronic runaway) and wasn't sure what to make of the plants.

We quickly made it clear for her that his "science project" was a mini marijuana crop. She was mortified and openly disappointed. Her son was a senior in high school and she thought she had gotten at least one of her children to the finish line with no major incidents. I normally was very heavy-handed when it came to drugs and demanded parents immediately get help for their kids before things got out of hand but her genuine surprise regarding her son's behavior made me rethink that strategy.

Her son was coming back in three days so we suggested she water the plants with a daily mixture of water and bleach. The plants would suffer a slow death and her son would just think he didn't have a green thumb. Her job was to pay attention to see if he attempted to grow a new crop or any other drug paraphernalia showed up in the home. Armed with this information, she had a better handle on the situation and could judge if her son was experimenting or heading down a dangerous road.

* * * * *

Jane and Lyle met us at the airport. I was to be the keynote speaker for their open house seminar. In the month since they came under the B.I.L.Y. umbrella,

325

they had formed a board of directors and had formalized themselves as TALK Parent Support Group practicing the Because I Love You philosophy.

When Jimmy and I went to Arizona, it was my first trip there. I had passed through years ago but never stopped to enjoy the sights. Arizona, that is Phoenix, or at least Scottsdale where Jane and Lyle lived, reminded me much of Palm Springs where I spent half of all my vacations. I loved it there. First of all, I am a sun worshipper. The heat sits very well with me so I felt a kinship immediately to their home town. We were prompted to dress very casual, like shorts and tee shirts for arriving and casual clothes for the opening of the new group. We felt right at home from our smooth landing, right to the front door of their home.

Speaking of their home, it was a ranch style one story with about 5 bedrooms and a great room which was attached from the living room, dining room, family room and to the kitchen. Much to the same décor that you would find in our desert resorts such as Palm Springs. They also had a great yard with a beautiful pool and cabana.

On our first night in the town, we had the opportunity to visit their parent group. Thirty or more parents were currently attending. I alerted them to prepare themselves for a huge influx of new parents. My experiences informed me, those parents who were looking for a resources and a free support group, would definitely be attracted to a B.I.L.Y. group opening in their community. The Phoenix parents were just like the parents back at home. They were struggling with chronic runaways, drug abuse and out of control behavior with their teens. Also like us, they were at their wits end and were desperate to regain the control over their kids and their lives.

When we returned to Jane and Lyle's home where we were staying for the weekend, we sat up talking until late into the night. Jane was a very classy brunette; I would say about 35 years old, well put together and I was sure that she was into an artistic lifestyle by the décor of her home. The paintings were awesome and I soon discovered that she was the artist for most if not all which hung generously about the home. Lyle was best described as a character from Guys and Dolls, being short, slim with a broad mustache and a receding hairline. His bark was much bigger then his bite and he had a never ending supply of jokes which kept

327

us in stitches all the time. He and Jane had a very successful Catering Company in Phoenix and were very well known in the community.

They had a son in an Ivy League College back east and a daughter who was a runaway very similar to Lesli's story and they had not seen nor heard from her in a few years. But they did hear she had a baby and was raising the baby on her own. She was the reason why they got involved in Tough Love. Jane and Lyle put a lot of work in the open house seminar and they had done a big push to get press coverage for the event. The open House Seminar introducing Jimmy and I and the B.I.L.Y. program was held in the library of Scottsdale High School. Jane and Lyle had done their homework so not only did we have about 150 parents, including teachers, counselors and some from the medical field show up, but we also had a few reporters there from the local papers. Lyle welcomed the crowd about 7PM and shortly thereafter, he introduced Jimmy who also spoke briefly in welcoming the crowd and then introduced the main event, me. I can entertain a small group of 6 or wow a mass meeting of hundreds. That is a gift that I am sure that I was born with and continued to pick up the pace with my involvement in B.I.L.Y...

I proceeded to tell the parents about me personally and why I started B.I.L.Y. and of course I then went into the humor and in no time at all, I knew I had won over the crowd. I had them both in tears and in stitches. I knew how to milk it and when to bring it to fruition. I even had the reporters come up to me and ask me if I was in show business or a comedy writer. Yeah, I wish I was. Perhaps in my last life, although this one was far from over and maybe B.I.L.Y. was my gateway to show business, a dream of mine since I was a little kid. I realized now I was entertaining people as well as informing and teaching. It was the entertaining part that helped to keep parents coming back each week. I instructed all my coordinators to be sure that they always broke the groups with a humorous story or clever consequence and send them home with a smile as well as learning the light at the end of the tunnel did not always have to be a train. My Malapropisms were always a good closing, too.

The reporters also sent photographers the following day to Lyle and Jane's home where we held a training meeting for their group leaders. The following day, we had a full page in the Scene section of the Scottsdale Progress newspaper. The title read "Support Group TALKS Tough

Love to Teenagers Because Of Love" It was a very positive article and because of it, their next meeting was swamped with new and excited parents. I hated to leave on Sunday but went home on a real high.

One of my fond memories of the TALK group in Arizona was the following year when six families from their group, joined us at our Communication Camp. I especially remember one family who had twin sixteen year old boys. They sent in their registration form very early but as the date approached, I received a call from Marsha, the Arizona mom, who was in a panic because she and her husband were not sure how they were going to present the camp to their boys. She was sure they would say no. I suggested she not tell them they were taking them to a B.I.L.Y. communication camp; just to say they were going to spend the weekend in Malibu by the beach. The boys were thrilled and really looking forward to the July vacation in California. They were into surfing and canoeing so it was an easy sell.

I will never forget that Friday afternoon when they arrived on the camp grounds. Their SUV was topped with two canoes, surf boards and the car was loaded with all kinds of beach wear and two very unhappy boys. I sent Dani, one of our sixteen year old popular girls from B.I.L.Y Too over to talk to the guys. She persuaded them to come out of the car and took them under her wing for the weekend. It didn't take too long for the boys to get adjusted and by the end of the camp; they had collected numerous phone numbers and told us they would return next year for our next camp. It was the overwhelming response from all the Arizona families and many returned the following years to our camps as well as frequent social visits. They even wrote a parody to perform in our talent show which resulted in a standing ovation.

CHAPTER EIGHTEEN

Ian Thanks You, Lesli Thanks You, Joycee Thanks You and I Thank You

At our next board meeting, we formally added our out of state location to our marketing material. The addition of the affiliate group forced us to talk about the precarious financial situation which we were currently in. Although our parents could attend free of charge, the board had expenses we sometimes had to go into our pockets to cover. Our book sales gave us a consistent financial baseline but as we continued to experience growth, paying rent at the various schools to have nightly meetings and covering Jimmy's salary, we teetered at empty on a monthly basis.

The idea to roast me at a fundraiser was mine. It felt like a better idea than the one the board had approached me with. They wanted to throw a dinner dance to honor me. As much as I loved to be in the spotlight, it felt unnecessary and diminished all the hard work so many other people had put in to keep B.I.L.Y. going. A roast felt like a fun way to raise money and reconnect with all the friends I had lost track of since I submerged myself in B.I.L.Y...

Over the years, my personal life had really gone through some big changes. I saw a lot less of old friends outside of the organization. Rick had given up dragging me out to the clubs and finally focused his attention on improving his relationship with Michel. I did manage to stay in contact with many friends not connected with B.I.L.Y. by phone but actual time spent together was only at anniversary and birthday parties. My involvement with B.I.L.Y. put me in a social circle where I didn't have to explain the ups and downs I experienced with my kids and therefore felt like a more welcoming place. With my B.I.L.Y. family, I was a good father, doing the best I could. I wasn't judged and seen as an expert in empowering parents. It felt much better than an incompetent sloth which my family somehow had a way of making me feel.

The Roast Committee went all out for this fundraiser. Brenda headed the committee. She was, by this time, one of my closest and dearest friends. She served on the Board of Directors, chaired on many committees including all those having to do with our camps. She was of course, part of our social core group.

In addition to all of this, there was a time when Brenda was having some financial difficulties and needed a place to stay. I had a spare bedroom where she asked if she could rent until she got back on her feet again. This turned into a few years of her staying in my home. Even during the times when I had several B.I.L.Y. kids that were transitioning from their homes to the real world of adulthood but were in no way ready yet. I was also able to obtain a position of employment at my work place for Brenda. There even was a time when her daughter Dani came back into her life after being a runaway and spent some time also living with us. Dani was like a substitute sister to Ian and soon became the best friend of Ann.

Brenda and I would spend hours just laughing. She was so much fun to be with and we remained close friends even when she moved away. I will always be indebted to Brenda for her many years of volunteer work with B.I.L.Y... She had an incredible talent of organizational skills. Something

I also have but need to rely on my Board to keep me grounded. Her older brother and I are also very good friends. Actually, we are really more like family then just friends. I will never forget the evening of my big roast.

The big Dinner Dance/ Roast was held at the Odyssey Restaurant in Granada Hills, California in their main banquet room with an adjoining large room where cocktails would be served and a Chinese auction would also be set up. The restaurant was on top of a big hill that overlooked the entire valley. The all glass windows invited the view. The invitations said cocktail attire but of course, Jimmy and I wore Tux's and I rented one for Ian. Everyone arrived dressed to the nines. Hors devours were served in the cocktail room and a sit down full dinner with some kind of Stuffed Chicken Breast was served as well as all the trimmings and a Chocolate surprise for dessert. A great band played before, during and then again after the roast. We sold out at a little over five hundred friends and family.

I was touched by the length they went to make the evening memorable and to also recognize the work I had done to make B.I.L.Y. the kind of organization I knew it could be. There was one surprise after another throughout the evening. Dina and Ted, two of our show business connections in the group, had secured a letter of regret for not being able to attend in person plus a signed picture from Ann Margret, for me. This was a bigger deal for me than the personal letter that President Ronald Regan sent to honor the event. I received that evening, a beautiful letter from him and Nancy as well as numerous letters and awards and framed documents from various government officials, from city council persons, and the mayor all the way through Governor, House of Representatives and the Congress. I was blown away with each presentation as well as a variety of Telegrams from others unable to attend. I never stopped smiling although my heart was still hungry to share that evening with Joyce and Lesli too.

Everyone in my life knew that Ann Margret was my fantasy. I had fallen in love with her when I first saw her on The Original Amateur Hour. Even when Joyce was alive, she used to tease me about my unrequited love and allowed me to have a picture of Ann Margret on my desk at home. I even played Albert Peterson, the leading role in Bye Bye Birdie at the Community Center which was also the movie that starred Ann Margaret. I sat on the stage with the biggest smile on my face knowing that if Ann Margaret had shown up, they would have had to call the paramedics.

On the dais with me was a swath of family and friends from the various stages of my life. There was Chad who was my oldest and dearest friend back from my school days, Ross from Marriage Encounter, Jay Cavanaugh from the IADARP Drug Rehab Program, Molly from The North Valley Jewish Community Center group and Sandy from B.I.L.Y. . Peter, who is Brenda's older brother and an old friend of mine from the Community Center, coordinated the evening and allowed each guest on the Dias to write their own brutal roasts. They were all extremely funny and everyone was very receptive. I am sure that Sandy's recollection of all my malapropisms was one of the highlights of the evening. Peter also wrote in a little music to the program that included the cast from a hit musical review that I preformed in at the Center.

It was a wonderful evening for my family and me. I was washed over with all kinds of emotion. Ian completely blew me away when he stood up and gave me a toast in

337

front of the packed room. This was the same child who could barely utter three words in front of the family. I was intensely proud of him. Ian looked like a movie star in his black tux with a red cummerbund and red bow tie. I was shocked when Jimmy called him up to the podium to offer a toast to me. Here was a young man who I could not get to talk in front of a group of 10 parents and now here he was in front of over 500.

I remember his short toast that went something like this. *"Ladies and Gentleman, Friends, Family and, B.I.L.Y. extended family, it gives me great pleasure to honor my father this evening. I am so proud of his accomplishments both in helping me to turn my life around and his never-ending devotion to helping so many families in crisis. , Dad I Love You, Everyone, a toast to my Dad"*

Of course everyone lifted their glasses and toasted me as the tears rolled down my eyes and, as I suspected, many others too. Ian walked over to me and gave me a big hug and at the same time whispered in my ear that he forgot to have a glass in his hands when making the toast so he held up an empty hand and of course we both laughed. He may have shared how proud he was of me but I couldn't have been more proud of him then I was that night. He had come so far and I told him he had ownership of this, not me.

I gripped the sides of the podium feeling so full, trying to clear my mind to make my closing speech. Hundreds of smiles and beaming eyes stared back at me. There were so many B.I.L.Y. parents in attendance from over the years.

Greg, the wheelchair-bound father, and his wife sat at a large table near the stage. They had a daughter that wouldn't do anything around the house or clean her room. His small group had come up with a clever solution to his long-standing issues. Six parents including me, showed up at their house on a Saturday morning armed with trash bags. We walked into her room while she was lying in bed on the phone. No one said a word and just proceeded to fill up the trash bags with her clothes and belongings strewn throughout her room. She screamed her head off like a wild banshee. Her mom and dad just sat there with a grin from ear to ear as we cleaned the room. When we were done, we carried the bags to our cars and drove off. Of course when the parents showed up to group the next week, their daughter was in full-blown crisis. She was angry with them for allowing strangers into her room to take her stuff and demanded her belongings be returned.

For the first time, her parents were feeling empowered and they stuck to their guns regarding their expectations that she clean her room and keep her space neat. It took her three weeks to realize they were not kidding. When she finally decided to go along with the program, she earned one bag of belongings per week until all her things were returned.

Standing back by the bar was the mom who took her son's toilet seat because he kept peeing on it and not cleaning up behind himself. Initially he didn't care until he realized that at some point he needed to sit down. It only took two days before they came to an understanding and his toilet seat was returned to him.

Seated a few tables back were a group of friends who I went to Grammar school all the way through High School with. Table loads of couples that Joyce and I experienced Marriage Encounter with and of course the many friends from the North Valley Jewish Community Center. All this, plus hundreds of my new extended family

340

of B.I.L.Y., was a real eye opener for my immediate family to witness. I cleared my throat several times and willed myself not to cry. There was nothing to cry about. My only regret of the evening was that Joyce and Lesli were not there.

"I didn't think I was going to be so emotional." I started. I remember my Thank You speech, starting out with a few digs to each of the people on the Dias that stuck it to me. Then in a serious way after welcoming everyone and graciously thanking them for their support, I stole a line from George M Cohan in the movie "Yankee Doodle Dandy". I lifted my glass to everyone and finished with, "Ian Thanks You, Lesli Thanks you, (I gestured above) Joyceee Thanks You and I Thank You."

A standing ovation with a thunderous applause ended our show and people began to leave but not before coming up to Ian and myself and raving about the evening and our accomplishments.

The fundraiser provided two very valuable things that evening: twenty thousand dollars and the validation that we were able to continue providing a much needed and sought after service to our community. Several years of dinner dances followed honoring various community leaders who were partially responsible for our growth.

For me personally, I am just at the beginning stages of my mission. I know in my heart, Joyce is helping to guide me on this journey.

CHAPTER NINETEEN

From Broadway to B.I.L.Y.

The attendance at all our groups continued to flourish. I glanced around the rooms each night at our various meeting locations and realized that we must be doing something right. The rooms continued to fill with a repeat of familiar faces plus a bouquet of new parents who were showing up each and every week. Unless invited into our core group of close friends, we had no idea what the occupation or living conditions were of any of our participating families. It wasn't a requirement on any of our parent information forms which every new parent had to fill out before going into orientation. We would often have a recognizable city official, sports figure, psychologist or someone from the entertainment field, but they generally would be covered with wigs and sun glasses. Many times they were court ordered. Last names were not required and in some instances, a different first name would be used. Since we practiced confidentiality, we never inquired much into the personal lives of our B.I.L.Y. parents, unless they openly provided the family dynamics.

I enjoyed doing the orientations for new parents' and noticed most of the celebrities and professionals seem to be from the more exclusive suburbs near some of our meeting locations. My coordinators would greet the new parents and issue the handouts, which contained a parent information sheet with a place for their names, addresses, phone numbers and emails. One of the dead giveaways when they would hand back the completed form in orientation, was it contained a made-up first name only with no additional personal information other then the issues that brought them to B.I.L.Y. It really wasn't necessary to know how they earned a living and almost all the time, the full stories came out once they felt safe in their small group environment.

I remember one famous Broadway star, whose orientation I did without recognizing her. Once I placed her in one of the small groups, I continued on with my paperwork and began my floating to each small group to see if there were any problems that needed my additional attention. After large group, I generally hung around with the small group leaders, just to check in with them on how things went that evening. The leader of the group where I had placed one of the new parents, asked me if I recognized the young mom who I placed into their group? I did not, until she told me who that person was. She also said that she was very open in her sharing and told her group that she was in the entertainment field. She continued to use the name of Jill but it was only a matter of a couple of weeks when everyone in her group recognized who she was. Eventually, someone in her group asked her if she was that person and she owned up to it. But by that time, we already had her hooked. She was a regular for about two years and rarely missed a meeting, except for the few times that she was doing a local TV show or had to fly back and forth to New York for auditions and personal appearances.

Jill had a 16 year old son who was having a problem with alcohol. Her ex-husband was frequently involved in their son's life and I did find out that he was also a practicing alcoholic. Jill was awarded full legal custody but her ex was allowed visitation every other weekend, if he chose. As expected, Jill and I became very good friends and I was even given a power of attorney when Jill had to go out of town for a couple of weeks. She did not

345

completely trust the housekeeper to take care of any issues with her son which could possibly involve his addiction problems. We had already discussed his going into a rehab if he didn't agree to attend meetings and stop drinking. Neither Jill nor I could convince Ted, her son, to stop his weekend drinking. He would hide bottles in his room and many a morning, Jill would be unable to get him up in time to go to school.

I was not one of Ted's favorite people and he did not appreciate the changes in Jill once she became an active participant in B.I.L.Y... Rules were posted in her home now and continually broken by Ted. She was extremely stressed all the time, with an open evidence of guilt. This was mainly brought on because of her frequent travels out of state when she had to leave her son with the Nanny and later on, with a housekeeper.

One Sunday evening, while Jill was entertaining on a cruise ship in the Greek Isles, I received a frantic call from the housekeeper. She asked me to come to their home as soon as possible. She said Ted was very drunk and wanted the keys to one of the cars. She had them locked up and was not about to release them to him. She informed me Ted was verbally abusive and she was afraid he might get

346

physical. I told her that I was on my way and she should call 911 if the situation escalated.

As I pulled up the long winding driveway to the front of their home, parked adjacent to the front double doors were two squad cars. I found some parking area behind the second car and hurried through the front double doors of the home, which were now wide open. As I entered the large marble foyer and proceeded to the living room. There sat the housekeeper in one corner of the room with an officer who seemed to be taking a statement or filling out a report. Another officer was on the phone, near the fireplace while two more officers were bookends to a cuffed Ted on one of the four large white plush sofas. Ted did not glance in my direction. The officer on the phone, motioned for me to approach him while at the same time, I took out my wallet and handed him my B.I.L.Y. business card as well as the power of attorney papers from Jill. He proceeded to hang up the phone and read the papers which I handed him. He was somewhat familiar with B.I.L.Y. and had also been filled in by the housekeeper of my position with the family and reasons why Jill had given me power of attorney, while she was performing out of town.

347

I asked the officer if it was possible for them to take Ted for a 72 hour hold, but he informed me that the situation at hand was not serious enough to require that action. He did suggest I get him into a detox- rehab such as Tarzana Treatment Center, which I was very familiar with. I also placed a call to Dr. Dave, to see if there was a bed available in the ASAP program. But knowing Ted, he would probably never stay for more then a few hours. The officers did not feel Ted was a threat to anyone so long as he stayed put in the house until he sobered up or until I took him to a rehab facility. They unshackled him, gave me a copy of the police report and bid us adieu.

Ted would not even look me in the eyes. He just said that he was sorry and just wanted to go up to his room and sleep it off. I tried reasoning with him but he would not listen to my requests. I reminded him of his mom's was instructions of taking him to a rehab should any problems arise and he shot back with, "I'll just call my Dad. He will come and take me out of wherever you try to admit me."

This was the first time that he ever brought up his Dad to me. I helped him upstairs to his bedroom, did a quick search of the room and was not surprised to discover a few vodka bottles under the bed. One was empty and the other was about ¾'s full. I told Ted I was going to spend that night in the living room on one of the sofas and I was a very light sleeper, so he shouldn't try anything stupid. I also told him I was going to call his therapist and try to get him in for a session, the next morning. He was okay with my suggestion and he just proceeded to pass out on top of his bed. I went down to the living room where the housekeeper was doing some straightening up. I asked her if she had Ted's father's phone number. She did and went to get it for me. When she returned, I was already on the phone with Ted's therapist and after I filled him in on tonight's activities, he agreed he would see Ted at 10AM the next morning. The housekeeper gave me Ted's dad's business card. I informed her I would be spending the night and I would be taking Ted to his Therapist in Beverly Hills, in the morning.

I glanced at the card but did not recognize the person's name, only the agency that he was connected with. I called his number and was surprised when he answered the phone. I introduced myself to him and apparently, Jill had already been in contact with him prior to her leaving for a two week gig. Actually she was due home in three days. I did have an emergency phone number for her but decided to take care of this without getting her upset. I explained to Mr. Saul Davidson, as his card informed me, the details of the evening with his son. I told him I thought it would be a good idea to get Ted into a 12 step program and possibly some in- patient time and was shocked with his reply.

"Bullshit" he responded, "You are not taking my son to any rehab. If you can't handle the situation, then bring him to me and I will take care of him. Those 12 step programs are a rip off"

"Mr. Davidson, they are free" I continued, "and as far as an inpatient program, your insurance covers him for 30 days" I replied.

He made light of his sons drinking and even told me he and his son would often go out and have a few beers when they got together. I reminded him it was illegal for his son to drink booze. He just responded with he remembers when his father used to do the same with him when he was Ted's age and he turned out just fine. I saw the handwriting on

350

the wall and just needed to get off the phone. I told Mr. Davidson I would keep him informed and also suggested he might want to attend one of our meetings in a different area from the one where his ex was attending. He just laughed as I said my good- byes.

The next morning, I was awakened by the beckoning aroma of freshly brewed coffee. I quickly freshened up as best I could, polishing off two cups and half a toasted bagel, provided by the housekeeper. I proceeded to take a cup of black coffee upstairs to wake up Ted. I was surprised to find him freshly showered, fully dressed and sitting in front of his computer, finishing some homework assignment which was due on that day. I reminded him of our appointment and he was not thrilled about it. However, we did manage to go and as I waited patiently in the outer office, he had his hour session.

After giving the therapist some business cards of B.I.L.Y., I dropped Ted off at his school, which was walking distance to their home. He promised to call me when he got home from school and as I pulled away, I watched him in my rear view mirror while he entered the attendance office. I had already called his school, while waiting for Ted in the therapist office, to advise them he would be late because of a doctor's appointment. They had my name on file and all went well. I was anxious to get home, take a shower and maybe even get a few hours of sleep, since I did very little last night...

When Jill returned on Wednesday evening, she called me to get all the details other then what she already heard from both the housekeeper and Ted. She was very upset. I suggested that she get Ted started in our youth group and she agreed. We also had a communication camp which was just a few weeks away and Jill asked if there were any spaces left? Of course I would find room for her and naturally, she would be placed in my camp family.   That camp was a huge success, as always, and a tremendous breakthrough for Jill and Ted. He agreed to go for help with his alcohol problems and shortly after the weekend, Ted was admitted to one of Dr. Dave's in- patient programs. Jill continued to come to group for several more months and then took a role in a Broadway play. She moved to Manhattan with Ted and we stayed in contact for several months after that. Every so often, when she appeared in town or in Vegas, I would try to get by to see her. On a brighter note, Ted graduated High School and then enrolled to an acting school in New York where he is currently pursuing a career in the theater. Just another B.I.L.Y. success to add to our collection.

Then there was the Tuesday evening when a young and very attractive mom signed in for my orientation. She stopped at the desk and picked up an information packet and wrote her name out on a name tag that we provided. I glanced at the tag and learned that her name was Ginger. She asked me if I would step outside of the library so she could talk to me privately. I proceeded to follow her to an area a few feet from the doorway. She asked me if I ever did one on one parenting classes in someone's home. I had never considered it as an option although I must admit over the years; I certainly did a great deal of sessions on the phone with parents who were in areas where we did not have a B.I.L.Y. group. I also was on call 24/7 for anyone who needed me in any of the groups.

"Was this for you?" I asked

"No" she replied. "It is for my husband who has been court ordered to attend parenting classes" She mentioned that he was a very famous R. & B. recording star and that he does not want to share these sessions with a bunch of strangers.

At first I was taken off guard and wanted to say we don't provide that service but I have to be honest here. When she told me who her husband was, I said I would be more then happy to meet with him at their home and discuss the possibilities of giving him some private parenting classes. She thanked me and returned into the library to join the other new parents who were patiently waiting for my orientation session to begin. She purchased one my program books and handed me a card with her name and phone number as she was leaving the library. I told her I would call her the following day and we could discuss the scheduling of our first home meeting with her and her husband. I was still not sure why he was court ordered although I did notice on her information form, that they had a six year old son together and he had an adult son from his first marriage.

The following morning, about 11AM, I called Ginger. She was very excited to hear from me and called her husband to come into the room. She told me that she was putting the phone on speaker so that we could all talk. He introduced himself as J.R. and thanked me for agreeing to provide him and his wife, private sessions at their home. I immediately set him straight that I had not yet committed to the private sessions and I needed to meet with him to discuss the reasons for the court order. He asked me if I could come right over and I told him that I was at work and the soonest I could see him would be Friday evening, since it was the first free night that I had. We agreed on a time and Ginger gave me the street address, which was only a few miles from my home.

Friday evening, I left my home at 7PM and continued up into the hills of the valley , winding around to a gated area where a guard slid open a window from his small office to inquire who I was visiting in that complex. I gave him the name of the family and also mine. After checking his guest list, where I assumed my name was already on, he wrote out a card for me to display on my dashboard and buzzed open the large Iron Gates. This followed with explicit directions and once again, I was on my way up another winding road to a cull de- sac and another large set of iron gates.

I rang the bell and answered the speaker as the gates began to open. I proceeded up a long driveway to a single story contemporary home with lots of windows and a view to die for. Ginger was waiting for me in front of the large beveled glass double doors. She gave me a hug and took my arm to lead me into what I would imagine was their large family media room. J.R. was on the phone while sitting in one of the large reclining chairs. He continued on with his call, which I found a bit rude. I walked over to him and extended my hand, which he shook and motioned for me to sit down. Ginger was embarrassed by his rudeness but I just took advantage of the time to glance around the room at all the Grammys, platinum records, various other awards and sheet music that was covering most of the wall space. Shortly thereafter, he did say to whomever he was talking to, he would call them back later.

"Nice to meet you Dennis" he offered and asked me if I wanted to have a beer or something. "I appreciate your taking the time to give me some court ordered parenting classes" he continued.

"I have not made that commitment yet" I responded and asked him if I could see the court ordered papers. Ginger left the room and returned with the report and I began to skim through to find child abuse was the reason for the parenting classes. There was one incident when J.R. spanked his son and apparently the nanny called Department of Children Services. This ended up in a court and the results were his having to attend some parenting classes.

It was at that time when his young son ran into the room and jumped on his Dad's lap. After a big hug and kiss from J.R., his son came over and asked me what my name was. I didn't notice any bruises as I cautiously glanced about his frame. He had on shorts and no shirt, so it was a relief not to see any visible marks. Ginger called for the nanny who came and picked up their young son to get him ready for bed. He blew kisses to Ginger and J.R. as he and the nanny left the room.

"I love that kid and would never intentionally hurt him" J.R. belted out.

"You just need to control your anger and spend more time with him" Ginger offered.

Well, I was starting to get a few details just by listening to the two of them shout back at one another. Finally, I interrupted and suggested I give J.R., an orientation and Ginger thought it was a great idea. She handed J.R. a pad of paper and told him to take notes, but I knew it was not going to happen.

Thus began six weeks of hourly sessions and the beginning of a new but brief friendship. Of course, they never offered to pay me for my time or even make a donation to the group, but I didn't care. My concern here was to establish a safe and responsible relationship between J.R. and his son. I really felt that J.R. and their young son had made some improvement with their increased time together. Each night, JR would spend at least on hour of one on one with his son, helping with school work, watching a video, playing a game or reading a book. Once or twice a week, J.R. would take his son out for a treat, sometimes with Ginger and sometimes just the two of them. The yelling stopped, at least for the weeks that I was seeing them. I even spent a few moments alone each week with their son, just to get somewhat of an update as to how J.R. was treating him. I really believed that J.R. was committed to his role as a father and was willing to follow all my suggestions. I provided him with the proper papers

358

he was required to bring to his upcoming court date showing his attendance in the B.I.L.Y parenting classes. Ginger was more then pleased with the way things were going with J.R. and their son but I could feel that something else was bothering her.

I was soon to learn that there was another problem, much more serious which eventually came out in what was to be our final session. J.R and his adult son had not seen each other for over ten years. I could feel tension that J.R. was experiencing when his older son became the topic of our conversation. It was apparent that the trouble in their relationship began with the divorce of J.R. and his first wife, who was the mother of his older son. Tyrell, J.R.'s now adult son, was 17 at the time of the divorce and his mother was awarded full custody. Apparently, there was some physical abuse involved that resulted in J.R. spending 6 months in jail. I couldn't pry too much when this came up. I needed more details and J.R. was not willing to discuss or disclose.

I spend an hour or so, the following day, on the phone with Ginger, while J.R. was at the recording studio. She proceeded to give me a more extensive detailed report on the relationship or lack of, between J.R. and Tyrell. She also expressed her desire to have them re-unite at some point and hoped I might be able to make this happen. Ginger was planning a huge surprise birthday party for J.R. at one of the big nightclub venues on the Sunset Strip. She told me she was planning on inviting me and also asked if I thought she should send Tyrell an invitation? I asked her if she was in contact with Tyrell and she told me that she made many futile attempts but their conversations were brief and very strained. She did believe the door to re-opening the relationship was slightly ajar.

"Would you mind giving Tyrell a call? She asked.

"I have no problem in talking to him, if you think it might do some good" I replied.

Ginger gave me Tyrell's private phone number and offered she would call him to alert him of my upcoming call, so it would not be a big and unwelcomed surprise. She also gave me details on the party as far as times and date. The following afternoon, Ginger left me a message she had spoken to Tyrell and although he was not convinced he and his father could ever re-unite, he was willing to listen to what I had to say. I don't recall the details of our phone conversation the following morning. I do remember there was a great deal of referencing my own personal situation with Lesli and how I felt about someday having a relationship with her. I found Tyrell quite responsive to my suggestion he attend his father's surprise birthday party and his presence would more then likely be one of the best presents J.R. would receive that evening. As expected, J.R. was completely taken by his son's unexpected appearance and it was very emotional to say the least. The party was spectacular. Ginger left out no details and I was mingling with some of the biggest recording stars in the industry. I was even introduced to Eddie Murphy and shook his hand. I couldn't wait to get home and share the details with Ian.

I heard back from Ginger, a few days later, that Tyrell and J.R. made some plans to see each other again and it was hopefully a new beginning of a much too long lost father and son relationship. Perhaps this also gave me some hope that someday Lesli and I would be able to put the past behind us and resume a much needed and desired father and daughter relationship.

Sadly, however, a few months later, J.R. was found dead from an overdose of prescription pain medication he had been taking due to a serious fall in a recent appearance in Las Vegas. I was devastated with this news but on the same hand, happy that Tyrell did get to reunite with his Dad before J.R. died.

.

CHAPTER TWENTY

My Best Friend Rick Passed Away

When the letter arrived, I debated most of the morning whether or not to open it. Over the last four years I had thrown a good number of Lesli's letters unopened in my desk drawer, but this letter arrived on a day when I was both worried and curious about her life. The curiosity had taken hold after Ian and I had come back from our vacation. Reluctantly, he informed me that Lesli was pregnant again and she was going to give her second baby up to the same parents who adopted the first child. As I listened to him stumble his way through her rational and due date I was surprised that I could still get angry about her poor choices. Although the idea of having the two kids together in one family was a positive move.

For some reason I knew the letter on the kitchen counter was going to tell me something I didn't want to hear but I felt compelled to open it. I grabbed my cigarettes and took the letter to the car with me. I sat in the driver's seat with the door swung open. I lit up and took a deep pull from the slender cigarette, flipping the letter over a couple times before letting it settle on my thigh. Why was I still wrestling with this? Lesli had long made up her mind and I was never a consideration so it was a waste of time to hope for something different. I picked up the letter as I flicked the cigarette across the concrete driveway. Inspecting the postal seal over the Liberty Bell stamp told me she was still in the Simi Valley. I tore the envelope open and pulled out the college rule paper. Lesli's perfect script filled every line of the paper.

Dear Dad,

I'm not exactly sure where to begin or how to say what I have to say but I guess honesty is the best policy, so here goes. I love you dad. You're my father and I love you. I want you to share a very special experience with me. Regardless of what has happened in the past. I am a grown woman and have made my share of mistakes but that's in the past and even though it hurts sometimes, I have chosen to leave it in the past. Daddy, Billy

And I have set a date. We are going to be married next June. I know that you probably have mixed emotions about the whole thing, but I am engaged, Dad, ring and all. I am so very happy. I love Billy more then I thought I could ever love someone. We want to be together forever. Someone has never loved me so much. We know that we may not be totally ready for this, but what couple is?

I want you to give me away at my wedding. It won't be a wedding if you're not there to share it with me. You told me once that when you hear my voice on the answering machine that you get a small tingle in your heart. Well think about that tingle now dad. There's only going to be one wedding and I want you to walk me down the aisle.

I know that it's a little less then a year away but I need to know. I know that it will probably be hard for you to make a decision but if you could be there for me, just that one special day in my life, it would mean the world to me. Please think it over and write soon. All my love and kisses... Lesli

Was she kidding? Give her away? I already gave her away and this was just the proposed frosting on a wedding cake. I tried to light a new cigarette, blinking rapidly as the anger started to take over. *How dare she write and ask me to do this for her?* I felt lightheaded. I put my head down on the steering wheel as the smoke from the unattended cigarette filled the car. A few moments passed when I abandoned the cigarette on the driveway and started the car. My pulse was still racing and I needed to talk to someone.

I pulled up in front of Michel's Condo. I hoped she wasn't busy as I rung the doorbell. I felt if I could talk to anyone about this it would be Joyce's best friend. A moment later, she answered the door. A look of concern registered on her face, the moment she saw me.

"Dennis, what's wrong?" she asked, as she opened the door wider for me to enter.

"She is getting married." I blurted.

"Who?" Michel continued.

In the middle of her immaculate living room I screamed! It was guttural and fierce. Michel watched me react like a mad man. "What is the hold that bastard has on her" I yelled.

I paced around the living room desperate to break something. "Lesli is getting married?"

Michel sat down on the sofa. I started laughing hysterically. I was falling apart. Michel watched me with concern but no judgment. Exhausted, I flung myself into the love seat.

"Four abortions, two babies she gave away, no high school diploma and now she is going to marry this idiot who lead her down this road," I shared with frustration as I put my head in my hands.

How could Lesli expect me to accept him in our lives? He sold her children and is ruining Lesli's life. I can not do it. I am spent. Michel was more worried about my reaction and afraid that I was jeopardizing my health. She tried to calm me down and eventually I sat there and listened to her wise responses. I knew what was happening in Lesli's life was not in my control nor was it because of my actions. It was her wants and desires. I was doing so well in letting go but she reminded me I needed to do some real soul

367

searching and be sure I was comfortable with my decisions. I knew what she was hinting but she was very careful not to advise, only to open the door to what were my options. This was very similar to what I have said to a parent who came to B.I.L.Y. with a similar story. I left there much calmer then when I had arrived.

When I got home, I called Ian and let him know about Lesli's plan. He was legitimately shocked. He was not a fan of Billy and he thought that she was crazy for even considering being attached to him for the rest of her life.

In my bedroom, I pulled Lesli's letter out of my pocket. The envelope was moist and bent around the edges. I had no intention of answering it. I opened my desk drawer and dropped in the letter.

I took on as many projects in B.I.L.Y. as I could. I wanted to keep my mind occupied and off of Lesli. The busier I became in other people's crisis, the less I had time for dealing with my own. I was so far into my escape hatch that it took me a couple days to return Michel's call with her horrible news that Rick had a brain tumor. He had been complaining about some severe headaches recently and finally went to a doctor who suggested an MRI. The results came in and we were all shocked to hear that he had a malignant tumor in the brain.

I felt guilty that I hadn't seen much of Rick in the last year. Pulling into Cedars Sinai visitor's parking lot, I thought of the last time I saw him. Rick had always been a picture of health and worked out every single day. Sure he used drugs occasionally and liked to suck everything out of life, but he was only thirty-two-years-old and always there for me.

Coming off the elevator, I saw a tense Michel sitting with her arm around Rick's brother, Marlon, who was completely shaken. His mother and a few other friends hovered over them while Rick was in surgery. The surgeon was doing an exploratory procedure to determine if the malignant tumor could be removed. I settled down in a chair next to Michel and touched her hand gently. She gave me a weak smile. I was glad that things had settled down between them. Rick was really in love with her but he was easily distracted and would

369

run off and get into other things when he felt too much pressure in the relationship.

To love Rick was to know he was a spontaneous man who did everything with intensity and lived life to the fullest. I remember in thinking back, about the first Christmas without Joyce. I was in no mood to go gift shopping alone so I'd asked Rick to go along with me for the company, to see about finding a black polo shirt for Ian. The plan was to head over to Bullocks in Sherman Oaks to pick up the shirt and a couple other gifts. Rick showed up at the house in his jeep with the roof off and no side windows. Before I could protest and suggest that we take my car, he bellowed that the beauty of living in Southern California was an 80 degree day in December.

The Sherman Oak's Bullocks didn't have the shirt in Ian's size so we headed over to the one in Beverly Hills because I really wanted to get him something he really wanted. The Beverly Hills store had no black shirts. I rummaged through the other colors deciding hopefully Ian would be happy with the fact the knowledge his financially strapped father made the effort to get him a polo shirt. Rick disappeared while I selected a white shirt and headed to the cashier. Rick reappeared with a big grin and announced he had found a store that had the shirt in the right color and size. I started to protest but decided to save my breath. I put the shirt back and we headed out to the jeep. We jumped on the freeway heading east.

"Where are we going?" I inquired.

"To get Ian his black shirt," Rick replied, as he continued on past the downtown exits.

Twenty minutes on the 10 Fwy it was clear we were driving away from the city all together. "Rick, where the hell are we going?" I demanded.

He gave me a big smile and yelled, "Palm Springs!" promptly turning up the radio to drown out my demand that we turn around. Ian did get his black polo and a whole lot more.

I was praying for something positive, when the two surgeons came into the waiting room and invited us to the private family meeting room. I could tell by the look on their faces, the news was not promising. After six hours, they had determined the tumor was malignant and inoperable. Marlon totally lost it as they delivered the bad news. They had relieved some of the pressure on his brain and wanted to start him on chemotherapy as soon as possible. Marlon kicked a chair and then stormed out of the room. Michel went over to his mother and hugged her as they both cried.

It was so unreal, like being in the twilight zone. We were all in a state of shock. The room expanded with grief and disbelief. I was numb, as we all waited until Rick got out of recovery, then I left. I wasn't ready to see him. I had to get to a meeting. I needed to crowd my mind with someone else's problem. I waited a couple of days before going back to the hospital. Rick was in good spirits and looked pretty good, considering his condition.

"I'm out of here tomorrow," he managed to respond.

His speech was slurred. Our conversation was brief and mostly about Michel. He asked me to promise to watch over her when he was gone. I told him I didn't want to hear that foolishness and he would pull through this, but in my heart I felt we were losing him.

A few minutes later a serious-looking Marlon came in with a camera, lights and a tripod. Rick was going to tape his will before he left the hospital. I couldn't handle that. I made my excuses and darted out of the room. I met Michel out in the hallway.

"Do you know he is taping his will?" I asked.

She nodded. "He doesn't want to wait too long. At some point he is going to lose his speech…his mind." Her voice cracked. I gave her a long hug.

I made sure I was going to visit Rick as often as I could. I was not going to use the excuse of being too busy. No one was saying it out loud but the chemo wasn't working and he wasn't going to last more than six months. When I saw him at his condo, there was always an interesting cast of characters hovering around him. I never saw so many manicurist and hairstylists in one place at one time. It was a comical parade. Rick had slowed down excessively.

He wore a Caesars' Palace baseball cap to cover his hair loss. When he saw me he would always take if off and tease me that I finally had more hair than him. Ricks favorite hat at the time was from Caesars Palace in Las Vegas. This was one of Ricks' hang outs throughout our friendship. He loved to gamble and he taught me his game of Roulette and to this day I always play and surround #32 which was his winning number. It has brought me luck also over the years. Because of Rick being a big gambler at that hotel, I remember going up to Vegas one time with a few friends and Ann Margret was appearing at Caesars at the time. I called Rick to see if he could do anything for us in getting us a reservation.

He not only got us the center front table right on the stage but also back stage passes to meet her. I was such a wreck that when we arrived back stage and she came over to us and said" Which one of you is Dennis?"

Everyone pointed to me and she took my hand and all I could say was "I Love You".

She smiled and thanked me and said "Why don't you introduce me to your friends" I looked up at them and could not remember their names. I was in shock or in heaven. She was beautiful. I called Rick afterwards and thanked him. I shared all about the experience and he was pleased the hotel took such good care of us...

It was only a few months before they took Rick back to the hospital. Rick never went back to work and he had a male nurse 24/7 while he was at home. I did visit him once at his place but I just could not handle seeing him in that condition. He was not the Rick I wanted to remember. They were pumping him with massive doses of morphine to keep him comfortable. I only went to see him once more while he was in the hospital. I couldn't do the deathwatch. It was too painful and brought back all the memories of sitting by Joyce's side, praying the death away.

Michel called me early on December 8th 1989 to tell me that Rick had passed away. Rick was dead, I sobbed, the receiver in my hand, long after Michel had hung up.

Ian and I arrived at Eden Mortuary, a half hour before the service. We went up to visit Joyce's gravesite. Rick was to be buried on her right side with Michel's plot on his right and my plot was on Joyce's left side. Rick had purchased the two adjoining plots that were available shortly after Joyce had passed away. I had picked up a dozen yellow roses, Joyce's favorite, to put on her plot. When we arrived at the site, we found the area was being prepared for the burial so we were unable to put the flowers down. When Rick first told me he had bought the plot next to our plots, I thought he was crazy. But now I was glad he could keep Joyce company, until I got there.

Marlon was a mess as he gave the eulogy. Watching him struggling to convey his love for his brother, broke our hearts. His older sister eventually had to go up and stand next to him to keep him upright. My own mind felt soggy. It was unbelievable that he was gone. He had been the catalyst for my recovery from my great loss. He got me back on my feet all while making sure I had some fun. We had some wild and crazy times which I would never forget. Listening to the Rabbi, I wondered if I should have tried to slow him down when

376

it came to his excessive partying. Maybe he would still be alive, although I knew there was no stopping Rick from doing what he wanted to do. When it came to Rick, it was his way or the highway.

We walked to the gravesite for the final service. Ian and I joined the long line of friends to shovel some dirt on to the casket which had been lowered into the ground. I tossed in the dozen yellow roses along with a small pile of dirt.

Ian and I had to return to work so we couldn't go back to the family home. I called Michel later in the afternoon. She sounded like she was holding up but I knew the grief comes in waves.

CHAPTER TWENTY-ONE

Lesli, For the First Time, Got Arrested

"Mr. Poncher, this is Billy Robles, Lesli's boyfriend"

My heart went right into my mouth. "Why are you calling?" I managed to get out as I sat down at my desk.

"Lesli got arrested," he said.

"For what?" I questioned. He mumbled something about a payroll check. "What?"

"I don't have any money and I thought you could bail her out," he offered.

"Not my problem," I said, and hung up the phone. She wasn't dead or hurt and that's the only reasons I would have been willing to get involved. However, I did have flashes of her being cuffed or behind bars in some cell. I was very concerned and decided to call Ian and inform him of my phone call.

"Ian, Lesli has been arrested" I began.

"For what?" Ian replied

"I don't know the whole story but Billy called for bail and said it had something to do with a forged check. Can you make some calls to get some details" I asked.

Ian answered" Let me see what I can find out and I will get back to you"

The wait was draining and I kept wondering if Lesli was okay and would she have to stay in jail for the night because I didn't bail her out. I started to feel guilty for my actions or lack of. Ian called me later in the evening and let me know Lesli had been released on her own recognizant and I have to admit, I was much relieved. . She had been charged with altering a payroll check from two hundred dollars to two thousand and then trying to cash it at a check- cashing establishment. Because of the amount, they had to verify it with the employer. When they called her workplace and spoke to the doctor, he instructed them to call the police and have her arrested. Of course Lesli didn't take responsibility for her behavior and blamed the "mix up" on the girl that made out the doctor's payroll and she had intentionally set her up by making out the check for two thousand dollars.

Two days later, after a B.I.L.Y. Too meeting, Ian let me know Lesli had moved out and once again left Billy. After her arrest, she had somehow managed to get out of doing jail time and was sentenced to six months of community service. She did lose her job. Once she wasn't bringing a paycheck into the house, her problems with Billy escalated. Eventually she left when she was able to land a job with a detective agency, which I thought was completely ironic, and moved to her own place in the San Fernando Valley.

Hearing all that was going on, I had to acknowledge that a tiny glimmer of hope still flickered inside me. I wanted this to be the end of Lesli wasting her life on the biggest mistake she had ever made, however, I knew better than to hang my hopes on any choices she might make. Ian was speaking to Lesli more often now that she was living closer to home. She had him convinced she

380

and Billy were ending their eight-year relationship. Lesli had given him back the engagement ring, which was no big loss. I heard that the diamond was so small you couldn't see it with the naked eye. During Lesli's entire relationship with Billy, she settled for less than she deserved and every one of his gestures fell short. Now he was dating other girls and she was concentrating on a career. It sounded too good to be true but I held on to a little bit of hope she would actually follow through and start changing her life. After all, it had only been three months since she had broken off with Billy.

Lesli gave me a call. It had been years since I heard her voice. Of course she wanted something and that was a new phone. Not having sufficient credit, she hoped I would co-sign for her. I couldn't help but laugh at her audacity. She had walked away from us and not looked back once, but she absolutely believed she had the right to ask for what she thought she deserved.

"You must be kidding" I quickly answered her request.

Of course, even after I refused, this was not going to stop my daughter. She forged my signature and had the bill sent to her apartment. It would be six months before I discovered that I had another phone in my name.

Ian reported that her apartment was tiny and she was having a tough time meeting all her bills. She had a friend who lived in the building and had suggested they share an apartment. Roy was heavily involved in the twelve step programs and about ten years older then her. Lesli described him as responsible and felt like he was the kind of friend she needed in her network.

Before I could entertain the idea that Lesli was starting to align herself with appropriate people, I received a call from her roommate Roy, in the middle of the night. Three months after he and Lesli had moved in together. He shared that he was madly in love with her. The more Lesli treated him like a trusted friend, the more he became possessive. He started to drink again and became abusive. Eventually, she was afraid to go anywhere because he started showing up in random parts of her day, uninvited. By now she was indebted to him financially and was scared to move out. Finally one night when he was at a meeting, she packed whatever she could and left him a note saying she wasn't coming back. He went nuts, resulting in a blizzard of calls to Lesli's family and friends in hopes of tracking her down.

He refused to believe that we had no idea where she was and called us several times a day. Eventually, I told him that I would file charges if the calls didn't stop. That's when the threats began. Since Roy wasn't the first person to threaten my life, I knew exactly what to do. I started to record his ranting and aggressive calls. He made it easy for me by leaving the rambling messages on my answering machine.

Ian finally heard from Lesli. She was oblivious to the kind of chaos that Roy was causing in our lives. She agreed to call him and demand he stop harassing us. He requested they meet face to face. She picked a restaurant, in case he became violent. She promised to call Ian if things got out of hand so he could pick her up.

The next thing we heard, she was back in the apartment with him. She rationalized she needed to get her stuff and this was the only way she knew how and the situation wasn't supposed to last more than a couple days. Her couple of days stretched into a few weeks, which lulled Roy into believing, she was staying permanently. His behavior improved and things settled down. As soon as she broached the idea of moving out, the phone calls began again and so did the threats.

This time I took the phone messages to the police and filed charges. I was not going to let Lesli's continued poor choice in people derail how I was living my life. We received a court date for early spring. Ian and I showed up at the San Fernando Court House early with tapes in hand. A nervous Roy was waiting outside on the steps. Ian was told by Lesli what Roy looked like and so we had no problem spotting him. He was close to 400 pounds with tattoos everywhere that skin showed. He had a shaved head and was rather scary looking. He wanted to talk to us before we went in to the courthouse. We quickly stepped past him without a word.

The courthouse lobby was filled with mostly young gang members of one ethnic group or another, a scattering of girls with babies and a few parents looking very distressed. The last time I was here was with a mother who was placing a restraining order on her daughter. Jillian had been through hell and had finally decided to take the reigns in her life. It broke her heart that her daughter, Suzanne, had been consumed by the drugs and preferred to live on the streets. The finally straw was the break in, by Suzanne's drug dealing boyfriend, that left her house destroyed and her youngest son traumatized. Jillian's restraining had come about two years after Lesli had been gone. That was the first time I really started to consider the idea perhaps sometimes you might never get your kids back.

After thirty minutes, we were called into an office with a judge and a legal secretary, who was taking everything down. I did most of the speaking and the questions were mainly directed at me and the relationship I had with Lesli. I asked the judge why Lesli was not also not there and she said Lesli told her that she did not want to be anywhere near Roy, ever again. We spoke somewhat of the events which had been going on that lead Lesli to where she was today. After the brief interview, she gestured for one of the tapes to be played. Roy was especially manic in this recording. On the tape, he cried for a few minutes, and then declared his love for Lesli before he abruptly hung up. The next call had him raging and threatening with what seemed like glass breaking in the background. In the last sample call, he apologized repeatedly for his behavior. He sounded like a little boy looking for his mother.

Satisfied with what she had heard, the judge instructed us to remain seated and not to address Roy directly once he was in the room. A sheriff then escorted him into the office. He shuffled toward a chair on the other side of the room. Ian and I kept our eyes on the judge. She requested that the tape be played again. The ranting and raving made Roy looked down at his hands that were in his laps. He looked mortified.

"Mr. Brown, is this you on the tape?"

He nodded.

"I will need an audible response," she demanded.

"Yes, ma'am." He answered clearly.

She pulled a form from a stack of papers on her desk and wrote aggressively across it. "Mr. Brown, I am giving you one year of probation. During that time you are not to have contact with Mr. Poncher, his son, daughter or anyone in their family network. Do we understand each other?"

"Yes, ma'am." he repeated.

"If you violate your probation, you will be immediately arrested and sentenced to eight years in prison" "Are you completely clear on all of this, Mr. Brown?"

"Yes ma'am" was his final response.

As we moved to exit the office, Roy put his hand out to shake mine. I brushed past him without a word. Ian and I made our way to the car. I couldn't help but wonder how Lesli continued to create crisis in our lives and she continued to go unscathed. Or did she?

* * * * *

Ian was working for a contractor now and installing sound systems in private homes. This was a hidden skill that came out of nowhere. He was working very hard and seemed a lot more confident. He was also seeing a lot more of Ann and needless to say, Rikki and I were thrilled. Marv maintained his stance of staying out of his daughter's love life but I knew he liked Ian and was happy with their relationship. Ann started dating Ian exclusively after the Halloween party. They were together every spare moment and most of the evenings Ian spent at her home.

A couple weeks after our fall family camp event, Ian pulled me aside. The camp had been outstanding. Marv, Rikki, and Ann had been in our camp family and some tremendous work and connections had occurred over the three days.

Ian was going to ask Ann to marry him and I wasn't really surprised. During camp it was clear that they were in love and there was a strong bond growing between them. What sticks in my mind the most about our family experience was in one of the camp workshops on Saturday evening in the Heart Workshop with our camp families. Rikki got in front of Ian and Ian broke down and told her that she reminded him of his mother. That she was a loving and caring mom and did all the things he remembered his mom did when she was alive. Rikki broke down first and then Ian followed and of course Marv, Ann and I were right behind them. The rest of our camp family followed suit.

This was such a break through for Ian who always fought back the emotions when it came to sharing anything about Joyce. We all reached for piles of Kleenex as the workshop continued.

Next in front of Ian was Ann. Ian looked into her eyes but could not speak. He was so pent up with emotions. They both started to sob and hug each other. All we heard over and over from each of them to each other was "I Love You"

We were all basket cases. Even though this was what I wanted from them both, my range of emotions caught me off guard. A wave of sadness washed over me. It wasn't fair that Joyce wasn't here for this tremendous milestone in our son's life. She would have thrown the most fabulous party for them. This was by far one of the happiest moments in my life. All the crap that had gone on with Ian was over and now he was a man that I could be proud of and respect. My constant regret was that Lesli was not with us so that we could celebrate this moment as a family.

The following Monday after the camp experience, we went to the safe deposit box, where I stored his mother's diamonds and allowed him to select one for Ann's ring. I was proud to pass on a legacy from his mother. We took the stone over to Darren who was a B.I.L.Y. parent and ran a wholesale jewelry business. Ian looked so grown up as he worked with Darren to select a setting for the ring.

After he received Marv and Rikki's blessing, Ian planned the entire evening. He was going to ask Ann to marry him. He had selected a restaurant on the beach for the special evening and planned to pop the question after dinner while they walked on the sand. My late blooming kid was a romantic.

Finally something wonderful was happening in our lives. I couldn't wait to share it with everyone. While Ian was preparing to ask Ann to spend the rest of her life with him, Rikki had the families over to their house for dinner. We didn't let on why we were having the dinner. We wanted that honor to go to Ian and Ann.

Around 10:30pm, I heard a car pull up in front of the house. Ann's kid sister, Nancy glanced out the window and announced Ann and Ian were coming up the walkway. My heart began to pound. I couldn't imagine that Ann had said no, but the suspense was killing me. My excitement caused me to jump from my seat and pace a little, although no one seemed to notice. As they entered into the den, their faces didn't give away any change in status. The guests greeted them casually and returned to their individual conversation. I couldn't look at Ian as he allowed a few minutes to go by.

Then finally, "Excuse me," Ian yelled over the din of voices. He had our undivided attention. "Ann and I would like to tell you something."

The guests settled down and turned their attention to the handsome couple that was standing at the front of the room. Ann stretched her hand out in front of her. "I am engaged," she squealed.

"To who?" Marv yelled out.

"To me," Ian offered, beaming with pride.

The family rushed them, eager to offer their congratulations. They oohed and aahed over the 1 ½ Caret diamond that looked tremendous in the elegant Platinum setting and Ann was clearly pleased with Ian's choice. As we toasted the young couple I realized, I felt pure joy.

Yet, once again, two members of my family were cheated of this beautiful experience. I so wanted to be able to share this night with Joyce and Lesli.

CHAPTER TWENTY-TWO

Oprah Winfrey, Are You Kidding?

The gentleman on the other end of phone was claiming to be a producer from the Oprah Winfrey Show. It took him a couple tries to convince me he wasn't jerking my chain. I wasn't a stranger to talk shows. Geraldo Rivera had a three-part series about runaways built around the work B.I.L.Y. was doing. The first show was filmed on the streets of Hollywood. It followed the story of Brenda, one of our B.I.L.Y. parents who was looking for her daughter. The second show was shot at our Woodland Hills location at Taft High School where they got the chance to see how the program was run. The final segment was filmed at a restaurant in Hollywood where we were hoping for a reunion between Dani and Brenda. I was never free from the reality while I was helping other parents reconnect with their children; my daughter had been completely out of my life with no sense if she would ever return.

Our first appearances created a big rating success and they invited us back a few months later. This time I had the opportunity to take six B.I.L.Y. kids with me. The audience was riveted by their stories of drug addiction, living under bridges, and making dangerous decision on a daily basis. I could tell by the look on their audience faces, these kids seemed like aliens when in reality teens of all walks of life were struggling and their parents were often unaware.

Appearing on the Oprah Show would expose us to our largest audience ever. This was such a great opportunity for us to explain our program and how we have helped thousands of families and continue to grow. The producer was booking a show on out of control teens. He had heard about the work B.I.L.Y. was doing and wanted to fly me out to Chicago. Even after I hung up, left with a list of items that needed to be faxed to him, I still couldn't believe it.

Three hours later, I had called every person I ever knew. I felt buoyed and important. So many things were going well, personally and professionally. Life had finally settled down and things felt more than manageable.

Landing in Chicago at midnight, I couldn't wipe the smile off my face. Over the last two weeks I had done a bunch of hand wringing and fretting they might call to cancel my appearance. Even when the plane ticket arrived from the show, I knew I wouldn't be relieved until I was physically in Chicago.

Making it through the gate, my carry on bag felt heavy probably because I had over packed. I still hadn't made up my mind what I was going to wear on the show. Since the producer booked me, I had been feeling like a scatterbrain. I'm sure they were still laughing about the message I left on the producer's answering machine. He had asked me to send over a short history of myself and how I started B.I.L.Y… I was to call him and leave him a message that the fax was on the way so that he could return to his office and pick up the fax. The message I left on his voice mail was that my biopsy was on its way. He called me back to find out if I was ill. We both had a good laugh when we realized that I meant my biography. Not a stranger to a malapropism, again I had found a way to litter them into my conversations at the most inappropriate times.

Exiting the gate I saw there were a few gentlemen dressed in black suits waving signs with names on them. A tall man, in dark glasses, had a placard which displayed **Dennis Poncher.**

"That's me," I said as I approached the Limo driver.

He greeted me and immediately took my bag from me. I followed him to the waiting black limo parked in a nearby lot. As we made our way to the hotel, I marveled at how beautiful all lit up and sparkly Chicago was. In a quick twenty minutes we arrived at the Hyatt Hotel. The driver took my bag and led me to the registration desk. I was instructed to be out front at 10:00am so that he could take me over to the studio.

The woman behind the registration was a young, very cute redhead and very friendly. I wondered, as she took a copy of my driver's license, if she was this nice to people who weren't going to be on the Oprah Winfrey Show.

My room on the twelfth floor was a one-bedroom suite with a beautiful view of downtown Chicago. The living room area was bigger then the one in my home with a huge maroon leather sofa and two matching chairs. The bedroom was behind closed doors and when I walked in there, the four poster bed was very inviting but there was no way that I was going to sleep even though it was about 1 AM. There was a welcome letter from The Oprah Show on my desk. The letter was on Oprah's personal stationary and signed by her. Of course it is framed and in a very conspicuous place in my home today. It instructed me to feel free to order either room service or take advantage of the dining room at anytime during my stay. On my bed was a menu for 24-hour room service and since I couldn't sleep and they were footing the bill, I ordered a full breakfast at one in the morning. By the time the food arrived I was propped up in the massive bed watching television and going over my notes for the show.

As I rolled over, stomach still filled, the clock blinked a solid 3:00am. After a three hour nap, I was back up, showered and fully dressed by 7:00AM. With time to kill, I took a walk downtown. Chicago was my home town but I was almost 5 years old when I left with my family and moved to California. I did go back once in 1956 when I graduated High School with two of my close friends who were also born in Chicago. I had very little memories of this town and it all was surreal for me. As I noticed the El which I seemed to remember as their rapid transit, I thought about movies where I had seen those particular scenes. There was a lot of traffic with the hustle and bustle of the morning rush hour and I felt very invigorated.

Back in my room, I packed since I was going to the airport right after I finished taping the show. I decided against ordering another breakfast and went downstairs to wait for the limo. Promptly at 10:00AM, the driver arrived and we took a short ride through the downtown area and made our way to Harpo Studios, which reminded my of the NBC building here in Burbank. I was greeted by a young lady probably in her mid twenties who worked on the Oprah's staff and it was obviously her job to make me feel welcomed.

I was ushered into the Green Room where three other guests were already enjoying a continental breakfast. There was a young teenage boy who looked to be about 16 years old and his mother sitting across the room on one of the couches. They were busy enjoying the snacks made available. Also there was a Therapist there but I don't remember his name. I introduced myself to each of the guests and was shortly ushered out of the room and into another room for makeup.

As they took me over to the makeup room, all the moving around reminded me of an efficient anthill serving a very powerful queen. I asked the lady doing the makeup if she could make me look like Brad Pitt but she said she was a make up artist not a magician. Back in the Green room, I received my final instructions with a few dos and don'ts about interacting with Ms. Winfrey. I was told I would be seated in the audience as back in those days, Oprah did her shows from there rather then up on a stage. I was to wait until she actually came up to me while on the air and introduced me and from that point on, I could shout out anything I felt was pertinent to her discussions with the theme of the day or any responses to any of the other interviews that she was walking around and doing.

The guests were then ushered into a large studio where various reserved seats were sectioned off and we were placed as the audience began to fill the studio. After a

399

brief warming up by another staff member, the airing began. Out walked Oprah to a thunderous applause by the audience. I kept pinching myself and could not wipe the grin off my face. I kept praying to God not to let me stumble when she came to me. The show moved on and there were so many times that I wanted to interject or disagree with many of the guests but I had to sit there patiently and wait for her to come up to me.

Finally, I heard her say, "And here's Dennis Poncher, from the nation wide non profit Parent Support groups known as Because I Love You."

Please knees, don't fail me now as I stood up and shook her hand. I spoke a bit of the group and why I started it and then she walked over to another guest and in the middle of her question, I shouted out something in disagreement and she returned to me. The parent had asked Oprah what she thought about grounding for a teen. Oprah thought it was very effective.

I then shouted out, "It's parent imprisonment. The audience laughed and she came back to me for my opinion. I said" Why in the world you would want to spend your weekend in the home with this child who would only make your life miserable. And if you did go out, he or she would either be right behind you or would have guests in the house that you would not approve of".

Once again audience applauded. Then she went to the next member of the audience who asked her opinion on drug testing and before she could answer, I was already shouting out that parents should have at least one drug test available at all times in their homes. This went on until the closing so I was certainly able to get my points across even of it was in such a short time and I had to push myself to be heard. As she continued to ask the audience for concerns she then turned to me and asked for my opinion. Actually, because it was in the last five minutes of the show, I think it had one of the most notable impacts.

Once we went off the air, the guests were directed to remain seated as the audience was ushered out of the studio. So many parents approached me and told me that they really enjoyed what I had to say and they were hoping someday there would be a BILY group in Chicago.

As the last of the audience left, Oprah walked around once again and individually thanked each of her guests. When she got to me, she smiled and said" Hopefully we will have you on again."

Landing at LAX, I was already planning for the landslide of mail that I knew we would receive as a result of my appearance on Oprah. We had learned our lesson from the last time that BILY was mentioned on a national level. Several months prior to my being on Oprah, a distressed North Carolina mother had written into both Ann Landers and Dear Abbey advice columns looking for help regarding her out-of-control son who was on the run. Both columnists within two days referred her to B.I.L.Y., noting that we were an excellent support group for parents who have difficult teens. They provided the post office box and our toll-free helpline.

Within in two weeks, we received over 10,000 letters. We routinely picked up 3 full mail bags a day during those weeks. Every letter was an appeal for help. We formed a committee of twenty parents to deal with the mail as we separated the letters by state. One committee answered the California letters, while another group packed up letters needed to be shipped to our out-of-state groups and I answered the internationally correspondence. For the remainder of the mail, we created a few standard letters designed to cover an array of issues: drug abuse, runaways, school issues, and mental issues. It took us three months to answer every letter. My home was always buzzing with parents working on letters.

Over the last ten years B.I.L.Y. had proven again and again that we were committed to helping parents and I was ready to do the same for the parents who were going to discover us through the Oprah show. We were ready to be a major resource as Parenting and Youth Groups. This media exposure snowballed into several more appearances on network TV shows such as Montel Williams, Dennis Prager, Good Morning America and various local news and cable shows.

The addition of our out-of-state groups in Pennsylvania was also a point of pride. At the beginning of the year, Shirley from a Tough Love group in Yardley, Pa. had reached out. The York's, had also burned them and was demanding more financial support from the parents, and the parents were no longer interested in dealing with them. They wanted to come under the umbrella of Because I Love You. Shirley and I had instant chemistry. I felt as if I knew her all my life. We had so much in common including our commitment for the preservation of families. Doylestown, Pennsylvania was the York's' home base so this was no small thing. A month later they flew me out to do a presentation to the interested parents. They were a smart and eager group and were looking for a more compassionate alternative than what was going on with Tough Love. There were fourteen groups within the Pennsylvania cluster and in the end with Shirley's guidance and persistence, all but two groups transferred over to us.

Many phone calls and emails led to four families from Pa. joining us at our next communication camp in California. The feelings I had, seeing those families pull into the camp grounds in their rental cars from the airport, were beyond words. When Shirley got out of the car, we hugged each other and we both shared some big tears. Of course those families were the stars of that weekend. It was another very successful camp and the following year, wouldn't you know it, we did our first east coast camp in the Poconos.

Three of us from the California camp committee flew out to Pa. for two days of training and one night for a traditional Haunted Hay Ride. We stayed at Shirley's farm complete with horses, cows, chickens and some fabulous home cooking, for two nights prior to heading out to the camp grounds. As anticipated, camp was fabulous. In addition, it was early October there and the changing of the leaves was a spectacular sight. I couldn't help but pack my suitcase with an array of the colorful leaves to bring back and share at our next meeting.

CHAPTER TWENTY-THREE

"No, No, Not Jackie" I Screamed

Our phones continued ringing off the hook, especially after my appearance on the Oprah Show. I remember one call in particular from Mitchell and Christine Block of Simi Valley. They had been searching for Mitchells' 15 year old daughter for the past four years. She had been living with Mitchells' ex somewhere in Las Vegas, when suddenly all forms of communication stopped and they moved, leaving no forwarding address. Mitchell had hired Detectives and contacted the local authorities in Nevada but no one was able to locate his ex -wife and daughter. Finally, Jackie called Mitchell from Arizona where she had run away and had an affair with a man who was much older then her. She told Mitchell that her mother changed their names and she still lived in Nevada. Jackie wanted to come and live with Mitchell and his new wife Christine. They were thrilled to hear from her and sent a ticket for her to fly home to California.

Jackie looked older then fifteen because of the wear and tear of drug abuse. The first couple of weeks, they seemed to have it under control but Christine had a feeling that Jackie was still using drugs. In no time at all, her suspicions became a reality when they discovered some cocaine under Jackie's mattress. They confronted her and she became violent. Mitchell called the police and they suggested he contact a support group which was held at Simi Valley High School, a few blocks from where they lived. Mitchell had already heard about B.I.L.Y. from his sister who happened to be an old friend of mine from college. Still no call was made to us until Jackie tried to commit suicide by taking an overdose of pills. They rushed her to the hospital and had her stomach pumped. One of the intake nurses on duty suggested they call B.I.L.Y. and finally Mitchell made the call and left a message on my voice mail.

I called Christine and Mitchell and listened to their crisis and could feel their pain over the phone. I told them about the ASAP program and assured them I would call to see if there was a bed available. There was and the same evening,

Jackie was admitted at Pasadena Hospital where ASAP held their in- patient programs. I also suggested that Christine and Mitchell start attending B.I.L.Y. and get them ready for when Jackie comes home. The success of any rehab program is not while the youth is in -patient where he or she is following all the rules. It's the changes that must take place in their structure and ready to enforce when the child returns home. I told the Blocks that we can help them to get ready for Jackie's return.

They started attending B.I.L.Y. meetings the following night and were ready to make all the right moves in order to help their daughter. After 30 days of in patient, Jackie was released to the Blocks and one of her conditions was she must attend the B.I.L.Y. youth group. She did not seem to have any objections and as a matter of fact, she really enjoyed the first meeting. From that day forward, Jackie began a whole new life style. She got very involved with the youth core group of B.I.L.Y. which included Ian and Ann. They in turn introduced her to Ian's best friend Alan who was a great guy with a terrific sense of humor. Alan and Jackie in no time at all, became a couple.

Everyone was drawn to Jackie in her small group on Thursday nights. She was about 5'5" and I would say no more then 110 pounds. I remember her as being very pale, wore very little make-up and kept her strawberry blond hair always in a ponytail. Jackie had a great smile and looked a few years older then she was. She did continue to have a problem in dealing with her depression but was attending an outpatient program from the ASAP Drug Rehab program and some 12 step meetings, occasionally during the week. Because of her growth and enthusiasm within each of the programs, she began to train as a junior counselor in the B.I.L.Y. youth groups.

Everything seemed to be falling into place including Mitchell and Christine's involvement in B.I.L.Y... They too began training as small group leaders and in a matter of a few months; they took over as coordinators of our Simi Valley location. They also became a part of our core group of friends and I saw them socially outside of the meetings. Their family successfully attended two or three of our communication camps. Jackie was becoming more and more popular with all the kids. She had a winning personality and joined in on all the planning of the picnics, bowlathons and parties put on by the youth groups.

I especially remember one of the social events that we went to was at Magic Mountain with the parent and youth groups. Jackie loved playing all the games and kept wining the giant stuffed animals. I remember we all had to walk around carrying these big monsters most of the day. When we finished, she had accumulated over 10 stuffed animals and insisted we drive to the Children's Hospital and drop them off there. I was very impressed with her generosity.

A few years passed and at one of my legendary New Years Eve Parties, at the stroke of Midnight, Alan got on his knees and proposed to Jackie. They had already been sharing an apartment as a test run for their future. Ian and Ann where in on it but the rest of the gang which included Christine, Mitchell and about two hundred others of B.I.L.Y. parents and Youth were happily surprised. Sadly though, in a matter of a few months, Jackie broke off the engagement. She told Alan that she was just not ready to tie herself down yet. She could not handle a committed relationship and felt smothered. Her real issues had to do with intimacy. Perhaps she began missing the drugs.

She left her great job working in a Dentist office and also left her support system, friends and her B.I.L.Y. group.

She moved to Bakersfield and began selling perfume on the road. I suspected that she was heading down a dangerous path. Once again she hit the drug scene only this time it was Methamphetamine. This all came as a shock to the youth group in particular because over the last two years she had been one of the most consistent and responsible B.I.L.Y. youth group leaders.

There was a dark side to Jackie and she seemed to be leading a double life. Perhaps some of this behavior was due to her erratic upbringing with her mom and the many years of not having her dad in her young life. She again returned back to L.A. and got in touch with her old druggie friends. Jackie had a way of sabotaging any successes that came her way. According to Mitchell, this was very common behavior for Jackie. Christine reinforced the fact about Jackie not being able to handle the good things in life.

She was 21 years- old now. Mitchell and Christine had lost all control over Jackie. Anything and everything which was positive in her life, she had written off. She would disappear for weeks at a time and no one knew how to get in touch with her. Finally the dreaded call came in just one month short of her 22nd birthday. Mitchell got the call.

"Mr. Block, this is the Mr. Harmon of the Los Angeles Coroners office. We are in Santa Monica, where we discovered the body of your daughter Jackie in a motel. She had taken a lethal dose of drugs"

Mitchell sat down on the floor of his condo and Christine held on to him as the Coroner requested that he meet them downtown.

They had a positive identification but needed him to sign some papers. He agreed to come down the following morning. Jackie had left a note saying *I am sorry, I just cannot do this anymore. I cannot continue to keep hurting everyone including myself.* . He hung up the receiver and began to sob in Christine's arms. She tried to comfort him as best that she could.

About thirty minutes later I received the dreaded call from Christine.

"No, no, not Jackie: I screamed. "Do you want me to come there now? I asked.

"Would you?" Christine continued, "Mitchell and I need you."

"I'll be there in about 30 minutes" I said.

I sadly hung up the phone. Immediately I called Brenda who was also a very close friend of Mitchell and Christine and told her the horrible news. She broke down sobbing and asked me to pick her up on the way to the Blocks, which I did.

By the time we got to their home, Mitchell's two other children and his sister had already arrived. It was a horrible scene. I remember Christine telling me Jackie always rejected help and turned her back on success. That was her demeanor. We stayed there most of the night and when we left, both Brenda and I were overcome with grief and sadness.

The news spread quickly about Jackie's death and my phone rang off the hook for the next few days. I was in constant communication with Mitchell and wanted to know if he needed any help with the funeral arrangements? Unfortunately I felt I had lots of experience in those matters. He told me he was having Jackie cremated and her ashes would be scattered in the ocean. He wanted to have a Memorial Service for her the following Sunday at Warner Center Park in Woodland Hills. He reminded me that Jackie was a free spirit and would have appreciated a celebration of her life in an outside setting.

Mitchell asked me to speak on their behalf. Painfully I looked over the large crowd gathered on that cool Sunday morning, each person holding a white balloon. I wanted to say something to comfort them. This was the first youth from the B.I.L.Y. Too youth group we had lost and I wanted to quell any fears there would be more to come. But dealing with the issues we dealt with on a weekly basis, kids have always been the wild card. Parents were only able to control what they could control.

Doing the eulogy for a B.I.L.Y. youth was probably one of the hardest and most emotional times in my life. I wondered if I would have ever received a call like that regarding Lesli, such as Mitchell did last Saturday evening. I shared some of the happy times we all had with Jackie

414

and also the sadness we were all experiencing in her loss. I kept the dialogue short and asked the crowd to release their balloons as a boom box played *This One's for You by Barry Manilow*. Sort of like an exercise at a B.I.L.Y. Camp. The crowd of over 150 parents and youth were all holding large white balloons. Silently we released the balloons as the soft breeze caught them and pushed them over the tree tops. We watched with broken hearts as they drifted westward towards the ocean.

I will never be able to pass that park without remembering the sight of 150 balloons floating to the blue skies above. Years went by and I managed to stay in close contact with the Blocks. I remember Christine telling me that they both remember what I told them on that first evening when Christine asked me if there was anything that they should have or could have done to prevent the suicide.

What I shared with them was what I learned over the years from many therapists that counsel teens; *you could not cause someone to commit suicide nor could you prevent someone from committing suicide.* She told me that was

415

what they most remembered and it kept them sane and able to sleep at night without the feelings of guilt. I miss Jackie and think of her often. So many have said she is in a better place now and not suffering anymore, I seriously question that and I still continue to mourn her.

CHAPTER TWENTY-FOUR

Lesli Returns

Ian wanted Lesli included on the guest list at their engagement party. I wasn't surprised her brother wanted her there, but I hadn't given it any thought as I was mailing out the invitations. Lesli had been out of our lives for so long, I no longer factored her into it even for something as special as Ian's wedding. Now I wasn't sure if I was ready to see her again. Ian was insistent and it was clear he was not going to back down.

It had been more than eight years since I had laid eyes on Lesli and over a month since I heard her voice on the phone. Our last blow up was because her lovelorn roommate Roy was calling me in the middle of the night, since she had rebuffed his attention. I questioned the poor choices in her life which were impacting mine. I hung up on her when she tried to make excuses. Now I was going to have to face her again at the engagement party after eight years, while 150 guests looked on.

I was only focused on giving Ian a wonderful celebration to honor his love for Ann. It was a very special time in our lives and I certainly did not want any problems between me and Lesli to spoil this affair. Rikki and I had worked very hard on every aspect of the party. I was grateful I had managed to save some money over the years and I was sparing no expense to give Ian and Ann this celebration. When Marv offered their home for the party, as it was larger with a much better layout for what we had planned, I accepted as long as I was able to take care of everything else, like the caterer, music, invitations, cleaning crew and what ever else we needed to make it a memorable event. By memorable, I meant without any crisis

On the night of the party, I was filled with mixed emotions as I left my house to go to Rikki and Marv's. I wanted there to help with the last minute details. The caterers were already there when I arrived and the rental company was setting the last of the chairs and tables in the yard. Rikki and Marv's house looked very festive. The musician arrived thirty minutes before the party was scheduled to start. As he set up on the makeshift stage, I was glad we had gone with live music. Everything was in place as the guests started to arrive. I positioned myself as far away from the door as not to deal with Lesli too soon. Ian had reassured me she wasn't bringing Billy or anyone that might embarrass us.

I was a nervous wreck but tried not to show it. I busied myself introducing family and friends and encouraging them to mingle, eat, and drink. There were so many happy faces and I was swollen with pride. Everyone was here to celebrate Ian finding love. Ann had been able to see him in all phases of emotions which were intense, sweet, earnest and loyal. The loyalty that he had wrapped his flawed sister in all these years was admirable.

Two hours into the party, Lesli arrived with her roommate. I glanced over at her several times, still very aware of my ambivalence to reconnect with her. Clad in a lovely black, low cut sleeveless cocktail dress, she looked beautiful, her dark hair hanging over her narrow shoulders. I did notice that she also looked thinner than I had ever remembered seeing her.

It was clear she was trying to make her way over to me, but every few feet she was stopped by family members excited to hug and kiss her. Over the years she had kept in touch with some of them. They had supported her side of our troubles and chastised me for being so unbending when it came to her.

Suddenly she was standing less than three feet from me. She moved forward and kissed me on the cheek. My resolve to keep her at arms length disappeared the moment she hugged me.

"It's so good to see you, daddy, I've missed you."

I hugged her tightly. "I've missed you too"

Our reunion was short-lived because her uncle came over and whisked her away into the crowd. My arms felt like lead at my side. I pulled myself together and turned to her friend who she had arrived with and introduced myself.

"Hi, I'm Lesli's father."

"I'm Megan. Lesli and I live together." I watched as a laughing Lesli accepted a big hug from her aunt Sydney.

"She seems a little too thin." I wondered out loud.

"She's been having some stomach problems. I think she has a doctor's appointment next week." Megan offered.

"How long has this been going on?" I didn't try to hide my concern.

Megan shrugged, maybe afraid she had said too much.

Armed with a bit of troubling information, I made it my business to corner Lesli before the evening got late and she left. The stomach pains had began after she started working at her second job at the Hilton Hotel. She was now working at a third job. No wonder she was having stomach problems, three jobs are too much for anyone. She said she was planning to take leave from the detective agency so she would have more time

421

to rest. With Lesli, I never knew what was true but this felt like a very serious problem in her life.

As I walked her to the front door, I made her promise to call me after she had returned from the doctor's appointment. She promised and gave me a kiss. I watched she and Megan make their way down the driveway and wondered if she had felt uncomfortable seeing me. Besides the concern around her health, I had tried to keep things as light as possible.

The party raged on until 2:00am. Most of the guests left around midnight but our core of families and friends hung out for another couple hours, critiquing the event and some of the loony attendees. Ann and Ian seemed happy about the party and thanked me several times during the evening for all the effort I had put into it and also thanked Rikki and Marv for letting us have the party at their house.

As I drove home, my thoughts drifted to Lesli and my concern about her health. She really didn't look healthy. I don't remember her ever having stomach problems as a child. I suspect all the stress and crap she had put herself through was finally doing a number on her. I regretted she had wasted all those years throwing her life away and now all she had to show for it was pain. I should have been thinking about the wonderful things upcoming with Ann and Ian but instead I focused on Lesli. It's been so long since I had a chance to worry about her while she was in sight.

* * * * *

The pain was diagnosed as Crones Disease. Lesli had tried her best to explain what the doctor had told her but she kept getting the facts jumbled up. The doctor gave her a diet she must follow and some prescription that needed to be filled immediately. I sent her over to Taft Pharmacy and told her to put it on my bill. The prescriptions were almost two hundred dollars. I was happy she hadn't resisted my offer to pay. When it came to the health of my kids, I would almost always provide. I guess I drew the line with abortions and adoptions.

As soon as I got home, I called my sister in-law Sydney because whenever someone in the family was sick, she was our go to research library. She had several medical books in her impressive collection. She was more than willing to read me everything she could find on Lesli's diagnosis. I did not expect her to tell me that it could be life threatening. The inflammation in her digestive system could spread to other organs and eventually overwhelm her body's functioning. It was something she had to live with for the rest of her life but if she kept to the prescribed diet, took the medicine, and reduced the stress in her life, she could have a good quality of life. My fear was she wouldn't be able to reduce the stress since she always seemed to be surrounded by it.

Even with the concern about her health, I still didn't talk to Lesli frequently. There had been a lot of years and bad feelings between us. I found it very easy to reconnect to the hurt and disappointment I felt when it came to her; I loved Lesli with all my heart. I never stopped loving her; it was getting back to liking her again that I was working on.

When Ian told me Lesli's co-workers at the Red Onion were throwing her a surprise birthday party I was ambivalent about attending. Of course Ian thought it was another opportunity for us to bury the hatchet.

I didn't want to go there alone so I took Brandie, the girl from my office who I had dated and still see everyday at work. Brandie and I maintained a close friendship. She was also very close with my kids, so I thought she would be a good date for the party. I figured I would be the only older person there. The staff plus some good friends of Lesli's were all around her and Ian's age. . When Lesli saw me, she started crying. The look on her face told me she too had been aware of that fragile space that we were occupying. I gave her a long hug. I was just going to accept this moment and let it be what it was.

Lesli was in a new relationship. Jon, the DJ at the Red Onion, seemed like a decent enough guy but I knew better not to get my hopes up when it came to her romantic life. I pulled him aside later in the evening and asked him how Lesli was doing heath wise. He assured me he was invested in doing what he could to make sure she took care of her health. He seemed genuine in his affection for her. Before I left the party, I made Jon promise that if Lesli got sick, he would call me immediately.

B.I.L.Y. was planning our 10th Anniversary party which, thanks again to Vanessa, was going to be held at the Police academy. Several parents worked on this event and it was a catered dinner with some entertainment provided by Sandy and some B.I.L.Y. parents and youth. B.I.LY. was providing this evening free of charge to all members past and present. We expected a huge turnout and of course, that's just what we had.

Unfortunately Jon got the opportunity to keep his promise a few nights before our big party. Lesli had let one of her attacks go too long, not wanting to wake Jon, but the pain had become unbearable. Jon rushed her to Tarzana Medical Center and called me. I arrived just as they were rushing her into surgery. I was surprised to learn that her condition was such; she might not survive the procedure. I immediately called my son.

Ian and I barely spoke as we waited for the surgeon to come out and tell us what was going on with Lesli.

426

After three hours, Dr. Peterson appeared in the doorway of the waiting room. Ian and I jumped up to meet him. Thank God, Lesli had survived. She had waited too long and they had to remove a portion of her colon and appendix. Both organs were extremely inflamed and an infection was starting to set in. He warned us, if she didn't take care of herself, she was on the path for more surgeries.

They let us go in to see her for a minute. She was pale as a ghost. Yards of tubes exited from various parts of her body. God, she looked like her mother did that last few days of her life. It was a real punch in the gut for me. The doctor had warned us that the first twelve hours were critical in her recovery. I was more than aware of those windows of hope sometimes closed with the person you loved the most on the wrong side.

"God Damn you Lesli" I thought, "You are not going to die. I will not let you leave me again". I softly cried to myself.

I insisted Ian go home. I would spend the night in the waiting room. I wanted to be there when she woke up.

Lying on the stiff couch, my mind wondered to all the months I had spent in hospital waiting rooms just like this one, fretting if it was the stay Joyce wouldn't come home from. That fear never goes away.

The nurse woke me up at 6:00am. "Mr. Poncher, Lesli is asking for you," the nurse alerted me. I jumped up and hurried to her room. I was not expecting her to be sitting up, much less with a face full of makeup and brushing her hair. Like mother, like daughter. For someone who had just had major surgery, she looked like a million bucks.

I sat with her for the majority of the day. Marv and Rikki sent their love along with a huge plant. Visitors and phone calls came all day. Jon called but didn't come to the hospital. I didn't share my annoyance with Lesli about Jon's absence. Making a big deal would only upset her.

When the doctor released her, I insisted she stay at my house and she agreed. Helping her to walk up the couple of stairs at my front door, I was very aware it had been nine years since she walked over the threshold

428

and it felt good. Ann was an angel and sat with Lesli most the day while I was at work. She had a steady stream of visitors including Jon.

On the evening of our big affair at the Police Academy, Lesli insisted that I attend. It was B.I.L.Y.'s 10th Anniversary Party and Lesli's best friend Shelly would spend that evening with her. I knew I needed to be with my B.I.L.Y. families that evening. It was great to see so many of the old gang. Jimmy opened the event and then introduced me to a standing ovation. I brought everyone up to date on Lesli's return and her recent hospital ordeal. The words became choked and the tears began to flow as Jimmy came to my side. There wasn't a dry eye in the house and I was so glad I had decided to attend and be there with my extended family. I felt truly blessed as I drove home to share the evening's happenings and good wishes for Lesli's speedy recovery.

That night, it was just she and I. We talked for hours but very little about the past. I wanted it buried and was hoping I would be able to put those stressful years behind us. I needed to move forward with my family on a positive journey and there was no room to carry the baggage of the past. Would I be able to forgive, perhaps? Would I be able to forget, probably not, since B.I.L.Y. occupied my life now and I was repeating the past over and over again in interviews, letters, speaking engagements and the like. I could feel my daughter coming back to me. I was also recognizing I couldn't keep holding her feet to the fire for things she did when she was a confused adolescent. I used the perceived shift in how we were relating to each other to ask if she would be willing to come to our next communication camp. She thought it would be a perfect way to bring things full circle. At the end of the week, she returned to her apartment. We were both healing.

CHAPTER TWENTY-FIVE

A Father/Daughter Reunion

There seemed to be a magical spell over Malibu.
We had no trouble filling all the slots for the weekend
and of course everyone wanted to be in my camp
family. They wanted to be a part of the emotional work
which was certain to happen between us. They wanted
to be part of the powerful father/daughter reunion.
Lesli felt very self-conscious with all the attention and
stuck close to Ian, who was doing security. I had
always been a facilitator in a camp family for the last
fifteen camps but felt that it was important for this
camp, I pass off that responsibility. Bruce, one of my
coordinators and good friends, had historically been a
great camp facilitator and I would need his strength and
compassion to get through this weekend.

Camp is a positive experience and no negative past
history is allowed in the workshops. This was going to
be a big challenge for me because I was hoping Lesli

would explain why she had made the choices she did for the last nine years. I was willing to try because I knew I wanted us to walk away from this experience, healed.

The first breakthrough for Lesli and I as well as for many other families was on Saturday mornings experience in the Meditation workshop run by Elizabeth, the minister from our first meeting place in Canoga Park. She was also the catalyst for my creating this camp. This particular workshop, we were put through a meditation experience which included our creating in our minds, a life size statue of ourselves on a beautiful path somewhere we created , which could be a park, the beach or anywhere we wanted it to be. Once the statue was created, we were able to crawl inside and look out without anyone knowing we were in there. We could see anyone approaching our statue. We would also share our feelings after each person left and what we wanted to say to them if they could have heard us. We had to deal with our feelings about family members approaching a statue of us as an individual and we were able to view and listen to the thoughts of the approaching members as they came down a path towards the statues we created.

First strangers would approach, and then a best friend would approach and next were the family members each individually. Finally we would approach our own statue with our thoughts and feelings. This was all shared by each member of each camp family after Elizabeth had walked us through the experience. Lesli was able to control her emotions as she shared about the stranger who enjoyed the beautiful statue that Lesli had created. Her best friend Shelly spoke to her of how proud she was that Lesli was finally on the right path and she knew Lesli would prevail. Her brother was her biggest supporter on the path and I was probably her biggest problem on the path. She began to apologize to me during the sharing but was cut off by Bruce who reminded her sharing was to be on positives. She continued on with how happy she was to have me back in her life and then she saw Joyce coming down the path.

When Lesli got to Joyce walking up to the statue, she broke down and it took a long time before she could compose herself. She told Joyce everything and how remorse she was for hurting everyone including herself. At this time, Bruce allowed her to continue without interrupting. It was one of the most emotional times in my life and I had to take two codeine pills to head off a master migraine after the workshop. It was truly a therapeutic cleansing for us as it always seemed to be for so many families.

Saturday, after dinner, we had our talent show. It was another of our successful shows. For me, it was one of the most meaningful shows. Lesli sang *"The Rose"* which surprised everyone with her great voice. Then she and I did *"Do You Love Me" from Fiddler on the Roof,* with of course different words which I wrote for the evening. It went over great and we got a standing ovation. I think we could have just read the Yellow Pages and got the same response. We were so much in the spotlight all weekend as everyone was praying for this experience to be the beginning of a great curing for us. Ian and Ann came up for the talent show and Ian taped it for us. He did not want to be a part of the whole experience because he did not want to steal any of the focus that Lesli and I desperately needed to deal with.

From that point on through the remainder of the camp, Lesli and I were once again reunited and it was as though somehow we were able to wipe away all the pain and turmoil of the past nine years and plan for a productive and happy future for our family. As we were leaving the final workshop, Trudi, one of the parents who was there with her son Robby, handed me this note.

Dear Dennis: Can words express real love? That's what I feel when I hear your name or B.I.L.Y. This group has changed my life or should I say given me life. Your children and B.I.L.Y. Too have done so much for Robby. It makes me feel so secure to know that you are here for him in time of need. I used to worry about you a lot but now I know that you have grown and learned to use the B.I.L.Y. tools to get you through the darkest of times. There is a light at the end of the tunnel and it's getting closer all the time. Have patience and you will be blessed. Thanks for being you and me thank God for your love, creativity and openness. Robby and I will always be there for you. Trudi.

As I finished reading this letter and handing it over to Lesli, another letter was handed to me from a parent who just joined B.I.L.Y.

Dear Dennis and Lesli: I wish to thank you both for choosing to be at the B.I.L.Y. camp this weekend. We have been adjusting to some very difficult issues and just being there was a real miracle for our family. My marriage was close to separation over the difficulties in adjusting to Maria's being a runaway, her drug usage, truancies and much more. She has just been home now for one month so I really didn't believe that this weekend would work for us. Thank God I kept focused. I followed your rule of not parenting this weekend. I tried to believe that it just might work for our family. I feel that your letter to each other was a break through for Maria and me. I know that she was truly touched as she clung to me a cried. Maria is truly fond of music and so the format was enjoyed as well as very moving for her. I loved each and every song also. Thus we move forward hoping to build on this stronger foundation and know that all will be well. Your story gives me so much hope. I tend to get very discouraged and at times have fantasies of running away myself.

Please know that you are doing a very beautiful and enlightening job at B.I.L.Y... You must preserve. I know that the challenges are great. I pray for your commitments and strength to continue. Peace, Joy and Serenity for you and your family from mine, always, Teresa.

More letters continued to arrive as we made our way back to the dining hall for our final lunch and good bye's. These letters are the fuel that adds to my fire. When anyone of my immediate family or friends who are not connected to B.I.L.Y., ask me why I devote so much of my time to this organization without receiving any pay, I simply take out a stack of letters such as the many I received that weekend. How fortunate I feel to be able to have this mission and be guided on this journey.

Dropped Lesli at her apartment, told her to get some rest and I would call her in the morning. I also was exhausted as I unloaded my car and brought my gear into the house. I walked directly to my room and lay across my bed. As tired as I was I couldn't shake the feeling of hope I felt in my heart. We had work to do but we had committed to giving each other a new beginning. I rolled off my bed and used the last of my energy to put my stuff away. I noticed a piece of paper sticking out of my camp book. It was a note from Lesli.

Dear Dad,

How can I tell you what I'm feeling when I sometimes don't even know myself. I wish things were perfectly wonderful between us but we're going to have to work at it. I do believe that we have so much to build on – our memories and our love most of all. I may not always understand why we have problems, or exactly how to make our relationship stronger, but I care enough to want us to try. I can't do this alone but we can do it together. I love you so much, Lesli.

I didn't think I had any more tears after camp, but there I was with a wet face. I pulled my desk drawer open and slid the note in with all the other letters she had written me.

CHAPTER TWENTY-SIX

Ian and Ann's Wedding

Ann and Ian decided on a May wedding. The morning of the ceremony Ian and the groomsmen got dressed at my house. They all looked so handsome in their black tuxedos. I savored every minute of that morning. Eating snacks and drinking champagne, I laughed with Ian and his friends. It was a thrill for me to see what a great group of friends, mostly B.I.L.Y. kids, Ian had developed and held on to over the years.

So many feelings were spinning through my head. Sure, I was excited for Ian and was anxious to share this day with all our friends and family, but there was also a blanket of sadness. Joyce was not here to celebrate with us. Everyone says she will be here in spirit but that's just not the same. I wanted to walk down the aisle with her. I wanted to hold her hand and feel her touch once again. I wanted to savor the aroma of her cologne. I wanted to relish her laughter and watch as she had the special dance with Ian.

This is so unfair but I must push aside these wants and deal with the haves. I have my son and daughter back in my life again after so many years of turmoil. I have created a support network, gradually spreading across the states. I have hundreds of new friends and a most welcomed extended family with Rikki and Marv. In a few hours I will have a most beautiful and loved daughter-in-law. I am truly blessed by all of this.

"Dad, the limo is here" Ian shouted as the guys gathered their belongings and headed out the door.

Ian and I were the last to walk out. As I checked the lights and double locked the front door, Ian turned to me with tears in his eyes and softly said. "Thanks Dad for all that you have done to bring me to this day. I am just sorry that Mom won't be here to share it with us"

Would he understand or have the same feelings as me when I answered back "Your mom will be here in spirit" I tried so hard but in vain to hold back my tears.

We arrived at the Calabasas Inn at 2:00PM., where Rikki had transformed the Inn into a scene from a storybook. All year long, she had reviewed every bridal magazine and decorating book she could get her hands on. As a result, she had a thick sample journal that would revival any professional event planner.

Ann and Ian had requested to see one another other privately for the first time in the Bridal Room. A few minutes later, they came out laughing and holding hands. There was no doubt they were ready to take this leap.

Wild flowers in an array of colors decorated every space. The Chuppah (traditional Canopy) covered in greenery and vibrant flowers. Behind the canopy was a huge waterfall and hillside that was breathtaking.

I could barely contain the pride I felt, walking down the aisle with Ian. Three hundred well-wishers beamed back at us. Lesli, who looked healthy and whole, was lovely in her purple bridesmaid dress as her cousin Jake escorted her down the aisle. I had no idea if I would ever get the opportunity to walk her down the aisle as a bride, but I was extremely happy that she didn't miss this wonderful moment for her brother.

Rikki and Marv were stunning as they walked Ann down the aisle. Rikki was especially outstanding in her purple flowing gown with a beautiful detailed sequined top. I couldn't ask for a better set of in-laws for my son.

Ann was radiant in her gown, a princess style with layers of lace and satin. A teary eyed Ian watched her as if she was the only person in the garden setting. As I watched them take their vows under the Chuppah, I knew this couple would make it. They had a family who would support them through all the ups and downs. Doves and White Balloons filled the air as a Cinderella white horse and Carriage awaited the young couple for a ride to the reception area.

As Marv took Ann out to the center of the dance floor for the Father/Daughter dance, he insisted that I bring Lesli to join them. The band played *"Daddy's Little Girl"* and it was one of the many tearful and joyful highlights of the evening.

The reception went well into the night. I can't imagine a more special and beautiful affair. I was still feeling euphoric when I got home. Remnants of Ian's preparation, earlier that day, were spread around the house. I picked up a plastic container which had held his boutonnière. I tossed it into the trash. In many ways, I was still processing the fact my little family had made it to the finish line in one miraculous piece. I held on to the hope that Ian and Lesli would be okay but over the past nine years I had prepared myself for a possible loss – especially of Lesli.

Out of habit, I pushed the play button on the answering machine as I picked up around the house. I could see there were at least twenty calls waiting for my attention. Most, I assumed would be congratulations from folks who weren't able to attend the wedding. I was caught off guard when I heard the crying. A strained woman's voice, sounding overwhelmed and verging on hysterics, rushed from the blinking machine.

"Mr. Poncher...I'm so sorry for calling so late but I don't know what else to do. My daughter...she wont listen…her boyfriend, he's trying to ruin her. He is running a drug lab and she won't stop seeing him."

More of her tears continued as I listened to the rest of the rambling message, grabbing up a pen to write down her information. Her daughter's guidance counselor had told her about B.I.L.Y. and had given her my number. She was desperate and alone. She left her home and work number and her address, imploring me to call as soon as I got her message, no matter how late. Looking over at the clock, I loosened my bow tie. It was just after three in the early morning. I'm not sure why I picked up the phone. She called after midnight so I guess I thought a parent so upset was still going to be up.

She answered on the first ring. "Rachel?" I assumed that was her daughter's name and she was waiting to hear from her.

"This is Dennis Poncher, Ms. Brown."

A new flood of her tears rushed over the phone line. "I don't know where she is. None of her friends will tell me anything." For some reason, I couldn't help smiling.

444

How well did I know this hopelessness which had lived in my gut for years?

"Ms. Brown, if you want, I can come over now and we can talk."

"You would do that for me?"

"Absolutely," after getting her address, I picked up my car keys off the dining room table, "I should be there in about fifteen minutes."

"Mr. Grayson said you would know what to do."

"Philip Grayson?"

"Yes."

"I'll see you shortly."

Life has a funny way of working things out. Not five years ago, Philip Grayson had not been shy about voicing his doubts about the effectiveness of B.I.L.Y., casting me in the role of a troublemaker, unnecessarily stirring up parents.

It turned out Ms. Brown lived only a couple miles from our Granada High School meeting. I was happy that it would not be a hardship for her to get to our support group. It was important to reduce as many of the barriers for these stressed out parents as possible.

As I climbed out of my car and started up the walkway, I wondered what she would think of me making a house call wearing a tuxedo. Maybe I could use it as my testimony that things can work out and she will survive, just as I had and the thousands of parents who had walked and those yet to walk through B.I.L.Y.'s doors.

EPILOGUE

Our immediate family began to grow in June of 1994 with the birth of Ian and Ann's daughter. Her name is Joanne Nicole, named after Joyce. Soon after, Ian and Ann purchased their first home in West Hills. In 2011, they added another addition to round off their family with the birth of their son, Garret Michael.

Lesli started to hit the personal appearance circuit with me. I took her to share with me on some Radio and TV talk shows as well as some local speaking engagements. I was finally able to step back and allow her to take the spotlight. She was a chip off the old block and could hold an audience in the palm of her hands. No notes, just like her old man.

She left the Red Onion and returned to her old job at the Detective agency. She was still taking two buses to work everyday even though she finally got her drivers license.

Lesli was committed to saving up for a car. Cindy, one of the girls in my office, asked if anyone wanted to buy her late model Nissan that was in great shape. She was getting a new car and needed to sell this one. I had a mechanic friend of mine check it out and when he told me it was a good deal, I purchased it. Cindy promised to drive it out to Marv and Rikki's on Christmas morning where we would be opening all our gifts with the family. I gave Cindy some money to have her boyfriend detail the car and also gave her a giant red bow to tape on the top of the hood when they parked it in front of the house.

After we had finished opening all our gifts and had a delicious breakfast, I asked Lesli to help me take her gifts and mine out to load up my car. The rest of the family knowing what was about to happen, all followed us out the door. As Lesli started to head towards the driveway where my car was parked, I told her to put hers in the car with the red bow parked in front of the house.

She screamed. "Is that mine?"

She started to cry and so did the rest of us. The car had a full tank of gas because I knew she would be gone for the rest of the day. It was a real joy to be able to do this for her and she so deserved this after so much heartache, for so many years. We all watched as she found the keys in the glove compartment and drove off to show her car to all her friends and family.

Lesli also was able to add to our family but this time, it was a future husband. She met him at a local studio hangout where he was tending bar. He was a college graduate and also a triplet. His family resided in New York with the exception of one of his brothers who lived here in California. Since his family was located in the East Coast, their wedding was going to be my sole responsibility. No problem, I would just borrow all of Rikki's notes and proceed from there.

Six months prior to the wedding, Lesli and her soon to be husband, Todd, announced to the family their plans to relocate in Portland, Oregon. So once again, Lesli was leaving me, only this time it was for something we were all pleased about. Sure I will miss her, but at least it was not back to New York or even further away. So after a fantastic wedding with once again about 300 of our closest friends and family, we bid adieu to the new Miller family.

After their few years of adjustments and the purchase of their new home, I got the call from Lesli I was finally able to instantly and positively react too.

"Daddy, I'm Pregnant", Lesli shouted through the receiver.

As the excitement subsided and the calls to all the family and friends were completed, my thoughts reflected back to the day in the Limo when Lesli said the same phrase to me.

Thus began numerous trips to Portland and soon the birth of Jocelyn Delaney Miller. She too, was named after Joyce. Unfortunately after some years, the marriage of Lesli and Todd went array. They had a civil breakup and Lesli moved out of the home with Jocelyn to a nearby apartment. Things are on a friendly basis now but it did take some time and work to get it there.

During all these happenings, B.I.L.Y. was also experimenting continuous growth. We had a fantastic web site and were receiving hundreds of letters and emails each week, along with constant requests to open groups in other states. We also were getting more Tough Love chapters requesting to come under our banner. Soon we had new groups in New, York, New Jersey, Texas, Georgia, Wyoming, Missouri, Idaho, Maryland, and Kentucky with more on the way

In 2000, B.I.L.Y. was running smoothly and my family was calm, so I decided to re-connect with some old school friends by having a small reunion party of Junior High school guys who were in an off campus social club. I started planning it in the later part of 2000 and the party's date was October 1st 2001. I knew I could pull this off by myself so I began with the sending of a handful of announcements to hold the date. Word spread and requests began to arrive by email, snail mail and telephone calls from additional old friends that wanted to be a part of this reunion party.

Well, my plans for a small intimate reunion at my home ended up with 307 RSVP's that will be attending. I had to tent my front and back yard and had parking attendants, caterers', gourmet coffee spots, dessert tables, three bars and a disco. When it got closer to the event, I contacted a few friends who were coming, to help me with the greeting table and to pass out name tags.

The day before the party, I developed Double Pneumonia. I had trouble breathing and my doctor wanted me in the hospital. I told him it was impossible because I was throwing this huge party at my home and all the ducks were in place. I somehow convinced him to send over some oxygen and a breathing machine with the promise to go to the hospital the morning after the party. I invited a few friends over for decorating the night before the party and I sat on the couch as I directed the staff.

Everything went well in the set up and I went to bed about 10PM with the hopes of feeling better in the morning. No such luck. I awoke and could hardly breathe. I was scared and I called Ian to get over here and take me to the hospital. They admitted me immediately into Intensive Care. I made Ian promise to go back to my home and stay there the rest of the day while things were getting set up and also to film the entire evening just in case I could not get back home for the evening festivities.

It was the last thing I remembered until I woke up four days later from a coma and saw Ian and Lesli at the foot of my bed. I knew I must have been very sick when I saw

Lesli there from Portland. In addition to the Pneumonia, my Pancreatitis flared up and was completely out of control. I was a very sick puppy. But I pulled through and six months later I had a second reunion party at the Calabasas Country Club for those who still wanted to party with me. Another big turnout and it was the talk of the alumni community for years to come. I sort of spoiled it for many future reunions as most people would say, we already saw everyone at Dennis' parties.

I was able to change their minds when my high school had its 50th class reunion in 2006 and of course, I was the committee chairman. We had it at the Universal Sheraton Hotel with over 400 friends. One of my classmates knew someone in the accounting department at the hotel and was able to swing the Presidents Suite for me to stay in on the big evening and after the affair. I checked in early that afternoon so I could get dressed there. The bell hop showed me to the room on the 20th floor while insisting on carrying my bag. When he opened the door to the suite, I was shocked. It had a huge marble foyer with a gigantic circular bar and eight leather bar stools. To the left, a large dining room with a glass circular table to seat 12 people and behind that, a full kitchen. Off to the left, a much larger living room with four huge sofas and a few chairs to try to fill some of the open space. The rooms were surrounded with floor to ceiling windows with a spectacular view. The bedroom and gigantic master bath were behind the dining room. I could definitely get accustomed to this life style.

I immediately got on the phone to thank Peter, my fiend from school who got me the room no- charge and told him to go to Smart and final and pick up some cases of water, cold drinks and beer plus some chips and dips. I told him to come early and change here, because we would definitely have an after party in the suite. We did. Some fifty of our closest friends joined us after midnight until the wee small hours, laughing and reminiscing. It was a big success but I am burned out now. Maybe I will do one for our 75th birthdays.

On a Friday morning in July of 2006, I was working on the computer when I received an instant message from an Anonymous sender. It read, "Hi, I'm looking for Lesli Poncher, do you know her:"

I answered back that I was her father and asked who that person was? There was no answer and they disappeared from the screen. Later in the day, I told Lesli of the message and we both thought it was probably an old friend looking for her since they were using her maiden name. Remember, this was before Face Book.

Well, later in the same evening, while on my computer, Anonymous reappeared with this statement. "Hi, remember me? I was the one looking for Lesli Poncher"

I responded again, only this time I asked who this person was and was no way prepared for the reply.

"I'm Lesli's biological son and I am sitting here with Lesli's biological daughter. We need to get in touch with her tonight. We recently were told we were adopted and today, while our parents are out of town, we uncovered our adoption papers with Lesli's name. We have been searching the web until we got in touch with you. We would like to talk to her before our folks return tomorrow"

Can you even imagine how shocked I was? It was midnight and yet I still called Lesli, who immediately got on the internet and began a chat with her two biological kids. She remained on line for the next three hours while I held the receiver and listened as she repeated the messages going back and forth. She told them she would call in the morning when their parents returned and if they were okay with her having some kind of a relationship, Lesli would make plans to see them.

The following morning she had a great phone session with the adoptive parents and was on a plane the very next morning, where she met and spent the day with her 16 year old biological son and 18 year old biological daughter. Since that time, they see each other a couple of times a year and are on the computer at least once a week. I did have the opportunity once, to meet them both and that was a real emotional experience. I don't expect to have any continuing relationship with them but I certainly have no problem with Lesli and their relationships.

Perhaps now I would be able to open the envelope that Lesli presented to me at our Camp Reunion experience. In one of the workshops she said," In this envelope are the last baby pictures that I was able to handle before I let the adoptive parents know that I did not want them to continue sending them. It was way too hard for me to hold the pictures of two children that I had given birth to but may never have the chance to physically hold them in my arms."

456

I told Lesli that I may never open the envelope because I felt that would be too emotional but thanked her for thinking of me.

About six months later, Lesli made a trip down here and finally introduced Joyelyn to her half brother and half sister. It was a very heartwarming reunion. Jocelyn was only six years old at the time but was very excited about having new siblings.

In October of 2009, I received a phone call from Paulette, a lady in Edmonton, Alberta Canada requesting information on possibly opening a group in Canada. She had found our web site and was having some issues with her daughter and needed some support. When I told her we were not yet in Canada, she asked me what it would take to get a group started up there. We spoke for a long time and I also told her to review all the information provided on the web site under "Starting a New B.I.L.Y. Group" then to get back to me with any questions or concerns.

To show you how incredible this was; earlier the same morning, I got an email from Diane, a mom in Canada who was having some serious problems with her teenage daughter and was asking if we had any groups in Canada.

"I am so sorry, but B.I.L.Y. is not yet in Canada. Why don't you give me your name and phone number and I promise to call you or have someone call you when we do get a group going in Canada. By the way, where about in Canada are you located" I responded

"Alberta" she emailed back.

"Where in Alberta" I continued.

"Edmonton" she proceeded and added her name, phone number and address. I wished her good luck with her daughter. I also advised her to check out our website for some great references. Naturally, I also threw in a few possible solutions to get her to start making some positive changes.

I was blown away when Paulette told me that she was from Edmonton and I excitedly told her about my conversation with Diane also from Edmonton. She promised to call her after we got off the phone. It turns out that Diane lived about ten minutes from Paulette. They communicated that afternoon and decided to work together in getting B.I.L.Y. started in Edmonton.

Paulette and I had instant bonding and within a few weeks, she had all her ducks in a row. Then she hit me with "Would you fly up here and train our future group leaders and myself, if we paid for your trip?"

"Are you kidding? I would love that. Just tell me when and I will be there" Plans were made and the opening was set for February 15th 2009.

"By the way Paulette, what's the weather like there in February?" I inquired.

"Usually, with the wind chill, minus 40 degrees" she casually replied

Don't even ask what I was thinking when she told me the temperature. You need to know, I have the heat on in my home once the temperature outside drops below 60 degrees and that's plus not minus. "Will you be picking me up in a dog sled?" I kiddingly asked.

Well, after a few trips to the mall for layers of clothing, I flew into Edmonton on the 12th and we did a big community meeting to introduce B.I.L.Y. at a church with a huge turnout. Also included on the Dias were some dignitaries of their local government and a player from the Edmonton Ducks. The opening was a welcomed success and the group continues to flourish. Paulette and I have created a very close relationship even though she is so far away.

On their one year Anniversary they had planned a Variety show fund raiser that was being chaired by Russ, Diane's husband. I few months prior, I got a call from Russ asking me if they paid for my trip, would I come up for their big show? Of course I answered with a quick yes. He told me that it was going to be a surprise for Paulette and his wife Diane. I was not to tell anyone of my upcoming visit. I arrived shortly before Showtime and was hidden back stage. Russ was the M.C. and after welcoming the large audience of supporters, he called Paulette and Diane up to the stage to thank them for assisting him in running the fund raiser. He said he wanted to present them with some flowers and asked for the florist to come out from back stage. Hidden behind two gigantic bouquets of flowers was none other then me. When I lowered the bouquets and they saw it was me, I thought we were going to have to call the paramedics. The screams and tears went on for a few minutes before Russ was able to introduce me to the wondering audience. It was a wonderful and very successful surprise. I stayed at Russ and Diane's home and spent a few days with Paulette and her family.

Paulette and I email each other constantly and I look forward to making another trip up there again someday and hopefully it will be in the summertime.

B.I.L.Y. continues to grow and we have recently introduced a new web site (www.bily.org) which has had very favorable responses. There's a new section on our web site called *Dear Dennis,* where I can answer questions and concerns from parents throughout the country, especially those where there are no B.I.L.Y. groups available. It saddens me to know there are so many families out there with little or no support and in such need of a group like B.I.L.Y... My mission is still in progress and I hope that someday I will be able to broaden our villages in order to offer a support group in every community. The need still grows and I feel truly blessed that I am able to continue on my journey.......

Made in the USA
Middletown, DE
24 February 2021